Theatre of the
Ridiculous

Theatre of the Ridiculous

A Critical History

KELLY I. ALIANO

McFarland & Company, Inc., Publishers
Jefferson, North Carolina

ISBN (print) 978-1-4766-7403-2 ∞
ISBN (ebook) 978-1-4766-3472-2

LIBRARY OF CONGRESS CATALOGUING DATA ARE AVAILABLE

BRITISH LIBRARY CATALOGUING DATA ARE AVAILABLE

Front cover photograph © 2019 Creatista/iStock

Printed in the United States of America

*McFarland & Company, Inc., Publishers
Box 611, Jefferson, North Carolina 28640
www.mcfarlandpub.com*

Acknowledgments

There are a number of people that I must thank for assisting with the completion of this book. First off, I would like to thank the faculty of the Theatre Department at City University of New York Graduate Center, especially the executive officer during my time there, Jean Graham-Jones, as well as my dissertation committee, David Savran, Edward Miller, and most especially my chair, Jim Wilson. I also want to thank the late Daniel Gerould for being my mentor during my time at the Graduate Center and believing in my work from the start.

I also owe an incredible debt of gratitude to Joe E. Jeffreys at New York University's Tisch School of the Arts for inspiring this work and for being willing to take the time to review my manuscript and offer thoughtful commentary on it. The Ethyl Eichelberger chapter is especially indebted to his assistance.

I would like to thank my family for all of their support throughout this process, especially Nancy Borriello; Gloria, Frankie, and Franco Benfari; and the entire Cotellessa clan for their positivity and encouragement of my work. Thanks to my dad for supporting my education. This work is in loving memory of my mother, Joy Aliano; my grandmother, Iris Cofsky; Mary Cotellessa; and Gloria Cotellessa.

Robert Hooghkirk is the most wonderful theatre-going companion imaginable and I am grateful for his willingness to explore Ridiculous performance with me. Diana Ingles deserves my immense thanks as she was the one who pushed me to pursue academia initially and consistently sat through whatever weird performances I was into at any given time. Without her, none of this would have been possible.

Finally, and most importantly, this book belongs to Henry Borriello as much as it belongs to me. Without his love, I would never have been able to complete it.

Table of Contents

Preface
Uncovering a Ridiculous Past

"The Ridiculous may be defined as a mistake or deformity not productive of pain or harm to others...." [1]

This book is haunted—haunted by a past that is often overlooked but which regularly leaves its traces on the contemporary stage; haunted by a cache of artists decimated by the AIDS crisis, no longer able to write their own story into the history of American drama; haunted by a downtown New York City landscape that has been buried beneath decades of decay and rebirth, gentrification and so-called NYU-ification. It is haunted by a past that I neither experienced nor even lived through, yet, from the moment of my first encounter with, felt drawn to. I needed to return to these Ridiculous sites, though long since replaced with all sorts of other storefronts and theatres, apartment complexes and chic restaurants and bars. I had to understand where these places were in order to try to comprehend who these people were. Their historical place and time somehow seemed to define the kind of art that they created and therefore who I thought them to be.

I have often felt quite close to these artists, though most I have never seen in person, much less ever met. The question I was most often asked as I described this project was whether I ever saw any of these productions live. My common response, "I was three when Charles Ludlam died," makes it clear that I could not possibly have lived this history for myself. This landscape was not my own, these artists were not my contemporaries. Yet, Ludlam, especially, felt like my kindred spirit, a kid from Long Island who ran off to the city to try to make his mark in the New York theatre scene.

Ludlam found his place below Fourteenth Street with a motley crew of great visionaries and unintentional creative geniuses alike, all looking to

1

make art for its own sake—the pleasure of performing as an end almost entirely in and of itself. I found a less forgiving Downtown Scene in the early 2000s when I began my New York City theatre education. Rather than an "Underground Playground," to riff on Stephen J. Bottoms's terminology, there was a rigid hierarchy of theatrical spaces and productions already in place; rather than room to experiment and play for its own sake, there was a need to innovate in order to capitalize and turn profits. Upon discovering the Theatre of the Ridiculous, I discovered what I wanted was not the theatre scene of my own youth; rather, I was trying to recapture a moment that had long since passed. My *Midnight in Paris* will forever be the hope of a late 1960s era cab turning past Sheridan Square, picking me up and whisking me off to a Greenwich Village more than a generation my predecessor.

Writing about the Ridiculous, then, is, at least in part, a journey to the past. While its lasting impact on the American stage is quite significant, experiencing the movement itself, in its own historical moment, demands an archaeological reconstruction of something that defies reconstruction. There is so much about the Ridiculous that is purely a product of its own time: shows could be put on just about anywhere because rents were quite inexpensive by today's standards; artists were to be found everywhere, because New York seemed the only logical place to run off to, especially for these predominantly gay male individuals; countercultural ideas were in the air, with Civil Rights, Women's Liberation, and the burgeoning Gay and Lesbian Rights Movement all hitting their stride during the decade preceding the height of the Ridiculous Theatre. A perfect blend of factors came together to make this movement possible at this unique historical moment. While inheritors of the Ridiculous form are quite prevalent in today's theatrical scene—Taylor Mac, for example, recently won a MacArthur "genius grant" Fellowship, and is well-documented by Sean F. Edgecomb as a keeper of the Ridiculous flame[2]—Ridiculous plays from the height of the form's productivity—roughly, the mid–1960s through the mid–1990s—have only recently begun to be regularly revived and studied.

Unlike other theatrical "-isms" and styles, the Ridiculous has been largely overlooked in surveys of the history of the theatre. In this sense, Ridiculous Theatre truly does haunt studies of American drama; it is almost present, just barely perceptible, yet just as often dismissed, forgotten, or outright ignored. Consider this mention in the supposedly seminal theatre history textbook, Oscar Brockett and Franklin Hildy's *History of the Theatre*; on a listing of well-known off–Broadway theatres that "went bankrupt in the 1990s," the Ridiculous Theatrical Company is said to have been "founded by Robert Ludlum"[3] who is actually the author of the Jason Bourne novels, not a queer playwright/actor/director. Thus, even Charles Ludlam, perhaps the only major theatrical figure, in terms of national recognition, to come from the Ridiculous era, is mistaken for someone else. The memory of this movement is vague and prone to errors.

On the other hand, this is an easy editorial mistake to make: their names sound alike and it would be simple enough to conflate him with a more recognizable figure with a similar name. However, such a statement begs an important question: why has Ludlam remained largely overlooked in academia, despite his remarkable achievement in the American theatre of writing, directing, producing, and starring in 29 of his own original plays? Is his work so inherently strange—or perhaps "queer"—that it cannot play to a mainstream audience? Such a case might be made for certain Ridiculous artists— Jack Smith, for example, created extremely esoteric and abstract works that even this so-called Ridiculous connoisseur cannot exactly claim to "get"— but Ludlam's plays, by and large, are farces, and a play like *The Mystery of Irma Vep* (1984) is still regularly performed. My goal, then, became not to answer why the work was overlooked, necessarily, but instead to find a way to reinsert the Ridiculous, as a theatrical form, back into scholarly discussion.

The Ridiculous might most clearly be seen by 21st-century audiences through its legacy of inheritors and descendants. As Edgecomb expertly argues in *Ludlam Lives!*, there is evidence of the lineage from Ludlam and his contemporaries to certain performers and aesthetics of the contemporary moment. He traces the impact of the "Ludlamesque" through "queer legacies," which, he says, "may appear to borrow traits and formulas of patriarchal and essentialist constructs at first glance (such as the father/son model), but the queer version of this model is antiprototypical and taboo (the 'father' may be romantically/sexually/incestuously linked to his 'son')."[4] In exploring these taboos, the Ridiculous allows for experimentation and, because the Ridiculous is so often overlooked in histories of the theatre, it has many innovations still left to be explored. The Ridiculous may be a product of the past, but its legacy can be

> a catalyst for social change. The continuance of the Ludlamesque Ridiculous thrives not on reverence and revivalism, but rather anarchic reinventionist approaches that synonymously honor and deconstruct the original intentions and characteristics of Ludlam's theatre of the era of post-gay liberation. This subversive practice allows the Ridiculous genre to transform as a medium that is a direct reflection of and reaction to shifts in contemporary queer culture.[5]

Indeed, Edgecomb has shown us that the Ridiculous Theatre aesthetic, in new and innovative ways, is still alive and well and that without the Theatre of the Ridiculous, as Charles Ludlam practiced it, much of our contemporary theatrical scene would be markedly different.

Therefore, to ignore or overlook this movement is not only a shame for our pleasure in performance but also because it skews our understanding of how the plays, performances, and even the theories from the 1990s onward came to be. Many of the groundbreaking elements seen in later artists' works were actually developed in and by the Theatre of the Ridiculous; the Ridiculous has haunted the study of American experimental, as well as mainstream, performance for decades without enough fans of the theatre realizing it. Tony Kushner did not create *Angels in America* in a vacuum; he was deeply influenced by Ludlam, who was deeply influenced by Jack Smith, and so on. In order to understand contemporary drama, especially "queer" or "experimental" drama, the story of the past must be told in full.

My project here, however, is not to consider the impact of the Ridiculous on the contemporary theatrical scene alone. Rather, I am interested in journeying back to the roots of the Ridiculous, in order to uncover *what* it was, in its own historical moment: who its key players were and what aesthetic elements they brought to the style. I argue that the Theatre of the Ridiculous constitutes a specific theatrical movement, one which contains very specific aesthetic markers that have heretofore not been recognized or categorized as specifically Ridiculous. A study of this aesthetic is not only crucial for the theoretical framework it will provide us for studying subsequent artists and their contributions, but also, and perhaps more importantly for Ridiculous studies, for the deeper understanding that it will give us about this particular historical period and its artistic output.

This theoretical framework must, then, embrace time and place as part and parcel of meaning; this will allow these theatrical ghosts to come alive in their own distinct place and time. The Ridiculous created, in a pre–AIDS epidemic world, an example of a "queer subculture," which, as Jack Halberstam argues in *In a Queer Time and Place*, "produce[s] alternative temporalities by allowing their participants to believe that their futures can be imagined according to logics that lie outside of those paradigmatic markers of life experience—namely, birth, marriage, reproduction, and death."[6] In the same way that queer subcultures defy a traditional heteronormative "life story," Ridiculous play texts eschew the logic of a climactic plot structure or focused character development, which traditionally serve as a kind of formula for playwriting. Instead, the Ridiculous embraces its own unique, anarchic, narrative form as a playful space in which all sorts of performativity are possible. In order to allow these imagined futures to come alive on Ridiculous stages, these artists used a series of very specific aesthetic elements that, when grouped together, challenge heteronormative dictates and social norms. Ridiculous Theatre allows the adult to embrace the child-like wonder of play by assuming and dismissing varied gendered and non-gendered identities, in works meant to indulge their fantasies of stardom and glamour.

Important markers of this theatrical aesthetic, then, include playing with the constructs of gender, fooling around with theatrical conventions, and the melding of highbrow and lowbrow culture. To achieve this mélange-aesthetic, one key to the Ridiculous is an interest in what I will refer to as a style of "remix," much as it is practiced in contemporary hip-hop music; this includes various practices of borrowing, referencing, quoting, or sampling from other people's works in order to create a complex cultural layering of elements from all strata of society. This mixing of cultural elements creates a varied performance landscape as opposed to a singular artistic style. In addition, borrowing from all areas of culture allows the borders of these Ridiculous spaces to be fluid; anything and everything can be welcomed (and/or mocked) in these performances. To be truly "Ridiculous," a work must not just have one or two of these features: it needs to be built of all of these elements as its key components of artistic expression. While Ludlam quipped, "The Ridiculous is a convenient name. Each time you do a play, it expands the definition of Ridiculous."[7] Ridiculous Theatre, as a form of artistic practice, has a shape and form all its own that deserves to be noted as a particular dramaturgy and performance style.

The Ridiculous style embraces an aesthetic of failure, a key component to my definition of the work as queer. As Halberstam theorizes in *The Queer Art of Failure*, "Heteronormative common sense leads to the equation of success with advancement, capital accumulation, family, ethical conduct, and hope. Other subordinate, queer, or counterhegemonic modes of common sense lead to the association of failure with nonconformity, anticapitalist practices, nonreproductive life styles, negativity, and critique."[8] This interest in failure is precisely at the heart of the genesis of the entire Ridiculous Theatre project. Of directing Ronald Tavel's *Shower* and *The Life of Juanita Castro* in 1965, director John Vaccaro "recalled his reaction when he first read *Shower* and *The Life Juanita Castro*: 'I read them and my friends read them, and they said: DON'T do these! They're HORRIBLE! And they were. Precisely why I wanted to do them.'"[9] The Ridiculous embraces—even celebrates—the detritus of culture with the same gusto that it is willing to create performative landscapes in which nothing is sacred, in both cases subverting conventional wisdom and cultural hierarchies.

To this end, the performance style of the Ridiculous privileges humor: being able to laugh at whatever is being depicted. As Ludlam wrote in his Ridiculous Theatre manifesto, "You are a living mockery of your own ideals. If not, you have set your ideals too low."[10] Therefore, everything is fair game to serve as the punchline of a joke; nothing is held too sacred, nothing is above reproach in the world of the Ridiculous. Being successful, in a traditional sense, is not the goal; rather, as Ludlam's "Instructions for Use" in his manifesto, "Ridiculous Theatre, Scourge of Human Folly," prove, the challenge is merely to try new things in performance. "This is farce not Sunday school," he writes. "Treat the material in a madly farcical manner without losing the seriousness of the theme. Show how paradoxes arrest the mind." It may be necessary to take something serious in a Ridiculous play, but do so in such a way that will enhance the humor. Or create a play that takes itself so seriously that it cannot help but be funny. Working in the Ridiculous mode should be enjoyable, while still allowing for the possibility "to scare yourself along the way."[11]

Indeed, this delicate balance between humor and seriousness is present in the richest of Ludlam's scripted farces, especially those of the 1980s. However, even in the more anarchically comical Ridiculous plays, such as those by Tavel or Smith, there is a sense of reverence present, but it is usually reserved for popular culture. In performing great icons—particularly female ones—there is a sense of invoking those individuals' spirits while still allowing the persona of the performer to be simultaneously present in the scene. This double awareness is reminiscent of Halberstam's understanding of the "ghosting" that occurs in representing some transgender characters, "allowing [them] to haunt the narrative after death."[12] While not all of these famous figures were actually deceased, they were not always fully "alive," as characters, in the world of a Ridiculous play; rather, their essence was evoked, both to break the sense of a realistic world within the drama—the play is inherently self-aware of the culture of which it is a part because of the inclusion of such allusions—and as a way for the performers to play *at* being these individuals. The Ridiculous is a playground in which its practitioners can raise the detritus of culture into new life through their plays.

The Ridiculous, then, was breaking with traditional theatrical conventions of realistic acting and an imagined fourth wall. However, doing so was not unique in the late-1960s; a slew of experimental theatre companies, including explicitly political companies like The Living Theatre, took up the challenge of defying mainstream culture and social norms through their artistic expressions. What makes the Ridiculous unique, then, was the manner in which it took up challenging the status quo. In *Playing Underground*, Stephen J. Bottoms designates this work as "underground," suggesting that this indicates a "relative disregard of 'agendas,' whether political or aesthetic"[13] as well as an "'underground' disregard for conventional wisdoms and categories, and … playful blurring of borders between artistic 'isms.'"[14] Bottoms contends that work from the Downtown Scene during this period, which includes all manifestations of the Ridiculous being addressed here, is interested in how to alter the conceptions of how to make art, not in promoting or condemning particular political agendas, platforms, or ideas. From this perspective, these artists positioned themselves outside of the system entirely, rather than standing opposed to the system (as might be implied in the term "countercultural").

One way to consider the work of the Ridiculous is to highlight the artists' interest solely in making art and their aesthetic choices, which went against the grain of the mainstream culture, as their only attempt at action.

Indeed, Ridiculous Theatrical Company performer Lola Pashalinski best sums up the Ridiculous's political valence: "politics doesn't exist only in direct political theatre, but also in aesthetics."[15] The Ridiculous was not didactic nor was it meant to promote or condemn a specific political agenda. The Ridiculous has important stylistic markers that we can highlight—an interest in gender performance, a mixing of cultural material from all strata of society, a preoccupation with the act of performing as opposed to a polished finished product of performance—as being indicative of this political potential. In *Queer Political Performance and Protest*, Benjamin Shepard suggests playfulness as being at the heart of important political performance activities throughout the last two decades, with "creativity, pleasure, and play in urban protest in general, and queer-community building practice more specifically"[16] being central amongst these practices.

This emphasis on pleasure and play is a clear marker of the queerness of the Ridiculous, as is its insistence on cross-gendered performances in each of its plays. Jill Dolan states, "To be queer is not who you *are*, it's what you *do*, it's your relation to dominant power, and your relation to marginality, as a place of empowerment."[17] Queer is preoccupied with one's actions, not solely with one's identity or essential qualities. In this way, queer is engaged with performance because performing is active; it is a way to engage with power structures and one's position in society.

Play is no longer just for fun; it can have a more profound significance and meaning. As Stefan Brecht contends in *Queer Theatre*, Ridiculous plays are about viewing the "process" of performing, not a polished finished product. Brecht explains that you are "seeing an activity as such—a doing, perhaps a making—rather than the doing or making of something. We are not so much seeing a play as the making of a play."[18] The emphasis here is on the process of performing, not the product of a performance, which could be seen as a kind of failure in a traditional conception of the theatre-making as an artistic practice which must produce a definitive production of a text.

The notion of failure, particularly as Halberstam theorizes it, is at the heart of how I am defining the Ridiculous as queer. This construction of queer embraces camp; as Halberstam contends, "in true camp fashion, the queer artist works with rather than against failure and inhabits the darkness." Embracing this sort of "negativity" is, for Halberstam, "a queer aesthetic."[19] For Ridiculous Theatre, this is their playground: instead of emphasizing the creation of a completed theatrical text or production, Ridiculous performances embrace an anarchic, almost improvisational form. Bottoms describes the acting process at the Play-House of the Ridiculous as "the unbridled

expression of his performers' outrageous personalities … introducing a kind
of improvisatory onstage chaos." This anarchic production style meant that
"the execution of a piece could vary substantially from night to night, as performers pursued ad-libs and spontaneous impulses, sometimes taking the
performance careening off on tangents from its scripted backbone. 'It was
chaos,' Vaccaro notes, 'but it had its parameters; it was directed chaos…. And
we had such fun!'"[20] Clearly, these productions would seem to "fail" as accurate translations of play texts on stage.

However, what they succeeded at was something exciting and new: a
form of performance fascinated with the liveness and ephemerality of the
performative moment, embracing the inherent anarchy of performing (or
playing) in the first place. By failing to create "great" plays or theatrical productions, in a traditional sense, Ridiculous Theatre created something brand
new: a queer form of expression unconcerned with mainstream society's need
for clarity of expression by "mak[ing] peace with the possibility that alternatives dwell in the murky waters of the counterintuitive."[21] Ridiculous Theatre asks why must a performance be a successful representation of a
particular text? Why can't playing on stage itself be a kind of reward? Remember, *The Life of Juanita Castro* (1965) has as its opening stage direction, "This
play should never be rehearsed."[22]

In answer to these queries, a Ridiculous performance embraces failure,
as Halberstam theorizes it, particularly "some of the wondrous anarchy of
childhood and disturbs the supposedly clean boundaries between adults and
children, winners and losers…. [Failure] also provides the opportunity to
use these negative affects [disappointment, disillusionment, and despair] to
poke holes in the toxic positivity of contemporary life."[23] These performers
were free to play at (and with) their roles, creating something that could only
exist in the place and time of its presentation; to study it is to try to interact
with a spirit, something almost present, partially recalled, but only previously
alive and only corporeal for a brief moment. There is never a concrete finished
quality to a Ridiculous play; it was always something in process of coming
to life, even when it was being presented to audiences. If, as Bottoms
describes, "precision and subtlety in the delivery of texts were usually the
first casualty of the Play-House's unhinged approach,"[24] no polished finished
products were to be found there.

Because of this intentionally "unpolished" quality, the body of work
associated with the Ridiculous is often labeled "camp," as these are plays in
which the actors "ham it up" and low cultural material is presented alongside
of or in place of high art. According to Fabio Cleto, calling this work "camp"
implies something deeper about the plays. Cleto argues:

> Camp is a mode of perception … that cannot in its enactment leave out an element
> of performance on the part of the … object, the decoding of which emphasise [*sic*] its

failure in performance, nor on the part of the subject, whose perception is in itself an act of performance, with its necessary audience and its allusive, winking narcissism. Vice versa, camp as a "style" of performance doesn't exclude—quite the reverse: it presupposes—an element of perception, an encoding and decoding of the self and the world as stage, and of failure of intentions.[25]

The crucial point here is about failure: camp productions are *meant* to fail. The emphasis is on the act of reception on the part of the viewer; he or she must recognize the failure not as something negative, but rather as being significant to the work's overall meaning. Ridiculous plays always possess a slightly unfinished quality; at one point in *Irma Vep*, for example, it is clear that one actor is playing two roles, wearing elements of each costume on a distinct half of his body and jumping back and forth. There is no attempt at theatrical realism, which could be seen as a failure to convince the audience of the reality of the world presented on stage. Yet, the point of the play is not to deceive the audience into accepting the on-stage action as a window into the real world. Rather, Ludlam's play is all about performance: his actors *playing* on stage for the delight of his audiences.

The interest in play, or what might be seen as an unfinished or amateur quality of Ridiculous productions, then, allows us to return to the concept of failure as a formative one in understanding the Ridiculous as queer and thereby radical. Halberstam suggests, "The history of alternative political formations is important because it contests social relations as given and allows us to access traditions of political action that, while not necessarily successful in the sense of becoming dominant, do offer models of contestation, rupture, and discontinuity for the political present."[26] Therefore, this interest in the act of performing, as opposed to the creation of finished works of art can be seen as potentially progressive. Ridiculous performances allow characters, who are often built of fascinations specific to a queer sensibility, to come alive for a certain period of time, but these manifestations are not completely convincing transformations. Instead, they are a kind of haunting: audiences can sense the evocation of the popular culture icons on stage but need not be fully convinced of their reality nor of some sort of representational transformation on the part of the performers. These figures come to life through a shared reverence between performer and spectator and in this sense, create a queer community, a radical act, through the site of performance.

Therefore, throughout this discussion my understanding of queer will be built on three key components. The first of these of the idea I raised in this book's first line: this sense of haunting. I will not talk about death and mourning specifically, nor am I preoccupied with exposing otherworldly figures. Rather, I am queering the concept of ghosting in order to address the way in which the Ridiculous reconfigures the cultural archive by raising the ghosts of its own particular icons and heroes, particularly Maria Montez. Like the web series *Queer Ghost Hunters*, which seems on the surface a silly subject for a show, this practice actually "manages to uncover some interesting queer history in the process" and gives the opportunity for all involved to become "'part of a community,'"[27] which, in the case of the Ridiculous, is based on a shared cultural lexicon of icons and idols. To understand how this ghosting comes to life in performance, I will privilege the concept of camp as Cleto described it, bridging it with Moe Meyer's understanding of a "processually constituted"[28] queer self, as a way to unpack the Ridiculous's particular performative take on identity, which allows the performers to draw attention to the on-stage action *as* performance. The final queer element is born of this camp perspective: an emphasis on failure, as Halberstam theorizes it, not as a negative quality but rather as a radical subversion of the heteronormative status quo, an element that is present in all of the aesthetic choices made within the Ridiculous plays. In this sense, Ridiculous Theatre is an empowered and empowering underground theatrical form that allows its practitioners and audiences alike to challenge mainstream culture.

This theoretical frame will provide some specificity when discussing the Theatre of the Ridiculous as a unique theatrical movement. Clearly, the term "ridiculous," as a way to discuss performance, goes back to the earliest days of theatre criticism; Aristotle's quotation that opened this chapter proves this. Yet, while this could suggest that Ridiculous Theatre is not an anomaly, it is unfair to the form only to understand it through the lens of theatre more broadly. Ridiculous Theatre is its own brand of theatre-making; while its inheritors and long-term legacy is fascinating, it deserves to be studied in its own right, through the lens of its own place and time of creation. The purpose of this book, then, is to provide a kind of roadmap to uncovering the Theatre of the Ridiculous, to insert this movement into the discussions of American theatre, so that other aspects, artists, and sites associated with it may continue to be unearthed and brought to light.

To do this, I begin by exploring the works of Charles Ludlam as a kind of high-water mark for Ridiculous Theatre production. His works contain all of the elements that I deem necessary for a work to be considered Ridiculous: a worship, bordering on obsession, with popular entertainment and celebrities; a practice of remixing allusions from both high and low culture; and a freeform approach to gender representation on stage. From here, I travel back in time and consider two of Ludlam's key influences: B-movie star Maria Montez and her number-one fan, experimental filmmaker and performance artist Jack Smith. Smith allows for connections to be drawn between Ridiculous Theatre and Pop Art which leads to my next chapter on John Vaccaro and Ronald Tavel's Play-House of the Ridiculous. I then consider Ethyl Eichelberger, whose work with gender sets the stage for much contemporary drag performance. Finally, I consider the legacy of Theatre of the Ridiculous, both its immediate adaptors and inheritors and a broader collection of artists whose work seems indebted to Ludlam and his contemporaries. Indeed, this overview is meant to show that much of the contemporary theatrical landscape would be quite different without the contributions of Ridiculous Theatre.

ONE

"A Ridiculous Triple Threat"
Charles Ludlam and the Making
of a Ridiculous Aesthetic

For those unfamiliar with the form of Theatre of the Ridiculous, the simple place to start would seem to be in defining the term "Ridiculous Theatre." That project, however, is more complicated than it may appear to be on the surface. There are actually varied definitions of what the Ridiculous is and what it means to be a Ridiculous artist; the interpretation shifts depending on which Ridiculous practitioner or company one is discussing. For Charles Ludlam's company, one particularly useful explanation appeared in a 1979 article for *Omega One*. Here, Robert Chesley suggests, "The Ridiculous Theatrical Company is not like other theater. It has qualities all its own, which appeal not at all to some people and which others find immensely appealing."[1] Like many so-called definitions of the Ridiculous, this statement evades answering the question, suggesting that the Ridiculous is something unquantifiable that often operates as an acquired taste. Yet, Ridiculous practitioner and expert Everett Quinton would argue, "It [Ridiculous Theatre] is among the most important times in American theatre. It has shaped what the theatre is today.... The Ridiculous does want to change the status quo."[2] It seems that the meaning of the Theatre of the Ridiculous may be hard to pin down with certainty, but the work associated with it is of great importance, for aficionados and regular theatregoers alike.

Even Charles Ludlam, the great Ridiculous playwright, avoided answering the query of "what is Ridiculous Theatre" directly. In place of a clear explanation, Ludlam once quipped, "The Ridiculous is a convenient name. Each time you do a play, it expands the definition of Ridiculous."[3] Obviously, such a comment does not provide much to go on in terms of what the Ridiculous, as a title for a style of performance, might mean. What it does prove is that pretty much anything—any topic, any punch line, any actor playing any role—might be fair game in this mode of performance. This gesture, which

13

emphasizes trying things out without the burden of strict guidelines to follow, is performative and clearly exposes the queer quality of Ridiculous practice. As David Savran explains, "In its [queer's] contemporary use, it suggests a mode of excessive and self-conscious theatricality that has long been linked to sexual deviance.... [Queer] is a performative designation, one that privileges doing over being, action over intention. Queerness, in other words, is constituted in and through its practice."[4] The Ridiculous, too, can only be understood through action; it comes alive in the "doing" of putting on a play, privileging the act of performance. Its definition, then, is always in flux, adapting and reconstituting itself to fit the newest performative acts within its framework.

This openness to the inclusion of anything in a Ridiculous play resonates with the aesthetic being defined as camp, which, in Ludlam's own words, "became a sly or secret sense of humor that could only exist to a group that had been through something together; in this case, the gay world."[5] Its camp qualities remind us that the Ridiculous is a distinctly queer form, meant to appeal to and thereby unite its otherwise marginalized, principally gay male, audience members. This community forming was based on "a rigorous revaluing of everything. What people think is valuable ain't valuable. Admiring what people hold in contempt, holding in contempt things other people think are so valuable—it's a fantastic standard."[6] The Ridiculous is built on a process of inversion, taking what was "low" and raising it to the level of "high art." In attempting to unravel the complexity of the definition of camp, Fabio Cleto notes that "camp recognizes they [artificiality, failed seriousness in certain performances] are 'bad,' but this is precisely the reason why camp adores them."[7] Indeed, Ludlam proclaims, "If nobody wants it, come to me! Let my theatre by the repository of all forbidden theatrical conventions!"[8]

Clearly, there is a kind of cultural and structural anarchy to Ridiculous Theatre, as it seems open to the inclusion of a wide array of indiscriminate forms, ideas, stylistic elements, and references. In his own personal notes, Ludlam created an outline on the subject of Ridiculous Theatre, entitled "Essaying Ridiculous Theater: It Helps to Be Simple-Minded," suggesting a privileging of pleasure—if you like it, include it—without a great deal of intellectualizing or clarifying. In this list, he suggests that the Ridiculous finds its ancestry in sources as diverse as avant-garde works by Alfred Jarry and Antonin Artaud; P.T. Barnum's aesthetic of "putting on a show" and his "attitude of giving the audience an eyefull"; and "silent films" due to their "super-expressive acting technique." He also saw the Ridiculous's "Anti-Ancestry" as being directly tied up with reacting against the Theatre of the Absurd. Ludlam sees Ridiculous Theatre as an "antidote to the theater of the Absurd, beyond the circular construction of morbid existentialism." Ludlam goes on to explain, "This non-discrimination state of innocence which I call simple-mindedness which is at the heart of the creative act is indistinguishable from idiocy or insanity hence the name Ridiculous Theater."[9] Ludlam saw Theatre of the Ridiculous in conversation with a great lineage of both popular and experimental performance. Although this is not *quite* a workable definition, these notes at least give a context for analyzing and discussing what Ridiculous Theatre is—and what it is not. Clearly, the Ridiculous responds to both the experimental and the commercial performance that preceded it, but it takes what it wants from these forms and discards the rest, in such a manner as to challenge the nihilistic tone of its direct artistic predecessor.

Breaking with the past and attempting to create art that was relevant to his own historical moment places Ludlam's work in the lineage of experimental artistic creation. According to Quinton, "I didn't think Charles wanted to change the world. I think he wanted to change the theatre."[10] Therefore, like many practitioners of the historical avant-garde, Ludlam *did*, in fact, write a manifesto for Theatre of the Ridiculous. To what degree we can—or, indeed, we should—take this document seriously remains to be seen. In this supposedly defining statement, if the manifesto is meant to be taken at face value, Ludlam writes as his seventh axiom: "The theatre is a humble materialist enterprise which seeks to produce riches of the imagination, not the other way around. The theatre is an event and not an object. Theatre workers need not blush and conceal their desperate struggle to pay the landlords their rents. Theatre without the stink of art."[11] Ludlam saw theatre as a way to make a living while still being a place for creation. In this statement, he seems to value the commercial entertainment aspect over an aestheticist view of the form.

This quotation, lifted from the only manifesto to be written about Theatre of the Ridiculous, could reflect Charles Ludlam's unique take on writing theatre. On the other hand, this document also could be seen as nothing more than another ridiculous mockery, ridiculing both the gesture of manifesto writing and the form in which Ludlam found himself working. Ludlam was critical of the avant-garde and did not consider himself nor his work amongst their ranks. In order to address the distinction between his Ridiculous practice and its historical predecessors, Ludlam writes, "The avant-garde is wrong and the audience is right. The audience is supposed to know what is going on. If artists fail to communicate, it's their fault, not the audience's."[12] Ludlam considered his work much more accessible to audiences and he dismissed the privileging of "newness" at the heart of the avant-gardist project. "Everything new isn't necessarily better,"[13] Ludlam contends, reminding us that working within a relevant mode of a particular historical moment can be as—or even more—powerful than simply innovating for its own sake.

To some extent, Ludlam was working within a previously established artistic mode, and not the inventor of such a form. Indeed, Charles Ludlam, while perhaps the preeminent name associated with the Ridiculous, was *not* the pioneer of Ridiculous Theatre but merely was an inheritor of it; when he broke from John Vaccaro's Play-House of the Ridiculous in 1967, he took the title "Ridiculous" with him as much out of spite as out of artistic intent,[14] "apparently never seeing the self-deprecation in using the technical noun as an adjective," according to the Tavel archive.[15] And yet, no single figure in the complicated history of this theatrical movement would come to be as associated with the form as Ludlam. His Ridiculous Theatrical Company created 29 works in the mode of Ridiculous Theatre, as much adhering to the above-mentioned manifesto as directly mocking it in their performances.

Thus, Ludlam has often been seen as the quintessential source of Ridiculous Theatre, in terms of both theory and practice. His papers were collected after his death into a volume that still acts as a kind of theory of Ridiculous Theatre, entitled *Ridiculous Theatre: Scourge of Human Folly*, in honor of the manifesto he had written. In addition, when in search of a definition of the Ridiculous during the heyday of its popularity, scholars were likely to inquire how Ludlam would sum up the meaning of Ridiculous, in terms of theatrical practice. For instance, Gautum Dasgupta interviewed Ludlam for *Performing Arts Journal* in 1978, asking him to define the Ridiculous:

> It has to do with humor and unhinging the pretensions of serious art. It comes out of the dichotomy between academic and expressive art, and the idea of a theatre that re-values things. It takes what is considered worthless and transforms it into high art. The Ridiculous theatre was always a concept of high art that came out of an aesthetic which was so advanced it really couldn't be appreciated. It draws its authority from popular art, an art that doesn't need any justification beyond its power to provide pleasure. Sympathetic response is part of its audience. Basically for me, and for twentieth-century art, it's always been a problem of uncovering sources; it proceeds by discoveries…. It's really an exercise to try to go beyond limitations and taste, which is a very aural, subjective and not a very profound concept for art. And to admit the world in a way that hasn't been pre-censored…. Ridiculous theatre is in color; it's hedonistic. Different artists define it their own way, but basically it's alchemy, it's the transformation of what is in low esteem into the highest form of expression.[16]

Here, Ludlam privileges the Ridiculous practice of taking elements from low culture and elevating them to the same status as that which is borrowed from high culture. He sees how his art form was born of the popular culture that surrounded his day-to-day life as an American and allowed the shared interest in this popular culture to serve as the backbone for his style of theatre. Ridiculous Theatre is always tied up with enjoyment and with pleasure in performance; it allows both its performers and its audiences to indulge in what they like and to see those things as being culturally valuable.

This quotation from Ludlam does wonders to illuminate how to understand Ridiculous Theatre. Ludlam's description is applicable beyond just his own Ridiculous plays. He understood how this drama was constructed and how an audience might make meaning from a Ridiculous play. Therefore, it may be impossible to understand the Ridiculous without first understanding Charles Ludlam and his contributions to the style. This may seem counterintuitive, as his theatre was not the site of the initial genesis of Ridiculous Theatre. Although it is not possible to claim that the style was born in Ludlam's spaces, his sites of performance can be claimed as the locations in which it was perfected. Ludlam was able not only to synthesize the various complex elements that I see as being key markers of Ridiculous performances into his plays, but was able to do it with panache, creating a sizable canon of plays that, by and large, do stand the test of time.

Throughout Ludlam's 29 plays, all three of the components that I deem critical to Ridiculous Theatre are present: the plays are heavily influenced by the popular culture, particularly Hollywood cinema, of the early to mid–20th century, to the point of being almost communal sites of worship for the ghosts of these popular icons; Ludlam engages in a practice I call "Ridiculous remix," in which references to and quotations from high and low cultural artifacts are blended into a unique original play; and gender is always problematized through the presence of at least one cross-dressed performer, with an emphasis on all character portrayal as a kind of "putting on drag," highlighting the performative nature of gender both on stage and, by extension, in life. In these ways, Ludlam is the apotheosis of Ridiculous Theatrical practice, for better or for worse. He is the artist most remembered and the one who made the greatest impact on the larger American theatrical scene.

Therefore, my "tour" of the Ridiculous Theatre begins with Charles Ludlam, for a time comfortably situated at One Sheridan Square in Greenwich Village. It was here, from the 1970s and on into the 1980s, that Ridiculous Theatre, as a practice of art-making, would come into its own. Ludlam became the master of the style that he inherited, borrowing and usurping from the other artists around him—as well as from all aspects of the larger cultural scene and educational background to which he had access—to build a unique style of both playwriting and performing. By bringing together all of the key elements seen elsewhere throughout the landscape of the Ridiculous, Ludlam was able to create both an artistically innovative, and an infinitely "sell-able," style of dramatic production.

Despite often being excised from histories of American drama (or mistaken for popular fiction writers), what Ludlam did was truly exceptional. He not only became a kind of contemporary American Molière, but his works also display a culmination of techniques used throughout the queer Downtown Scene until this point to create a unique and flexible theatrical style. The plays of Charles Ludlam embody all three key elements of Ridiculous Theatre: they are all deeply indebted to the popular culture of the 20th century, notably in his first work, the pastiche drama *Big Hotel* (1966); they include a remixing of elements borrowed from all strata of culture, particularly prevalent in what I refer to as his "late-style" dramas, *Le Bourgeois Avant-Garde* (1983), *How to Write a Play* (1984), and *The Artificial Jungle* (1987); and, in performance, they demand a defiance of the norms of gender performance, always including at least one character played in drag. Nowhere is this practice of what I call "gender mashup" more pronounced than in his classic portrayal of *La Dame aux Camellias* or *Camille* (1973).

The Ridiculous, in my estimation, must be a product of the blending of practices of popular culture ghosting, reference remixing, and a queer approach to gender identity. This is because the radical qualities of the Ridiculous—that is, the way in which it speaks to and with its historical moment of artistic production—is embedded in these aspects. The ghosting has queer radical potential as it signifies that the detritus of culture may not be so disposable after all; rather, the popular may be worthy of its own ritual worship. Ludlam's *Big Hotel* displays this in its unrelenting assemblage of cultural icons; it allows the theatre space to be one in which Ludlam's preferred cultural ghosts are allowed a moment of distinction and importance. This ghosting also allows for practices of textual layering to be employed as dramaturgical tools. These "remixed" plays undo hierarchies of cultural power in provocative ways, showing that a reference to a television commercial is as useful, if not more so, than a reference to a classical work. Gender performativity is a key aspect of this remixing; the layering of gendered identities into a single character's construction suggests both the instability of gender as a signifier as well as a further undoing of cultural and social norms.

By looking at this particular cross-section of Ludlam's works, I establish that he did incorporate all of the major elements of the Ridiculous into his work. His practice of privileging certain cultural icons and modes of expression in his Ridiculous dramaturgy are clear indicators of the queer camp aesthetic in which he, and the Ridiculous more broadly, were working. As Andrew Ross explores in his essay "Uses of Camp," "In the gay camp subculture, glamorous images culled straight from Hollywoodiana were appropriated and *used* to make sense of the everyday experience of alienation and exclusion in a world socially polarized by sexual labels."[17] Ludlam does this expertly, reappropriating and refashioning imagery and identities from the cultural lexicon to his own queer ends. In this way, scholars are correct: Ludlam is a key figure in Ridiculous Theatre production. He not only synthesized these elements but did so in a way that created plays that are still readable—and potentially producible—today.

Ghosting of Popular Culture: Big Hotel

Certainly, one of the first aspects of the Ridiculous that becomes evident upon reading or seeing one of these plays is the seemingly never-ending use of quotations and allusions. As Ludlam noted, there was room for nearly everything in the Ridiculous; nothing was sacred and nothing was above mockery. To write a Ridiculous play, one could, and should, quote from anywhere and everywhere, building his or her play from whatever references he or she felt were generative.

Ludlam took this notion of quoting to the extreme, especially in his early works for the Play-House of the Ridiculous. For the first three years of his playwriting career, Ludlam's plays were grand-scale pastiches, referencing and alluding to everything and anything from pop culture to 1940s starlets to off-color humor and word play. Ludlam's notebooks (one spanning 1967–1970 and another 1969–1973) show an interest in the collage form even for recording personal thoughts. The first notebook covers everything from personal musing about relationships and marijuana to reviews of performances he had seen to reflections on his company's practices. Some ideas are recorded as complete passages; others are more associative, recording single words or small diagrams to get a point across.

For example, Ludlam recorded a particular tarot reading, possibly a study for the 1969 play *The Grand Tarot*,[18] a play which is an apotheosis of pastiche playmaking. The play can be performed in any order; the tarot deck would be dealt before the performance and "the order in which they [the cards] fall determines the order in which the scenes will be played."[19] Although the structure of this play was later standardized, just this concept for play presentation suggests a deep commitment to collage as an organizing principle. In addition, the later notebook in the Ludlam collection shows his quotation collecting in action; he variously quotes from many different sorts of sources, sometimes on the same topic, interspersing his own thoughts and bits of his own original dialogue throughout the notebook.[20] Even the construction of Ludlam's own diaries was a process of collaging, suggesting that Ludlam not only saw collage as an organizing principle for dramaturgy but for life as well.

As a way to structure a work of drama, however, collage is not an easy one for spectators to make sense of. There is a tension in the structure of Ludlam's early plays, one that pulls against the rules of traditional dramatic construction and even rubs against itself, full of structural and story-telling inconsistencies. Quinton sees these early plays as emblematic of "the 'theatre of anger,'" a term he uses to define some of the Ridiculous works.[21] He recognizes the confrontational quality of these sprawling, early scripts. No attempts are made at developing a tightly or fluidly scripted drama over the course of these plays, nor is there any sort of attempt at dramatic consistency across events. In early Ridiculous theatre, form mirrors content—everything that can be included is included and everything that can be questioned and/or mocked is subject to such treatment. The best example of this early playwriting structure is Ludlam's first play *Big Hotel*.

Ludlam did not structure this play as a story-driven, action-based drama. Rather, *Big Hotel* is constructed from a series of references to and from other works. In his review of a 1989 production, Frank Rich puts it best, stating, "As for the narrative, forget it."[22] This play, written for John Vaccaro's Play-House of the Ridiculous, may be the best example of Ridiculous composition-by-quotation format. Rather than writing a closely-knit narrative, the play is a mélange of various references. Rick Roemer recognizes that "although *Grand Hotel* was the overall inspiration for *Big Hotel*, the direct references to the film are few. The obvious one is, of course, the hotel as a thoroughfare through which an odd assortment of people travel, bringing with them danger, murder, intrigue, and glamour."[23] *Big Hotel* operates as a kind of parade of characters through this hotel. The audience could watch the play as a collage of references—some familiar and some more obscure. It is a celebration of classic films revered by the artists involved in the play; the play operates as a large-scale pastiche rather than as a traditional drama. No specific dramatic throughline ties the actions of the play together. Rather, characters appear almost at the will of the hotel—or the playwright—and engage in on-stage interactions.

The point of this play is less the story or the action than what Ludlam was getting at in creating such a grand, sweeping pastiche as this. *Big Hotel* contains an apologia on behalf of its playwright, right before the action in the hotel commences. Within this self-referential speech, Elwynn Chamberpot states, "Truth says, of old the art of making plays/Was to content the people; and their praise/Was to the poet money, wine, and bays./But in this age a sect of writers are,/That only for particular likings care,/And will taste nothing that is popular./With such we mingle neither brains nor breasts;/Our wishes, like to those make public feasts,/And not to please the cook's taste but the guests.'"[24] Ludlam, as playwright, speaking through an agent character (whom he did not play), is basically stating that his interest is to please his audience, which will be made up not of the high-class critics of culture, but of the common people. Because of this, then, the play that follows is filled with jokes, double entendres, and popular culture references meant to suit his particular audience.

In this play, Ludlam is paying homage to the shared cultural interests of his company of performers and their audiences, many of whom were gay men, like himself. Therefore, his play indulges their shared cultural interests—they likely privileged the same afternoon Hollywood icons as Ludlam—

and who, ideally, therefore would recognize the film icons and tropes being employed during the production. *Big Hotel*, then, is a kind of "memory play," tapping into the shared cultural database of film scenes that Ludlam and other movie aficionados like him would have seen in their youths. In *The Haunted Stage*, Marvin Carlson suggests that theatre "is the repository of cultural memory, but, like the memory of each individual, it is also subject to continual adjustment and modification as the memory is recalled in new circumstances and contexts."[25] Indeed *Big Hotel* suggests a queer archive; as Robert Mills puts it: "Queer-history exhibitions will adopt a style of presentation partly modeled on scrapbooks and collage; in place of the representative 'object,' they will appropriate fragments, snippets of gossip, speculations, irreverent half-truths."[26] All theatre, to some degree, is ghosted by the culture that created it. Ludlam decided to shine a light on his shrine to popular culture, using this play as a place to present many of the films and stars that he—and the larger community of gay men of which he was a part—had idolized throughout his life.

Yet, according to Roemer, "[*Big Hotel*] was originally just a notebook filled with various lines, quotes, etc. that Ludlam carried around with him, never intending to create a play out of them. It was [Play-House of the Ridiculous director John] Vaccaro, however, who persuaded Ludlam to fashion them into a play."[27] Ludlam may have wanted to keep his collection of quotations to himself, but Vaccaro clearly saw how presenting these references, celebrating them on stage, would make a work of drama relevant to their times. In his review, Rich sees the play as "an unofficial manifesto of the Ridiculous artistic creed [with its] collage of transvestite clowning and classical references,"[28] a list of Ridiculous criteria not far removed from my own. There are a number of plotlines—the main one focusing on Norma Desmond, played in drag by Ludlam, facing problems with both her career and her agent—that all include references to "many familiar names of American films of yesteryear—Norma Desmond, Trilby, Svengali, Lupe Valdez and Maria Montez."[29] To untangle the story of this play is less important than to recognize the large degree to which it indulged in the worship of 20th-century Hollywood cinema.

Indeed, if the Ridiculous is ghosted, then it is by Hollywood film more strongly than by any other influence or source. There is certainly a trajectory to be traced from other popular forms, such as vaudeville and the American book musical, to the Theatre of the Ridiculous, but these influences are far less pronounced than the admiration for 20th-century Hollywood cinema. In this early work, particular stage images are foregrounded, usually drawn from the cinema, and the cast of characters could read as a list of famous film icons. When asked why he was so interested in including particular film icons in his plays, Ludlam stated:

It is a tool for understanding what we are doing, the kind of things we are doing. You see, even if you imitate another actor—unless you are an impressionist—even if you try to imitate him absolutely, what comes out will be original. You can't do it. So I think learning from other actors is useful, especially when you use them as a reference for a completely different type of thing. It is a question of collaging them in a new way…. Mae West never made a movie with Gene Kelly.[30]

Ludlam's dramaturgical style is committed to the notion that something new can be made by mixing varied references to already existing material.

The reference to Maria Montez in *Big Hotel*, in particular, is key, as she was a force throughout the Ridiculous scene. Ronald Tavel, Jack Smith, Ethyl Eichelberger, and John Vaccaro all mentioned her as an influence on their work or an aspect of their aesthetic at some point in their discussions of their Ridiculous creations. Ludlam was no exception; in this play he created "the so-called 'Cobra Cunt Ceremony,' which referred to *Cobra Woman*, the Maria Montez cult classic.[31] The scene was designed in homage to Montez as a High Priestess—portrayed in *Big Hotel* by [drag performer] Mario Montez—who selected sacrificial subjects to be thrown down a volcano."[32]

This scene allowed for the involvement of lots of "performers" and "artists," or, more precisely, anyone who happened to be around for a particular performance.[33] This production, though considered uneven by Joseph LeSueur in his *Village Voice* review, did include "a wildly imaginative theatrical effect [that] makes the climactic, otherwise disappointing Babylonian sequence worth waiting for."[34] I assume that LeSueur is referring to the "Cobra Cunt Ceremony" that Kaufman described, as the stage directions for it call for "MOFONGA [the Maria Montez role] *dances wildly, seriously pointing to each member of the cast in turn. When selected, the actor screams, 'No, I don't want to be a dishwasher,' and is thrown into the flames of the Firepit Restaurant by perfumed slaves with oiled bodies. Finally, all are sacrificed, and the slaves too throw themselves into the flames.*"[35] If done with any theatrical flare—and what Ridiculous play would not be—then this scene would not only be a spectacular on-stage effect but also a fairly realistic rendering, even if a parody, of the climax of Maria Montez's famous film *Cobra Woman*.

In light of this evocation of screen goddesses and their films in his plays, Ludlam claims in *Scourge of Human Folly* that one of the motivations behind his style was to engage audiences in new ways. One method for this was creating a collage-style play like *Big Hotel*; the lines could be "put together in different ways every night to see how they could work."[36] In this way, the audience was forced to actively think their way through what they were seeing. Ludlam admitted that, to a spectator, the plot would be unclear: "We knew what the plot was, but I don't know if the audience did."[37] It would be up to those in attendance to attempt to make meaning out of that which they saw, to impose narrative to the series of vignettes.

Ludlam, however, wanted to take his interaction with audiences even further, especially since he was creating a work of theatre that indulged their shared cultural past. This direct engagement with the audience was what made the worship of the cultural ghosts in the Ridiculous unique from the ghosting that happens throughout world drama. Ludlam would "pull people in off the street and shove them up on stage."[38] He was asking his audiences to participate in some way, whether that was by literally volunteering as a performer in the worship scene, or as a spectator at a ritual, who is never quite passive, as the religious proceedings include all in attendance. Ludlam states, "Our goal was that the audience would become part of the theatre, that the theatre would expand to encompass the world. It was almost a religious idea."[39] These early Ludlam plays were rituals as much as they were plays and what they honored was the cinema culture of the early to mid–20th century with which these individuals had grown up.

Theme is not what is valued in *Big Hotel*; performance and spectacle are. The play is preoccupied with theatre and, because of this self-awareness, can be seen as metatheatrical. The characters of this play are, to a large degree, recycled from elsewhere, be that Goethe's *Faust* or *Sunset Boulevard*. Because of this, they draw attention away from any sort of "reality" of this hotel and throw into relief the fact that this is a performance. As Carlson elucidates, "Like the recycling of narratives, the recycling of characters is based upon an assumption that the theatre audience is itself recycled, an assemblage of people who, like the ghostly king, are 'appearing here again tonight' and thus carrying in their collective memory the awareness that drives the theatre experience."[40] As the performers are aware that they are in a drama, the audience in turn is aware that what they are seeing is a fiction, one built from stories and characters of which they are aware from other sources. Metatheatricality is a key component of Ridiculous theatre; all of the artists considered here were interested in breaking with Realism as a form of theatrical representation. In its place, they were interested in exploring performance as an artistic mode in and of itself, not as a representation of some sort of objective or observable reality.

In his work, Ludlam was willing to use elements of popular culture, sampling and remixing them (and celebrating them) in order to make something original. Roemer, for one, suggests that *Big Hotel* "has no meaning behind it and was not intended as political or social statement; it must be taken at face value."[41] Although I agree that this is not an explicitly political drama, what it is able to accomplish in its reverence for popular culture and its direct engagement with its community of spectators, could be seen as quite radical in dramatic production. This play "laid the groundwork for the other plays to come" insofar as it suggested that any and all popular culture references were sensible source material for a drama and that anyone and everyone in attendance for a performance has an active role to play.

By using their plays to worship the icons of their particular cultural past—as products of the film-going middle-class America of the mid–20th century—Ridiculous artists like Ludlam were able to give value to the popular, which was otherwise overlooked in the "high art" strata of culture. As Carlson notes, "The simultaneous attraction to and fear of the dead, the need continually to rehearse and renegotiate the relationship with memory and the past, is nowhere more specifically expressed in human culture than in theatrical performance."[42] In these forgotten Ridiculous productions, the characters from 20th-century film are transferred to the stage and receive their due worship. The ghosts of the particular fascinations of the gay male community—such as Maria Montez—are able to be "archived" in this queer way, given new life on stage through Ridiculous play-making. Although these icons would exist perpetually on film, these productions provided the Ridiculous artists a chance to embody these personalities and bring them physically to life on stage. Culture is not divided into "high" and "low" in these Ridiculous plays; everything is worthy both of being honored and, of course, of being mocked.

Remixing in the Ridiculous: Le Bourgeois Avant-Garde, How to Write a Play, The Artificial Jungle

Ludlam saw his Ridiculous form as "an adventure, an exploration of the irrational deliberately unfashionable."[43] As a playwright, Ludlam took on the task of celebrating elements of culture that had otherwise been derided or eschewed in the intellectual theatre. Indeed, throughout the duration of Ridiculous play-making, borrowing from all aspects of the cultural landscape was a key component of their dramaturgy. References to high art—like the Faust sequence at the start of Big Hotel—were consistently blended with "low" culture references, like Maria Montez's B-movie Cobra Woman. Big Hotel was an early version of remixing, using pastiche as a style of dramaturgy. Many lines are derived from outside sources and can be traced back to those sources. By being blended together, all of these references create a unique original artistic product, such as in the concept behind musical and new media remixing.

This type of play making, what I call "Ridiculous remix," would become a mainstay at the Play-House of the Ridiculous, where Big Hotel was first performed and where Charles Ludlam began his career. Ludlam, too, would continue to experiment with forms of adaptation, quotation, and pastiche in his plays for the Ridiculous Theatrical Company for the duration of his career. All of his plays have at least one major reference to another work and are sprinkled with allusions to other cultural elements. This practice can be understood as radical; not only did Ludlam allow elements of so-called low culture into his plays, he constructed works in which they were valued, even worshipped, alongside of, or in place of, more highly respected cultural products.

That being said, by the last decade of Ludlam's career, he was creating much more strictly plotted farces than the plays in the sweeping collage style of *Big Hotel*. This "late style" (I consider it late both because it came at the end of Ludlam's life and because it appears to be a culmination of the aspects of his earlier theatrical experiments) shows Ludlam moving toward a more farcical vein, using more "highbrow" references, mixed with "lowbrow" allusions. By this time a style known as Ridiculous Theatre had begun to emerge; in a 1976 profile of Ludlam, the author notes "anarchic humor, non sequitors, broad farce, good and bad jokes, bawdiness both verbal and visual, and breakneck pacing" as all being elements "that one generally associates with the Theater of the Ridiculous."[44] By the 1980s, this format had been entirely synthesized into a coherent method for writing comedies. A play like *Le Bourgeois Avant-Garde*, for example, is less a Ridiculous mockery of the Molière comedy *Le Bourgeois Gentilhomme*, and more a contemporary adaptation of it.

This play, along with *How to Write a Play*, a briefly performed, but tightly constructed and highly comical work, as well as Ludlam's final completed drama, *The Artificial Jungle*, exhibit a flowering of the form of dramaturgy that began with the pastiche dramas of the Play-House of the Ridiculous into a true method for creating play scripts. *How to Write a Play*, it seems, both mocks the idea of creating a Ridiculous Theatre play while exploring what might actually be the method for doing so. *The Artificial Jungle*, on the other hand, is an exemplar of what this method of play-making can create, a perfect blend of a literary classic—*Thérèse Raquin*—and a Hollywood film—*Double Indemnity*—into a unique and tightly plotted original play, punctuated here and there with references to other works. Not only, then, does this play serve as Ludlam's final drama but it also suggests what Ludlam's Ridiculous Theatre might have become, if he had lived long enough to break into the mainstream theatre.

These three plays expose the development of "Ridiculous remix" from the broad stroke pastiche-style of playwriting used in *Big Hotel* to the methodical plot structuring of *The Artificial Jungle*. In a sense, Ludlam's dramaturgy builds on practices of "remediation," as defined by J. David Bolter and Richard Grusin. In their book of that title, they argue, "The process of remediation makes us aware that all media are at one level a 'play of signs.' Media have the same claim to reality as more tangible cultural artifacts; photographs, films, and computer applications are as real as airplanes and buildings."[45] Indeed, for Ludlam, films in particular are the cornerstones for art-making; his plays all include some reference to Hollywood cinema within them. Yet

Ludlam takes this interest in media a step further, remixing these elements into a unique, original product.

I am applying the term "remix" here in the way in which it is used in musical and Internet studies. Robert K. Logan, in his section on "Remix Culture" in *Understanding New Media: Extending Marshall McLuhan*, expands upon the Wikipedia definition of remix which "defines a remix as 'an alternate mix of a song made using the techniques of audio editing'" by adding "the contemporary practice of creating new cultural artifacts by remixing prior cultural elements to create something new."[46] Basically, a remix creates a unique artistic work from the works of others, like Ludlam building his play on the plot of a Hollywood film and filling it up with characters and lines borrowed from all over the cultural map, as he did in *Big Hotel*. In his later plays, Ludlam engages in a much more precise remixing practice; he uses one or two major works as the basis for the plot line, and then mixes that story with all sorts of other references. Unlike in *Big Hotel*, in a work like *Le Bourgeois Avant-Garde*, he does not allow the story to meander. Rather, he focuses on the development of one major plot and maybe one or two subplots, as opposed to many individual character threads.

In light of this tighter dramaturgy, it may seem that the Ridiculous loses its radical edge. Yet, Quinton proposes a "new theory" that "the Ridiculous is not self-conscious. It wants to comment on the world."[47] How better to contribute to that process of commenting than to do so on one's own style of work? In *How to Write a Play*, Ludlam "remixes" the entire idea of the Ridiculous, putting it up for mockery as much as any of the content covered throughout his Ridiculous plays themselves. In this work, the driving narrative is that of a man named Charles who needs to write a play and it is remixed with all of the crazy distractions that will ultimately serve as the source material for his drama. Ludlam was sophisticated enough of a playwright not only to remix elements of the surrounding culture but even to remix the little sliver of culture which he was in the process of creating.

Finally, Ludlam's *The Artificial Jungle* seems most indicative of late style composition, as articulated by Joseph N. Straus in "Disability and 'Late Style' in Music," at least insofar as late style is meant to link modes of artistic production with the creator's own debilitating physical and/or mental state. Ludlam became very ill after the opening of the production of what would become his final full-length play; it is hard not to draw parallels between his condition due to AIDS and the nihilistic content of this play. Yet I believe his late style began to develop as early as the mid–1980s, with *Le Bourgeois Avant-Garde*. Late style, for Ludlam, did not mean depicting his illness on stage; rather, it meant moving away from the sweeping epic collage style of his early works toward a more tightly plotted, and more accessible, while still heavily metatheatrical, style of farce.

Le Bourgeois Avant-Garde

For Ludlam, remixing was a marker of his dramatic style from the beginning; there is no denying that *Big Hotel*, in addition to being ghosted by the cultural past to which it pays homage, is also constructed from borrowed ideas layered together to create something original. However, Ludlam did not stick to this sort of dramaturgy for long. As early as 1970, he began writing more tightly plotted works, beginning with *Bluebeard*. This play, as well as every subsequent play Ludlam wrote, still heavily relied on references to other works. Yet, these plays also focused around a central plot line, with specific characters whose actions drove the plot forward, as opposed to the coterie of characters found in Ludlam's earliest works.

The shift in style toward the use of a tightly structured and developed plot would reach its apogee by 1983; in that year, Ludlam wrote a well-structured, straightforward, Ridiculous adaptation of Molière's *Le Bourgeois Gentilhomme* entitled *Le Bourgeois Avant-Garde*. It is clear that Ludlam took much care in crafting this play; there are numerous versions of the script amongst his papers as well as annotated pages from Molière's original.[48] Being true to his source material was obviously very important to Ludlam as he crafted this daring and hilarious commentary on the artistic community of the era in which Ludlam and his Ridiculous Theatrical Company were creating their work. In his feature on Ludlam for the *New York Times* in 1983, the same year that this play first opened, entitled "The Eccentric World of Charles Ludlam," Sam Shirakawa highlights how this play both pokes fun at the contemporary art scene while still allowing Ludlam the space in which to innovate. Shirakawa writes, "But while the play roundly sends up the strained but vapid innovations of some of the SoHo gallery crowd, Mr. Ludlam himself contends that there is not nearly enough innovation in contemporary theater."[49]

Le Bourgeois Avant-Garde is a quintessential example of the Ridiculous style at its most polished and one of Ludlam's more acclaimed productions. Among the accolades that Ludlam received, one is a citation from the *Villager* for *Le Bourgeois Avant-Garde*, which reads, "A dazzling romp through Molière's comedy which probably had the master's ghost dancing through the halls of the Comédie Française with delight at this cutting satire of cultural pretension."[50] Ludlam's great success here is in being true to the spirit of the original, using the same sort of satirical edge that Molière used to mock the bourgeoisie to take on his own era's pretentious community of experimental art aficionados. This play is metatheatric, filled with references to other works, and imbued with high-spirited celebration.

In this play, it is art and its creation, especially experimental forms, which are being mocked; in the opening sequence a Composer and a Choreographer split hairs over definitions of artistic movements. When the

Composer asks, "You mean you are a Futurist?" the Choreographer replies, "No, the future was over by the early thirties." The Composer then proclaims, "Well I am a *Post*postmodernist."[51] The debate is a clever mockery of the categorization of art and artists and the sometimes seemingly arbitrary distinctions among artistic movements. Ludlam's last note in a collection of documents associated with this play's construction is a scrap of paper with one word on it: "Post Talent."[52] Ludlam clearly saw that innovation also can be a clever disguise for a lack of actual artistic ability.

This critique of the avant-garde is key to making sense of Theatre of the Ridiculous more broadly. While I am arguing that the Ridiculous form was theatrically innovative and experimental, Ludlam himself was very vocal about being anti-avant-garde. He had his own understanding of what the term "avant-garde" meant and did not associate his own practice with it; in his own papers, he writes, "I am considered avant-garde but I don't consider myself avant-garde. The avant-garde is ahead of its times and I am of my time, of the perfect moment."[53] From this perspective, Ridiculous Theatre is meant to be *of* its time, providing a commentary on the norms and ideals of that particular era.

In addition to presenting cutting contemporary commentary, however, this play is also a faithful modernization of the Molière work. Instead of finding a middle-class man aspiring to the upper class, Ludlam's comfortably middle-class Mr. Foufas wishes to be "avant-garde," to be on the cutting edge of art and culture. To this end, he, too, wishes to better his position by marrying off his daughter to someone of the class to which he aspires. As with the Molière play, with the help of a nosy servant and some hijinks, the truth is revealed and the young woman is reunited with her rightful love.

By bringing in references to so much of the experimental scene, most of which "is abstract," Ludlam was able "to illustrate his opinion by showing that [avant-garde art] doesn't really mean anything at all and is, more often than not, pure pretense."[54] For example, Mr. Foufas is asked to "deconstruct" a letter, basically to approach it as one would a Dadaist poem, in which the order of words is meaningless. Mr. Foufas ends up with "'Beautiful—your—eyes—for—dying—am—of—I—fair—love—mistress,'"[55] a mix of words rendered meaningless by their lack of meaningful order. Much of the avant-garde and its artistic "pieces" are exposed for what they are—nonsense—as are their critics, pompous know-it-alls who actually don't know much of anything.

In addition to this mocking of the avant-garde (in a sense, a gesture of taking something considered "high art" and disparaging it as if it were low), Ludlam is also able to "blend" other cultural references into his "Ridiculous remix." Most of these, however, tend toward "high culture," such as references to Peter Brook and his imaginary language Orghast or a reference to the

"Black Mountain School," a nod to John Cage's educational institution, Black Mountain College. Although there are some off-color jokes, such as references to flatulence,[56] the overall work is faithfully rendered as a jab at the experimental art scene told through the framework of the Molière farce.

This work is a classic example of Ridiculous remix, if not for the way that it blends high cultural and low cultural references but for the ways in which it mixes academic aims—exposing the silliness of the avant-garde and exploring how a 17th-century work might be relevant to the contemporary moment—with the usual sorts of joyful elements—word play, topical references, and slapstick—built into the Ridiculous Theatre as a form. For Frank Rich, in his *New York Times* review, "'Le Bourgeois Avant-Garde' bills itself as 'a comedy after Molière,' and that's about the only line of the evening that's not a joke."[57] Rich recognizes that this is a play for theatre insiders, while being willing to mock those for whom it is designed. Rich writes, "If you're not up on the latest tides in theater and dance performance art, you may get lost. If you are in the know, you may be offended—which is, of course, the point."[58] Kaufman agrees that this play is principally designed to poke fun: "As with all of Ludlam's work, this division of aesthetic goals embodies a conundrum: Serious intentions are leavened—if not disguised—by the overriding conceit of the Ridiculous, which begins with inversions, ends in paradox, and, in the process, mocks all that it surveys, including the Ridiculous itself."[59]

How to Write a Play

In *How to Write a Play* (1984), Ludlam is able to deconstruct (without losing meaning) his own process of play making, bringing to light the true "ridiculosity," to borrow Roemer's term, of Ridiculous play construction. Indeed, Ridiculous play construction is a unique form of writing. As was the case with *Big Hotel*, it can involve stringing together quotations and references, or, as in *Le Bourgeois Avant-Garde*, it can implement techniques of adaptation, such as pastiche and parody. *How to Write a Play* presents a wholly different form of Ridiculous remix, one that takes on the task of remixing the Ridiculous itself. The premise of the play is simple: a character named Charles is under pressure to complete a play and is continuously distracted by crazy occurrences, such as a millionaire who has fallen in love with Charles in the guise of alter-ego Galas[60] and wishes to express his devotion to the beautiful woman he saw in that play or a dancer wishing to show off her "bump and grind" skills as an audition for Charles's company, that interrupt his process.

This play not only squeezes in an incredible number of jokes, but many of the jokes poke fun at Ludlam, his style, and his plays, as opposed to anything from the surrounding culture. Charles begins by indulging his own tools of procrastination, perhaps a jab at his own actual playwriting procedure, and then interacts with Everett, meant to be Everett Quinton, Ludlam's lover and collaborator for the last years of his life. When asked to choose a fabric, Charles picks one and is told by Everett: "Good. I'll use the other." The point of this distraction? Everett explains, "Because you have absolutely no taste. And if you like it, then the other one must be the right choice."[61] Ludlam is willing to mock himself in this play, as well as his process, his style, and even his taste in costumes. Nothing in the Ridiculous is above mockery, not even the artists themselves.

The series of events that follow are entirely ridiculous. For example, one encounter involves a woman reunited with her husband, delightfully named Ima Poussy, for the first time in fifteen years, who, rather than berating him for leaving her, exclaims, "Fifteen years ago you went out to buy a bottle of horseradish for the gefilte fish and you never came back! I've been waiting, Ima. It's been a long time to be without horseradish. Where is the horseradish, Ima?"[62] What is the most important thing here? Not the marriage, but the condiment. Almost every moment is played for a punchline and the ensuing party of the cast of crazy characters is as "absolute" as "farce" can be, in light of the play's subtitle, "An Absolute Farce." Just as two tramps in Samuel Beckett's classic *Waiting for Godot* repeatedly recall they are "waiting for Godot," Charles consistently reminds those around him that he needs to write a play. Yet, this play is not focused on the action—it is not called "Writing a Play"—but, rather, on the instructions for completing such an activity. This work could almost be seen as a model, a manifesto in its own right, for how one might go about constructing a work of Ridiculous drama.

How to Write a Play is remembered as one of Ludlam's "more solid and delightful farces," though it was not much performed in his lifetime; "*How to Write a Play* never opened for review. Its three historical performances were attended predominantly by the company's most die-hard fans."[63] In reviewing Everett Quinton's 1993 revival of the piece for the *New York Times*, Frank Rich implicitly likens its plot to the early *Big Hotel*, describing "a steady parade of interlopers who insist on knocking on the exasperated hero's door as he tries and fails to write his play" in place of a forward-moving, narrative-driven plot. Rich finds the meaning in this strange assortment of characters and their associated gags; he writes, "'How to Write a Play' finds its greatest pleasure in celebrating the sheer artificiality of theater and the infinite ways its oldest and hoariest devices … can be revivified by fresh inspiration."[64] The play is, of course, about the writing of plays, both a metatheatrical reflection on the form of theatre art but also a metafictional recreation of Ludlam's actual writing process.

"Metatheatricality" as a practice and concept is key to understanding Ridiculous Theatre. According to Patricia Waugh, "*Metafiction* is a term given to fictional writing which self-consciously and systematically draws attention to its status as an artefact [*sic*] in order to pose questions about the relationship between fiction and reality. In providing a critique of their own methods of construction, such writings not only examine the fundamental structures of narrative fiction, they also explore the possible fictionality of the world outside the literary fictional text."[65] "Metafiction," then, is creative written work that it is aware that it is made up, aware of its own status as a creative product. With this knowledge, the work is able to analyze the form in which it was created through its content. Ludlam employed this technique in his plays, working in a form that is usually described as "metatheatrical," or called "metatheatre," building on Lionel Abel's seminal 1963 work of that title. For Waugh, "terms like … 'metatheatre' are a reminder of what has been, since the 1960s, a more general cultural interest in the problem of how human beings reflect, construct and mediate their experience of the world."[66] Indeed, Ludlam's plays expose a desire to use theatre not only to contemplate topics of interest to the playwright, but to theorize about the form of theatre and the process of making it as well. A play like *How to Write a Play* is as much preoccupied with understanding the form of Ridiculous Theatre as it is any other element within it.

This play might be difficult to revive now, as it is so embedded in both the culture of the Ridiculous (the references to plays like *Salammbô* and *Galas*, both written by Ludlam) and the personage of Ludlam himself (his relationship with Everett, for example, or the fact that his drag was never convincing). Still, the script explores the real possibilities of the Ridiculous by remixing the Ridiculous as a style. It shows that anything, even the form itself, can and should be turned on its head and laughed at. Ludlam states as the first axiom of his manifesto: "If one is not a living mockery of one's own ideals, one has set one's ideals too low."[67] No play better uses remix to exemplify this than *How to Write a Play*. When Charles realizes, "I'm completely dry. I'm burned out. It's writer's block. I haven't got an idea in my head! There've just been too many distractions!" Everett reminds him, "Why don't you just write about all the distractions and interruptions that happen to you when you're trying to write a play?" "That's a brilliant idea! I'll do it," cries Charles,[68] because nothing is more Ridiculous than real life.

The Artificial Jungle

By the mid–1980s, as can be seen in both *Le Bourgeois Avant-Garde* and *How to Write a Play*, Ludlam had moved toward a form of dramaturgy that was preoccupied with remixing, but in a strict climactic, narrative, linear structure. Building on that tradition, and becoming the culmination of it, as it would be Ludlam's last complete play, 1987's *The Artificial Jungle* is perhaps the most tightly plotted drama that Ludlam ever created, being true to both its sources and its overall nihilistic tone. Here the remix of sources is much clearer than perhaps anywhere else in Ludlam's oeuvre; as Frank Rich notes in his *New York Times* review, "'The Artificial Jungle' is Mr. Ludlam's omnibus reply to 'Double Indemnity,' 'The Postman Always Rings Twice' and 'Little Shop of Horrors'—with a little of Zola's *Thérèse Raquin* tossed in for added kicks in Act II."[69] The elements borrowed from each are fairly clear: Chester Nurdiger owns a pet shop with his wife, Roxanne, who falls in love with ne'er-do-well Zachary Slade. The two plot to kill Chester, as the couple does in *The Postman Always Rings Twice*, in order to cash in a life insurance policy on him, as in *Double Indemnity*. They commit murder by suffocating Chester and throwing him to the piranhas, which operate much like the carnivorous plant of *Little Shop of Horrors*. When the second act begins, the two seem to have gotten away with their crime, until Chester's mother, Mrs. Nurdiger, overhears them and is then rendered mute by the trauma she has just witnessed, as in *Thérèse Raquin*. Slade and Roxanne are overcome with the guilt of their crime and their romance is destroyed. By the end of the play, only Mrs. Nurdiger's eyes remain alive on stage. As this plot summary makes clear, this is a tightly knit *noir*-style melodrama with comical hijinks sprinkled throughout. Its climactic structure fixates on this small pool of characters, all clearly linked with one another by the action, and it does not meander in time, place, or story.

Ridiculous remix, then, can be said to have evolved from the early pastiche plays—*Big Hotel*, we recall, was originally nothing more than a notebook full of Ludlam's favorite film quotations—to being a seamless blend of varied source material, whether great literature or Hollywood cinema or classical drama, in order to create a unique dramatic work. In addition, however, we find something in *The Artificial Jungle* heretofore not seen in Ludlam's plays: a nihilistic approach to life. This seems to contradict Ludlam's stated "Aim: To get beyond nihilism by revaluing combat."[70] Rather than fighting his fate, Slade commits suicide, uttering words from Albert Camus's *The Stranger*, a classic work in the Absurdist vein: "I'm dying. And I look up at the stars, the thousand unseeing eyes that look back on this little speck of dust we call the world, and I ask—What was my crime compared to your indifference. I committed a senseless murder. But in its very senselessness it is in harmony with the universe, which is itself senseless and ultimately stupid. In an aeon or two, who will be left to accuse me?"[71] These lines show an acceptance of death, as well as the idea that what a person has done during his or her lifetime ultimately carries no weight. In a few generations, no one will remember what that person did or, most likely, even that such an individual ever existed at all.

This particular "remixed" element contradicts Ludlam's own description of his work, insofar as it related to the Theatre of the Absurd that preceded it.[72] Ludlam explains, "The Absurdists got bogged down in their own nihilism. We represent a positive nihilism, like the kind you find in Buddhism. Instead of negating anything we try to find its inherent value."[73] According to Ludlam's Ridiculous, then, life may be meaningless, but this fact should be a source of enjoyment, a way to justify finding as much pleasure in life as possible. Ludlam found the Absurd presentation of the meaninglessness of the world to be lacking; Ludlam points out, "Modern art up through Beckett is the reduction of form—the elimination of things. There's no way to go beyond Beckett, because you can't get any more minimal. You reduce and reduce until there's nothing.... I'm moving in the other direction, to a maximal, more baroque vision."[74] Ludlam was looking to create a universe full—in fact, almost overflowing—with things: both physical and linguistic. He wanted a world where conflict mattered and actions had meaning and significance.

This breaking with earlier theoretical concerns could signal that this work is a "late-style" piece from Charles Ludlam. A work can be designated as late style when it comes late in the timeline of an artist's career and is noticeably different in style or structure from the artist's earlier work. Late style is a concept often considered in music, in instances where a composer's last works differ significantly in content or structure from his or her earlier creative work. Yet, this notion of late style seems applicable in the dramatic arts, specifically in Ludlam's case. In "Disability and 'Late Style' in Music," Joseph N. Straus argues "that in the end *there may be nothing late about late style* in the sense of chronological age, the approach of life's end, or authorial or historical belatedness. Rather, late style may in some cases be more richly understood as *disability* style: a perspective composers may adopt at any age, often in response to a personal experience of disability."[75]

There are various markers present in a musical work considered late style, including "bodily features (fractured, fissured, compact, or immobilized) and certain mental and emotional states (introverted, detached, serene, irascible)."[76] In short, the music is analyzed and described in ways similar to the manner in which human conditions are considered. Ludlam uses a number of these elements in *The Artificial Jungle*; the play is structurally "barer, simpler, more attenuated" than earlier works; it uses a "direct and intimate mode of communication"; the characters to some degree are "introspective"; the construction of dialogue is "simplified" from the nature of the collage plays; there is a "direct" quality to the way in which the play deals with its existential theme.[77] The combination of these elements in a musical composition would mark it, in Straus's understanding, as a late style piece. Therefore, if Straus's methodology is used when reading a dramatic text, these same elements could be applied in order to categorize this play as a late work.

In Straus's concept of late style, the changes in musical composition are meant to be reflections of an artist's changing relationship to his or her sense of physical or mental ability because of some debilitating disorder. Straus explains how this reflection of personal concerns through the form of one's artistic creation is rendered in musical composition:

> We might simply assume that late-style works may involve internal contradictions, so that inherent tensions among these different characteristics are themselves a marker of stylistic lateness.... The traits associated with late style are largely evocative of disabled or impaired bodies or minds and their failure to function in a normal way. Many of the characteristics of late style suggest nonnormative physical, mental, or emotional states, and even specific disorders.[78]

Straus is describing the ways in which the musical elements that make up late style compositions mirror the realities of certain ailments afflicting the composers, whether these disabilities are physical, mental, or emotional. By looking closely at Ludlam's final dramatic work, there seem to be echoes of the AIDS crisis, as well as Ludlam's fear of his own mortality, reflected in the thematic elements that the play highlights.

Obviously, this is different from the kind of late style that Straus is suggesting; there is not apparent awareness on Ludlam's part of his ailment, though he may have had a fear of the disease. Thematically, though, *The Artificial Jungle* seems a departure from a sense of "positive nihilism" or a "baroque vision" that Ludlam stated to be his aims. The connection between the nihilistic feeling of this play and Ludlam's rapid decline in health and eventual death cannot be dismissed. Unlike the composers of which Straus writes in his "Late Style" essay, Ludlam did not construct *The Artificial Jungle* while being overcome with illness or disability. He would not officially be diagnosed as HIV-positive until November 1986, and the play had already opened in September of that year. As Kaufman recognizes, "Even though *The Artificial Jungle* was written and produced before Ludlam was diagnosed with AIDS, irony topples over irony when one recognizes just how much his last play appears to be addressing the status of his own health."[79] Ludlam was not writing about being sick, or "disabled," as the composers discussed in Straus's article may have been.

Unlike Aaron Copland, Straus's object of study, who wrote a late style composition while entirely aware of his impending loss of memory due to the onset of Alzheimer's, Ludlam did not write *The Artificial Jungle* as a response to his HIV-status. Kaufman reminds, "No one, including Ludlam, realized that he was already infected with the HIV virus, and that his condition would rapidly deteriorate over the course of the winter and the run of the play."[80] Ludlam may have reflected on themes and used structural elements that, retrospectively, seem to be musings on his physical decline, but he did not do so as a means to deal with AIDS, as he was not yet aware that he had the disease. However, there is the possibility that Ludlam could have suspected that he was sick or feared that he might get sick. The onset of the AIDS crisis in the 1980s would have made a preoccupation with mortality even more pronounced for Ludlam—people, especially those who were part of his extended downtown New York community, were dying. Although Ludlam was not sick when he wrote this play, AIDS had entered the cultural consciousness by this time, and certainly could have affected his selections of material. It is possible that Ludlam could have been remixing these fictional narratives with his experience of the world at this time, expressing his thoughts on what was happening through his choice of source material.

The Artificial Jungle is significantly different from Ludlam's earlier plays; its nihilistic tone sets it apart from other works that Ludlam wrote and suggests an inadvertent late style on his part. Still, its use of Ridiculous remix is remarkable; it suggests that this "late style" had begun its development as early as the beginning of the decade and only flourished fully in his last work. In his final play, Ludlam shows where Ridiculous playwriting may have gone if he had lived longer: there may have been more tightly constructed farces built from the perfect blending of sources that vary in cultural cache in order to reflect directly on the temper of the times.

Mashing Up Gender: Camille

Indeed, throughout the various Ridiculous sites—and even the larger Downtown Scene of which they were a part—plays were being constructed from mixing together references from other sources. The Ridiculous, however, added a key ingredient to this blending process; in addition to remixing cultural elements in their plays, they also included gendered identities that came across as being similarly remixed. Every Ridiculous performance included some form of cross-dressing. This "drag" performance was not merely men dressing as women or vice versa. It was a more complicated, and potentially radical, statement on the ways in which gender should not be seen as innate. A character's gender, in a Ridiculous play, is merely another aspect to be put on and performed. In this way, Ridiculous gender performance throws into relief the idea that within all individuals there is the possibility for any and all gender characteristics.

To achieve this end, crossdressing and playing against biological sex was often not a perfect transformation in a Ridiculous play. Rather, as Ronald Argelander argues:

staged transvestism or theatrical sexual role-switching has been treated in countless plays, films, and community "firehouse" reviews as a comic reaffirmation of strict sexual role division. "Drag" is denigrated by showing how impossible it is for a man to successfully create the role of a woman (and vice versa) except for the purpose of derisive laughter. At the Theatre of the Ridiculous, the laughter is not derisive. They entertain the idea that strict biological/social sexual division may be a cruel joke that nature/society is playing on humanity. For them, and in their performances, pansexuality is a reality.[81]

In fact, Ridiculous performers regularly avoided trying to pretend they were the opposite gender. Instead, they practiced a form of gender play that I call "gender mashup" because, like the contemporary Internet form known as mashup, this mixing allows its sources to be layered, as opposed to being blended, and even to be evident to the viewer.

Mashups are a unique form of created content in "the world of music and the world of web programming."[82] Yet, I believe that this term can have wider artistic application, so that it can include theatrical practices like the one through which Ludlam and other Ridiculous artists created cross-dressed characters on stage. For Brett O'Connor, "a musical mashup typically involves combining two or more different songs, often from very different musical genres, into one, resulting in an entirely different musical composition" and "a mashup in the computing world usually involves two or more web applications or parts of web applications combined to make something new."[83] In both of these cases, as in remix, combining elements of other works creates a new work. However, in the case of mashup, it is usually the mixing of two disparate elements that creates the final work, as opposed to a blend of a myriad of references, as in Ridiculous remix.

Gender mashup, then, is a construction built of two genders—usually male and female, though performance artists like Ethyl Eichelberger would complicate this mixture further—in which a new character is created from the blending of the two. This differs from traditional cross-dressing, a marker of world performance for centuries, in that there is usually no attempt to the fool the audience into believing that the performer *is* the other gender; he or she is only playing *at* it for the duration of the performance. In an interview with Ridiculous Theatrical Company collaborator Lola Pashalinski, Ludlam responds to her question "Why then insist on transsexual casting?" by saying, "Well, I believe that personality is an artifice and I think that role playing is the eternal message of the theater, it's its most profound theme. For us I think it wasn't so much that we took on wrong roles because of sexual identification but that we refused to take on any role, we wouldn't be one or the other sex because we saw that it was artificial, because we didn't make the clear conventional identification."[84] The Ridiculous artists made this abundantly clear; Ludlam's performance in *Camille*, for example, involved him allowing his chest hair to show above the neckline of Marguerite's fancy gowns.

This sort of playing with gender was different from the drag perform-ance that is associated with Ridiculous contemporaries at Andy Warhol's Fac-tory. Drag superstars Candy Darling and Jackie Curtis, for instance, not only worked in drag on stage; they lived in drag outside of the theatre. Ludlam found this practice problematic, though he enjoyed on-stage drag performing. Of Candy and Jackie, he writes:

> You give a performance and come offstage, and you've got to get into yourself and rest, reconstruct your own true personality again, indulge it. Only then can you go back and play the role again. But once you start playing the fantasy twenty-four hours a day, you may have obliterated your personality on a more or less permanent basis. A mask can be a protection to preserve what's inside, but in the case of Jackie and Candy—particularly of Candy—they were always being overly generous with others, giving so much they didn't leave anything for themselves.[85]

For Ludlam, drag was a performance mode, a way to create a character for the duration of a play. Ludlam may have misread how Jackie and Candy understood their own identities—rather than indulging a fantasy, they may have been asserting their actual gender identity—but Ludlam maintained that his cross-gendered work was only meant for the stage, not the real world.

Ludlam did regularly perform in drag; in *Big Hotel*, he played Norma Desmond, both as realistic film icon and as mockery of that type. Yet, in his second play, *Conquest of the Universe*, he would leave the drag performing to other players of the company and instead played the tyrannical leader. To call Ludlam simply a "drag performer" is a misrepresentation of his career; he performed male roles in the Ridiculous Theatrical Company productions more often than female ones. In fact, Quinton admits that he's "played more drag roles than Charles did."[86] Ludlam's contribution to acting was not his ability to perform in drag; rather, it was his profound understanding of how to blend realistic Stanislavskian acting methods with techniques appropriate for playing farce. Quinton describes Ridiculous acting "as walking both sides of the fence in the acting style. Play the story with all the honesty you can muster and then you find ways to lob jokes in."[87] The impact of a play like *Camille*, then, is in its ability to portray the story honestly and with emotion, while punctuating that with humorous bits.

What is striking in Ludlam's choice of parts is not that he often cross-dressed; it is that more often than not, he took the best role for himself, whether that part was male or female. The way gender mashup operates for Ludlam is as much as an ego-stroke for the lead performer/creator as it is as a way for the artists to present a commentary about the performative nature of gender. Returning to the concept of "metatheatre," Mary Ann Frese Witt sees metatheatricality operating in modern plays as a way to draw attention to the "performativity of gender," to borrow from Judith Butler. Witt writes, "Rather than mimetically representing the 'real' world, metatheater calls into question accepted notions of that reality, stressing instead the world's theatricality.... In both the seventeenth and the twentieth centuries, characters in metatheatrical plays show an awareness of themselves as performers, their performance, as it were, betraying their performativity," linking this discussion of theatre drawing attention to itself to Butler's understanding of "gender ... [as] a performance that is performative: the consciousness of gender as performance has the effect of revealing that the notion of it being either essential or foundational is an illusion."[88] Ludlam's performances not only draw attention to the machinations of performing, exposing theatre as a falsehood, but also highlight how this extends to gender, reinforcing the notion that gender is equally as false as any other traits of a performed role.

Because of his experience with Ridiculous remixing, playing Camille was a perfect fit for Ludlam; "Given all its tragic and campy excesses, the subject was a natural choice for Ludlam, who was becoming an expert at recycling what had long been considered culturally effete and turning it into something fresh and viable—or at least outrageous."[89] Indeed, what was most striking about this production was Ludlam's portrayal of the title role. In his review for the *New York Times*, Mel Gussow notes, "This is no facile female impersonation, but a real performance. Ludlam never forgets his gender, and neither do we.... Unlike transvestite actors who play females as if to the manner born, Ludlam in drag remains a clown."[90] Ludlam built on the mixing of culture by adding to it the mixing of gender: "his chest hair, which announced itself prominently beneath the *décolletage* or open neckline of his costume in the opening act" allowed Ludlam to play the role as he saw fit, not to trick people into believing he was something he was not, and to "pioneer the idea that female impersonation could be serious acting."[91] Ludlam was both making an important statement in this performance and indulging his own egotistic desire to play this part. Embedded in this performance of a dying courtesan was both the possibility for radical commentary and an actor's attempt to show off his own chops and receive accolades for them.

Ludlam's choice to perform the role in drag is politically significant. Ludlam himself contemplated the potential power inherent in the tale of *Camille*. He noted, "'Played seriously, "Camille" would be laughed off the stage today—it's so sentimental.... I don't ask to be taken seriously. I invite the audience to laugh at me from the first moment by showing my chest. I'm not tricking them like those female impersonators who take off the wig at the end of the act. Yes, I want the audience to laugh, but they should also get the impact of this forbidden love—it is really tragic and shocking."[92] Ludlam is able to co-opt this story and uncover deeper meaning within it. A key reason for this radical possibility in this performance is Ludlam's use of mashup: his mixture of male and female in the lead role as well as his blending of high tragedy and low comedy in the play's construction.

Camille, adapted by Ludlam and produced by the Ridiculous Theatrical Company in 1973, deals with human mortality. Ludlam's play is an adaptation of the work by Alexandre Dumas *fils* and concludes with the heroine's death, as the original work had. Ludlam himself noted the inherent radical possibility embedded in his Ridiculous, or camp, adaptation of the classic melodramatic text:

> I think my theatre is political, but what is political is perhaps misunderstood. Politics is about spheres of influence, and in that sense it is political.
>
> If a man plays Camille, for instance, you begin to think it's horrible, but in the end you are either moved or won over. You believe in the character beyond the gender of the actor, and no one who has experienced that can go back.
>
> In such cases, this theatre is political in the highest sense of influence. But as far as pushing for political upheaval goes, it's not true to the nature of art. Art is not meant to tear society down, it is meant to enhance it.[93]

Ludlam believes that the political effect of a piece is tied up with how the spectator feels when the work is over. Ludlam claims that he does not believe that art should be used as a tool for altering society, but that art can have a political effect on the individual. Quinton elucidates the power of the potential emotional effect of this play; after recollecting a conversation with Ludlam in which his partner told him that "he was doing the final scene and he heard a pocketbook open and the lady was getting her tissues out because she was crying," he realized that when he "[heard] the pocketbook open" during his own performance of the role in London "that he had achieved this thing that Charles had talked about…. When I heard that pocketbook open, I said, 'oh yes,' I can't tell you if I don't achieve anything in my life beyond that…. I'll always think of that as an accomplishment."[94] Quinton understands the key to this play, the impetus behind its impact, is the emotional reality of the story; the humor is meant to be layered on after.

The political effect of Ludlam's plays is embedded in the emotional power of the dramatic work. If the play can make its audience feel, then it can engage them politically. This is a radical definition of "political" because it is not about any specific political commitment at all. It is a politics that is not embedded in ideology or specifically engaged in debate on currently contested issues. Rather, this is an idea of the political that operates on the individual level, recouping the emotional faculties in place of the intellectual ones as the site of political efficacy. The ending of *Camille* is high tragedy, yet so over-the-top that it can move an audience to complete hysterics, whether they are of laughter or of tears. Like Ludlam's presentation of gender in his performance of Marguerite, it is a mashup of the tragic and the comic.

This potential for tears, as Ludlam noted, highlights the political capacity of the play. In these Ridiculous plays, meaning is made through the mixing of disparate elements together.

Ludlam's *Camille* is not political in a didactic sense, nor is it protest drama. Rather, it is a dramatic work which creates an emotionally vicarious experience for an audience member, and in so doing, forces its spectators, no matter their predispositions, to mourn the stage death of a man in drag. Consider the power of Marguerite's final speech:

> I am dying, but I am happy too, and it is only my happiness that you can see.... And so you are married!... Look at that.... What a strange life this first one is. What will the second be?... You will be even happier than you were before. Speak of me sometimes, won't you? Armand, give me your hand. Believe me, it's not hard to die. That's strange.... I'm not suffering anymore. I feel better, so much better than I have ever felt before.... I am going to live.[95]

There is a real celebration of life in these final lines; Marguerite is able to find happiness, even in this dark moment. The moment also involves a proclamation of the hope that someone may be remembered after he or she has passed. Yet this hope leads to ultimate despair; the dramatic irony is that the audience knows Marguerite will not survive even though she says she is going to live.

To see the full extent of how these lines can be taken seriously, rather than only as an over-the-top, melodramatic joke, consider them against Marguerite's last lines in the original text:

> And so I am [dying], Nichette. I can smile; for I am happy. You, too, are happy. You are a bride. You will think of me sometimes—will you not? And Gustave, too—you will speak of me together! Armand, come! Your hand! You must not leave me! Armand here, and all my friends! Oh, this is happiness! And Gaston, too! I am so glad you are come! Armand is here, and I am so happy! Oh, how strange!... All the pain is gone! Is this life? Now everything appears to change. Oh, how beautiful! Do not wake me—I am so sleepy![96]

Ludlam's adaptation is not all that different from the text of the Dumas original. Ludlam has co-opted *Camille* for his own Ridiculous aesthetic, but he also has rendered a loving and respectful adaptation of the Dumas text. As Linda Hutcheon points out in her book *Theory of Adaptation*, "An adaptation is a derivation that is not derivative—a work that is second without being secondary."[97] An adapted work can be studied in its relation to the original, but it is worthy also of contemplation in its own right, as it is in no way lesser than its source material. An adapted work of art is still an original artistic creation and therefore exists with its own set of creative objectives and artistic intentions.

In Ludlam's play, then, these beautiful concluding lines, meant to move an audience emotionally, also can operate politically in ways that the Dumas text may not. Ludlam dares his audience to sympathize with his tragic heroine in this moment. By sympathizing, a spectator is forced, however briefly, to reconsider his or her position regarding queer politics. If one could care for this man in drag, why not care for all men in drag? By extension, why not empathize with any individuals who could be identified as queer? This reconsideration of one's position, no matter its ultimate outcome (i.e., no matter if the person actually changes his or her stance) is a political action, as potentially powerful as any lecture drama.

Camille sums up a great deal of the aesthetic elements we associate with Ridiculous Theatre. In an article on the Ridiculous Theatrical Company written for *The New York Times*, Elenore Lester comments about *Camille*:

> This quintessential scene of late-19th century melodrama, with its Beardsley-esque undertones of death and eroticism, is played on a stage so small and crowded with papier mache backdrops it looks like a puppet theatre. Heightening the artifice is Camille with, of all things, a hairy chest, a bulbous nose and a fake falsetto voice. Through this grotesquerie, Charles Ludlam, director-writer-performer and creator of the Ridiculous Theatrical Company, releases the poetry that heretofore has been locked in banality.[98]

In this description, Lester captures a great deal of the Ridiculous performance style and aesthetic. There are elements from different strata of society being presented alongside a character that defies easy gender categorization. This is a classic Ridiculous play and one of Ludlam's masterpieces.

In many ways, *Camille* has been considered not only the apex of Ludlam's Ridiculous drag performance, but of all drag performance of the period. According to Alan Sinfield, "Ludlam, by playing the lead part in drag, transposed it to a gay man's point of view."[99] The idea is that Ludlam was not just playing the part because it was a meaty role that appealed to his sensibilities—what he claimed as the justification for playing it—but also because he was a homosexual man. Rick Roemer agrees, "Ludlam's attraction to this character was, no doubt, steeped in his homosexuality. Like most other gay men, Ludlam was made his entire life to feel like an outcast and a deviant. He felt an identification with and a compassion for Marguerite, who found herself marginalized because of who she was…. This kind of discrimination was something that Ludlam understood very well."[100] These scholars see this drag role as being iconic of Ludlam's desire to expose his own oppression as a gay man through his representation of an oppressed heroine. Chesley builds on this concept to suggest, "Yet in the work of the Ridiculous, as in many other areas of life, a viewpoint informed by a gay sensibility can possibly be seen as offering something of value to *all* people, regardless of sexuality."[101] There may be a quality of these productions that reflects a "gay sensibility," but that point of view is used to get at very universal human concerns, such as love and mortality, in the case of *Camille*.

My impression is that Ludlam was interested in the performance of the role and the effect that it produced on the audience. Of playing Camille, Ludlam states, "If we could only get that first scene of meeting her—that *shock* of meeting her, if you will—over with, then that pre-curtain association with sex as such, of female impersonation as such, might go away, and we could all become involved with the part as a part and the play as a play. It is not a question, really, of what man is playing the hero today or what woman is playing the heroine, but simply what is being played."[102] Ludlam wanted his audiences to value the performance as it was, as opposed to getting caught up in it as drag or what it had to say about gender. Ludlam actually dismisses any dichotomy between the concepts "heterosexual" and "homosexual," stating, "'I would not believe for a minute that we don't have all the possibilities within us,' Ludlam concludes. 'Because acting, theater—*art* would be impossible. There would be no common ground where you could communicate, with images or with anything, to other people.'"[103] Ludlam's claims here remind of David Savran's contention that theatre is "the queerest art": "In comparison with other arts (especially film), theater is queer in part because of its particular mode of address and its uncanny ability to arouse a spectator's mutable and mutating interests."[104] A single performance can reach different people in different ways, allowing a performance to connect with all of its audience members, yet do so individually as well as communally.

Ludlam saw the power in what he was doing in his mashing up of gender. Firstly, he was emphasizing performance above all else; Ludlam describes, "A man or a woman might be better at evoking a specific personality or making a definite point in the play. You get different levels of reality and unreality, and what ultimately happens is that the rigidity with which we look at sexual roles and reversals breaks down."[105] But Ludlam was also aware of what this might insinuate about performance beyond the on-stage space. Ludlam continues, "The most profound theme of the theatre is role-play—that roles are interchangeable, that personality is an artifice in life, and that it can be changed or interchanged. I believe that is the eternal message of the theatre."[106] These gender mashup performances throw into relief the performative nature of gender—and even individual personality—in ways that would not be heavily theorized for at least a decade after they occurred on stage.

Yet, despite the many ways in which this play has been considered groundbreaking in terms of its statements about gender, it is also designed for sheer pleasure. In addition to the use of drag, other elements mark *Camille* as a Ridiculous text. The play involves various *lazzi* and elements of slapstick humor, such as "*GASTON throws a pie in her [Prudence's] face.*"[107] Ludlam's play also is filled with a great deal of word play and jokes built into the dialogue. Playing on the double entendre of the word "faggots" (and taking into account the probable demographic of the audience and the 13th Street, New

York City location of the theatre), Marguerite asks, "Nanine, throw another faggot on the fire," to which Nanine replies, "There are no more faggots in the house." "No faggots in the house?" Marguerite exclaims. "Open the window, Nanine. See if there are any in the street."[108] This verbal repartee breaks the tension of this scene, providing not only comic relief but also a distancing from the emotional intensity of the moment. Ridiculous plays contain some telling markers of their style, such as self-awareness and metatheatricality, gender-bending, an improvisational style, and word play. The plays can be jam-packed with various performance elements and often present a mocking, but good-natured sort of humor.

The meaning of any performance of *Camille* was created specifically by the audience's emotional reaction; in this way, Ludlam continued to tap into the kind of ritual atmosphere created by his performances, which were always ghosted by the surrounding popular culture. Ludlam contends, "When the audience laughed at my pain, the play seemed more tragic to me than when they took it seriously. A solemn audience trivialized the event. This [irony] of *Camille* was the ultimate masochism. I went out there to try and have a happy ending every night and got knocked down by every peripeteia of the plot."[109] The audience's perspective on the play's genre and their subsequent emotional reaction imbued the play with its overall effect. If the viewers could laugh at Marguerite's pain, it proved her lot was more pathetic than if they could cry for her. The audience's emotional reactions are crucial to the play's interpretation. Therefore, the piece empowers its spectators.

The meaning of Ludlam's *Camille* is in the eye of the beholder, so to speak; an individual can interpret the work as he or she sees fit. Through their emotional reactions to *Camille*, spectators became meaning-makers in their own right. The gender mashup served as a part of the overall experience; if the performance had an emotional impact, in addition to the humor raised by the drag "shtick," then the audience would likely cry for Marguerite's demise. If the comedy reigned above all else, they would likely leave the theatre chuckling. It seems as though either outcome would have been acceptable to Ludlam, if not for critics of the play. So long as the audience was engaged— so long as the performance gave the spectators something to walk away with emotionally—then for Ludlam it was effective enough.

Conclusion

Ludlam understood that "the theater is an event and not an object."[110] This mentality is key to understanding what makes the Ridiculous what it is: it is a performative form, one that is engaged in using theatre in new and innovative ways without ever losing sight of the importance of entertainment in a theatrical experience. Ludlam's contributions to American theatre, experimental drama, as well as to comedy and farce should not be denied. Ludlam brought these comic styles to the modern theatre, showing that through dramaturgical techniques of collage and remix, and performative techniques of drag and mashup, everything that was old could be new again. In an interview with Ted Castle for *ArtForum*, Ludlam admits, "I would say that my work falls into the classical tradition of comedy. Over the years there have been certain traditional approaches to comedy. As a modern artist you have to advance the tradition. I want to work within the tradition so that I don't waste time trying to establish new conventions. You can be very original within the established conventions.... The drama is the form that I'm interested in."[111] Ludlam found ways for old forms of comedy to speak to a contemporary audience and actually seem quite groundbreaking and innovative.

Ludlam also accomplished a feat no other American dramatist has been able to do to date: running his own theatre, producing 29 of his own original works in which he starred and for which he served as director. No other theatrical figure is as commonly linked with the Ridiculous style of performance as Charles Ludlam is. From an interest in popular culture and erudite knowledge of the dramatic canon, he synthesized a dramatic form that left open many possibilities for how a performance could be constructed, especially gender performance. Ludlam wanted to see something new in American theatre. In his own notes, he jotted, "The theater is now filled with people doing things. The world is full of people doing things. Who needs to go to the theater to see people doing things? Doing this to impress the audience makes you a performing dog. This is sick, corrupt and egoistic. Better to do nothing."[112] Although, certainly, people do *do* things in a Ludlam play, these actions are often much more imaginative than what one might find in a more a conventional play from the period.

Yet Ludlam was not actually the sole creator of the movement. He fell into an intricate network of artists—many of whom were already associated with Warhol's Factory at the time the notion of a Theatre of the Ridiculous came into existence—attempting to develop new aesthetics in their live performances. In particular, these artists, like their Pop Art colleagues and contemporaries, were interested in how they could bring their interest in popular culture icons into the more "highbrow" form of live performance. As Andy Warhol would render the design aesthetics of Campbell's Soup Cans into icons of high art in painting, artists like Jack Smith would attempt to allow their reverence for a B-movie starlet like Maria Montez to be the source for great performance.

It is my intention, then, to cast a wider net on Theatre of the Ridiculous: to recapture the other artists who influenced and/or collaborated with Ludlam to create the style with which he would come to be almost exclusively associated. Ludlam's short tenure at the Play-House of the Ridiculous early in his career is where he honed his style of performing and learned models of playwriting. This site was born from the association of its initial lead playwright, Ronald Tavel, and Andy Warhol, for whom Tavel would write scenarios. Warhol's early associations with performance artist/photographer/filmmaker Jack Smith, who exposed him to experimental cinema techniques, heavily influenced Warhol and his entire Pop Art aesthetic. Smith himself was not born in a vacuum; his aesthetic owes a great deal to his worship, bordering on obsession, with 1940s starlet Maria Montez, a popular film actress, who lacked some of the pedigree of her cinematic contemporaries. Maria Montez serves as a kind of inspirational godmother to all of the Ridiculous practices to come. Because of this, her influence will be the focus of my next chapter.

Two

The "Godmother" of the Ridiculous

Maria Montez and the Ghosting of Ridiculous Theatre

"We need more sacrifices!" Maria Montez shouts in one of the most lavish scenes of her film *Cobra Woman* (1944). This rich, campy, B-movie was revered by Charles Ludlam and his contemporaries, despite the fact that it does not possess any of the markers that we might contemporarily associate with "great cinematic classics." Rather, as Max Gold points out for *PopMatters*, "It's a spectacle built of sheer camp. Full of golden thrones shaped like cobras, sparkling dresses designed by Vera Drake, and hyper-religiosity directed towards actual cobras, the film is soundtracked by yowling and occupied by the flailing of its extras. Ordinarily, where films use dialogue and action to further drama or to propel a plot, *Cobra Woman* is fantastical to the point where these become irrelevant."[1] Rather than being concerned with complex storytelling—or any modicum of cultural sensitivity—it is instead an indulgent, escapist spectacle, in the finest sense of the terms.

Generally speaking, *Cobra Woman* is not held up as one of the most significant films of the 1940s. However, when studying the Theatre of the Ridiculous, we find traces of it, and its star Maria Montez, everywhere. In this way, unlike many so-called "countercultural" theatres of the same period, such as the Living Theatre, which were built around shared political beliefs, the Ridiculous community is constructed around shared popular culture. These men created the sort of performances that they did because they were inspired by certain popular culture icons of the 20th century. For the Ridiculous community, both its participants and spectators, this insistence on representation of these oft-underappreciated celebrity figures served as a kind of performative archive of the cultural relics of most value to their unique queer sensibilities. As Jack Halberstam reminds in *In a Queer Time and Place*, "the notion

46

of an archive has to extend beyond the image of a place to collect material or hold documents, and it has to become a floating signifier for the kinds of lives implied by the paper remnants of shows, clubs, events, and meetings. The archive is not simply a repository; it is also a theory of cultural relevance, a construction of collective memory, and a complex record of queer activity."[2] The Ridiculous decided to allow their live performances, their embodiment of these historical personas, to create a kind of spiritual archive, to raise them from the dead and give them new life in their performances. No single performer was more influential to Ridiculous performance than Maria Montez, whose over-the-top glamourous costumes paired with her demonstrative acting style permeates the works of all of the major Ridiculous creators covered in this book. These individuals were fascinated by her films, which were often exotic epics and tried to bring that sensibility to life, literally and figuratively, in their performances. Montez, albeit unknowingly, is a key precursor to Ridiculous Theatre.

Because there are traces of Montez and her films everywhere in Ridiculous plays, the concept of "ghosting," as it relates to performance, is key to understanding the Ridiculous. It takes the Ridiculous reverence for popular culture to a much deeper level. A love of the popular is not just an aspect of these performances; it is an ideology, a driving force behind their construction. Charles Ludlam and his Ridiculous contemporaries were creating these shows so as to raise the ghosts of their heroes, especially those forgotten or ignored by mainstream society, like Maria Montez. They were creating their own fantasy world in which these icons not only still existed but could be embodied by the performer.

In addition, the Ridiculous artists were building a framework from their cultural past, one which other artists could then later reference, particularly fellow gay artists. Richard Dyer's analysis of film in *The Culture of Queers* applies as well to Theatre of the Ridiculous because of

> their access to filmic and lesbian/gay sub-cultural discourses. In other words, because they were lesbian or gay, they could produce lesbian/gay representations that could themselves be considered lesbian/gay, not because all lesbians or gay men inevitably express themselves on film in a certain way, but because they had access to, and an inwardness with, lesbian/gay sign systems that would have been like foreign languages to the straight filmmakers.[3]

These artists were already part of a shared community—their overlapping preoccupations with film stars like Maria Montez proves this—but they were also in the process of contributing to that community. The Ridiculous developed its own language of references relevant only to others who shared their particular sensibility. In this right, the Ridiculous was both part of a larger gay male cultural identity, and ghosted by that identity, while also building a new community through the shared cultural lexicon born of their cultural past.

In the Ridiculous, ghosting is not just an aesthetic tool; it is an actual element of the movement. These artists built on the works of their predecessors in order to assert their own cultural presence as gay men. In *The Meaning of Gay*, Todd J. Ormsbee writes, "The most common and perhaps most powerful way gay men sought a cultural heritage was their look to the past for a feeling of connectedness through a *gay history*, which would be both a history of gay men themselves and history with a gay sensibility."[4] Ludlam, for example, would claim Jack Smith as an artistic father figure; he was asserting a lineage for his Ridiculous aesthetic within his community of fellow gay male artists.

Maria Montez: Goddess of the Ridiculous

Maria Montez, on the other hand, could be seen as the spiritual mother for the movement that I am calling Ridiculous. To be truly Ridiculous with the capital "R," as opposed to simply stylistically similar, an artist must have been at least somewhat committed to the kind of Montez-worship associated with Smith. Rachel Joseph makes a compelling case for the ways in which Smith's emulation of Montez were precisely tied up with her lack of talent.[5]

Jack Smith brought Montez iconography directly into his art; in his most influential work, *Flaming Creatures*, this was through the presence of drag performer Mario Montez: "Smith convinced a young Hispanic Post Office worker he met late one night on the subway to act in the film in the guise of Maria Montez, the Hollywood star of the early 1940s films Smith so admired. The young man became a central image in the film and eventually adopted the name Mario Montez."[6] The significance of *Flaming Creatures* cannot be underestimated; films like Smith's *Flaming Creatures* and Ken Jacobs's *Blonde Cobra* (1959) "served as models for the pop art of the 1960s."[7] This work was seminal in the foundation of what would come to be called Pop Art and, eventually, Theatre of the Ridiculous.

The presence of Montez iconography in *Flaming Creatures* is not unique to this one work, however. The essence of Maria Montez, as it were, permeates all of Smith's artistic creations. He was constantly trying to "raise the dead" in his performances: Smith attempted to bring to life the film icons and the Hollywood fantasy-land that he had grown up witnessing in his local movie houses. His *What's Underground About Marshmallows?* (1981), for example, includes an extensive list of Montez's film performances, followed by "the first thing you notice as you enter the round socialistic movie studio … the temple of the sacred brassiere of Maria Montez."[8] Her undergarment was seen as "sacred" in this all-important cinematic site; she was the holy object to be worshipped. This sort of adulation of the ghost of Maria Montez is a powerful force throughout the Ridiculous.

Indeed, incarnations of Maria Montez are everywhere in the Theatre of the Ridiculous; Ludlam, for example, created an homage to her classic *Cobra Woman* with the "Cobra Cunt Ceremony" in his *Big Hotel* (1967). Yet the Ridiculous artists were concerned with doing more than just referencing her films. As Ronald Tavel suggests, "Other stars have provided an image in which to live: Maria Montez provided a vocabulary in which to robe and narrate some of the more memorably vanguard and radical art of our time."[9] Tavel's interpretation of Montez mirrors Smith's ideas about art. Smith writes in "Art and Art History":

> But the art ideas about art are so perverted that, uh, its [sic] become a guessing game—one year its [sic] confused with Katharine Hepburn's jaw line, another year— this year it happens to be uh, its mistaken for, um, a grosser kind of sleaze than has ever been imagined before. But they do think that it has something to do with sleaze, but I think that's one thing they are sure of … and uh, but this is such a useless idea of art, as a matter of fact, in this perverted time of art that we've evolved, uselessness is the most prized quality—the more spectacular and idiotic and useless the better.[10]

Rather than being preoccupied with "sleaziness" or mainstream film stars, like Hepburn, Smith wants to bring glamour back into art along with the commonplace. For him, as well as for most of the Ridiculous artists, there was no better icon of this remix of the common and the fabulous than Maria Montez.

Montez starred in a number of films during the 1940s, many alongside actor Jon Hall, that "were characterized by a visual and narrative thematic of magical exotica."[11] Her career was short, as she died in 1951. Her death, it seems, was almost as fabulous as her life; "in order to lose weight Montez began to bathe in scalding hot salt water and eventually died as a result of a heart attack caused by the extremity of this treatment."[12] Steven Watson believes that the manner of Montez's death was precisely what made Smith such a devotee. Watson writes, "The publicity surrounding Maria Montez's death caught Smith's attention. He started calling her 'the Marvelous One,' erected an altar to her in his cluttered apartment, and lit candles to her twenty-four hours a day."[13] Whatever its cause, Smith's love for Montez went beyond basic celebrity worship; this was something much deeper.

What was so special about Maria Montez? The Dominican performer, who failed as a stage actress before solidifying her career as a star in the cinema, possessed a "dissonant pleasure … whose performance maintains an intensity, rather than authenticity, of character."[14] Montez played every role with a great deal of energy, truly performing within the guise of the character, as opposed to becoming the persona being portrayed, as is done in more realistic performance. Smith was taken with the aspects of Montez that were most disposable; "'Trash,' he proclaimed, 'is the material of creators.'"[15] Like the proliferation of junk that would litter his stages, Smith allowed the worst, which were also the best, aspects of Montez's acting style to permeate his own performance techniques.

Therefore, there is a larger thematic quality that comes to light when one scrutinizes this obsession with a B-movie star. There is a kind of disconnect that is thrown into relief: the chasm between beauty and the grotesque, the thin line between art and travesty. Although most of the writers that Richard Dyer quotes in *Heavenly Bodies* share positive impressions about Judy Garland—another female star who serves as a gay male icon—he also includes a more negative interpretation of her image. Dyer writes:

> [Certain "gay fans"] can only read Garland in a gay way that is negative ("hysteria," "exhibitionistic")—they are recognizing a quality of emotional intensity that is in fact what the other gay writers also emphasize but they give it a denigratory label.... Garland could also be used in this subcultural discourse, more queer than gay, that spoke of homosexual identity in self-oppressive modes characteristic of oppressed groups—distancing, denying, denigrating. Aspects of Garland's career and performance could be seen as pathetic and God-awful, and gay men could as it were misrecognize themselves in that and hasten ... to disown it.[16]

Part of the appeal of Judy Garland could have been the more negative aspects of her career: the way in which she succumbed to the pressures of being a mega-star with "hysteria." Dyer suggests that for some this aspect of Garland's persona is uniquely appealing because it seems to reflect some aspect of the gay male experience; this becomes both a source of identification and a point of denial. To some degree, Montez worship operates similarly to Garland love; there is both a self-affirming quality in the positive aspects of her technique as well as a reflection of what some might consider a failure in quality. This is reminiscent of Jack Halberstam's construction of the queer value of failure.[17]

It is precisely Montez's failure to be a "great actress" that made her Smith's most favored performer and a symbol for all of the Ridiculous artists who built on this style of performance-making, as Joseph claimed. This interest in something that can be seen as both beautiful and trashy is linked directly to these artists' Downtown Scene setting. For playwright Ronald Tavel, for example, it was this mixture of beauty and rubbish that stood out in Smith's adoration of Montez and his love of his neighborhood. Tavel recalls:

> And, in a sense, Montezland was the Lower East Side Jack lived in, when we walked-a-nightaway SoHo before it was called that, silhouette-wet and deserted, or to the abandoned synagogue below Houston and beyond Norfolk, a Levantine carpet-borne enticement unbelievably there, with minaret window niches, gilt crescent arches, blue mosaic walls with artfully domed, empty recesses. He took me there when the moon was full, and he'd rush ecstatically down and up the dark, broken staircases into the breathless romance of its shattered towers.[18]

Montez, with her own flawed artistic beauty, was, for Smith, somehow iconic of his particular experience of his own Downtown Scene, of the culture in which he created his works of art. All of the elements of his geographic setting—both his neighborhood and his loft/theatre—were like Montez; they were both beautiful and damaged, remarkable and commonplace, magical and mundane simultaneously.

Maria Montez is most famous for her exotic dramas, such as 1944's *Cobra Woman,* a performance often referenced or parodied in Ridiculous plays, as in the aforementioned Ludlam play *Big Hotel.* The appeal of Montez's iconic *Cobra Woman* performance is most likely born of the clear disavowal of realism in her incarnation of the title character. She presents the scene in such a manner as to draw attention to the fact that this is a performance, as opposed to trying to make the audience believe in the reality of what is occurring on screen. Her accent is unrelated to the character she is portraying and her line delivery lacks any clear sense of dramatic motivation. Because of this, the serious dramatic moment—she is choosing people to be sacrificed to a volcano—comes across as humorous, precisely because of its inauthentic seriousness.

The scene is also delightful in its embracing of theatricalism. The set looks like a scenic construct; it does not give the illusion of being an actual location. Despite this, it is lavish and populated with throngs of people, including some well-oiled shirtless men. To add to the scene's spectacle, Montez, as the titular Cobra Woman, is also exquisitely glamorous, donning an ornate, gigantic golden headdress and an intricately detailed cloak. Many of Smith's "Baghdad"-style wardrobe pieces hearken back to this costume; golden thread, gemstones, and bright colors were all regularly used in his mode of dress.[19] The entire movie is epic in scope, bringing together the best qualities of melodrama and cinema into a sprawling and entertaining film.

Smith was not unique in his idol worship of Maria Montez. Even the academic-leaning Tavel takes the time to sing the praises of the Hollywood star, without whom perhaps none of the Ridiculous magic could have occurred:

> Enough has been said about the Theatre of the Ridiculous for me not to have to note that the paradigm she [Montez] breathed breath into by being, in no conventional reading of the phrase, a professional performer, was crucial to my decision to come to theater, and to what I'd have of it. What makes her so obsession-fomenting, and so the well-spring of iconoclastic and humanistic speculation is what she can do, display, and reveal in the "surround" of acting; it held and still holds whatever interest I have in theater, or need to have in film.[20]

What Tavel is suggesting, and what cannot be denied when studying the Theatre of the Ridiculous, is that film actress Montez was the single most important cultural influence on the performance aesthetic that would be used in Ridiculous productions. Her style of performance was these artists' model for acting technique and her standard of feminine beauty was the glamour to which they aspired.

This dedication to Montez could be mystifying for anyone who is not a Montez devotee. In fact, for anyone who has ever seen a Montez film, this may be surprising to consider. As Watson so elegantly puts it, "By prevailing critical standards Maria Montez's acting was abysmal." It was not her acting talent, according to Watson, that made her a box office success; rather, it was her exotic beauty that made her "Universal's biggest star during World War II."[21] Even her Internet Movie Database entry proclaims, "her pictures soon became immensely popular, even though she could not really act, could not dance and could not sing."[22] The Ridiculous artists often hold Montez up as the paragon of movie star greatness, yet for all intents and purposes, she failed to become a great actress by Hollywood standards. In this way, the Ridiculous reverence for Montez is a good example of a blend of cultural layers: a popular star whose "artistry" defied conventions was held up as the epitome of exquisite talent.

Ms. Montez was not just an influence on or an inspiration to Ridiculous artists; recreating her glamour and style and the fantasyland in which her movies took place was at the heart of why these artists chose to create performances and films in the first place. Tavel articulates this obsession best: "If anyone was a diva, she [Montez] was; when she sat in a room, that's who you looked at and no one else…. She is bringing this fantasy world, breathing life into it and making it a place for you to live in, you the oppressed and did you ever feel oppressed as a six-year-old gay boy. Did you ever."[23] Admiration for Montez went beyond even celebrity-worship. She somehow embodied these ostracized youths' desire for escape and for fantasy.

This reverence for Montez was not meant in some postmodern way, either in quotation marks or as a form of irony. Ludlam, Smith, Tavel, Ethyl Eichelberger, John Vaccaro, and others associated with the Ridiculous did in fact revere Ms. Montez as a screen goddess. In light of this fact, Douglas Crimp asks, "Did Smith love Maria Montez ironically? Was she, for Smith, so bad she was good?" and responds, "Certainly not, if we are to take him at his word."[24] Crimp engages Marc Siegel's reading of Smith's Montez worship, highlighting the importance of the ways in which she allowed her belief in the fantasies that she performed on screen to allow such fantasies the possibility of being manifest in the real world. In this way, for the Ridiculous artists, it was essential to capture her fantastical quality in their own performances. If Montez was indeed "the apotheosis of the drag queen,"[25] as Vaccaro contends, in her performance style, then these male performers wishing to become her in their own cross-dressed performances would have wanted to maintain a similar anti-realist acting style to the one that Montez used. Their performances would be a drag of a drag, if you will, a cultural blend of the performativity of performance.

The Ridiculous interest in an anti-realist mode of acting could indeed have been derived directly from their Montez idol worship, as Montez was the touchstone for talent among Ridiculous artists; "Smith also strove to emulate another aspect of Montez's work, one that he greatly admired—her acting style."[26] Smith called what he was doing the "Reptilian Acting Style," "an extension of the common sense approach of Lee Strasberg [that] would seem to be saying let's *not* pretend—this could affect thinking."[27] Based on Smith's description in this article, it seems that he wants to make acting more real by basically having his actors *not act*; the "technique rests on the premise that everybody is already a fine actor."[28] In this right, Montez would be the best actress; she did little that would be considered realistic acting on screen. In its place, she was very much herself in front of the camera, drawing attention to the fact that she was performing, delighting in the glamour and the presentational qualities of such an activity.

Perhaps this was why Smith and other Ridiculous artists saw her as the epitome of greatness on screen, not just because of her glamour and her on-screen charisma, but also because of her ability to command a scene simply by being present in it. She did not need to work at character—Maria Montez was compelling to watch simply by *being* herself, as opposed to *becoming* the character who she was portraying. Basing their acting technique on her performances lent a unique brand of antirealism to the plays of the Ridiculous. Jack Sargeant suggests, "Costume and the accompanying performance necessary to create the illusion of being 'other,' thus draws attention to the constructed nature of identity. Identity is not fixed, but in a continual morphogenic flux and is best understood as fluid, able to transform, to be in a continual state of 'becoming' rather than 'being.'"[29] These artists were precisely interested in the way character can be put on—or, put another way, the performative nature of identity—as opposed to creating the reality of particular characters on stage. Smith, Ludlam, *et al.* did not try to *be* Montez in their performances; rather they attempted to experience what it would be like to be in the process of "becoming" this film idol. Smith, for example, wanted to raise her ghost on his stage, to embody it for a time, and then to return to the real world once the performance ritual was complete. Ghosting, then, emerges as a key element of Ridiculous aesthetics, production techniques, and dramaturgy.

Ghosting and Audience Construction

Because of the presence of such pronounced practices of ghosting in the Ridiculous—to the point where productions, like those of Smith, could almost be seen as dream-like personal rituals—it becomes essential to consider audience construction. Plays like those put on by Smith were clearly not for the average theatregoer; that person would likely understand very little of what he or she was witnessing. Those who would enjoy a Ridiculous play would be those who understood the most references; i.e., cultural insiders to the particular culture that appealed to the Ridiculous artists. Audience construction (and education) is key to understanding what makes the Ridiculous a movement in its own right. It is not just that these performances were stylistically similar; rather, it is that they speak in a similar manner to audiences who understand the "language" employed.

This Ridiculous language is an intertextual one, built of references that appeal to this particular subset of society: the audiences who would come to see these plays. Ridiculous aficionados constitute a subculture of queer identity and, therefore, as Halberstam argues, demand that scholars, "...theorize the concept of the archive, and consider new models of queer memory and queer history capable of recording and tracing subterranean scenes, fly-by-night clubs, and fleeting trends..."[30] From this perspective, the recognition of cultural allusions and references—the familiarity with the particular on stage ghosts—defines this subculture and its archive is created in the performances themselves. This interest in citationality is a postmodern gesture; as Julie Kristeva explains, "an insight first introduced into literary theory by Bakhtin: any text is constructed as a mosaic of quotations; any text is the absorption and transformation of another. The notion of *intertextuality* replaces that of intersubjectivity, and poetic language is read as at least *double*."[31] Every text is created from text from other sources; meaning can be made both by understanding the product of this combination and by recognizing its sources. Ridiculous dramaturgy is merely an extreme version of this: Ridiculous play texts are constructs built from the mixing of various other sources. This intertextuality is what creates the tapestry of the Ridiculous performance; being able to comprehend it is what makes one a citizen of the Ridiculous community.

Therefore, the practice of referencing outside source material in their plays is a way of meaning-making for this group of artists. The nature of the cultural elements they chose to include was unique to this group; they invoked certain cultural images, such as Maria Montez, and discarded or avoided others. For the Ridiculous, this practice was not casual; it was always linked to an attempt to "raise the dead" and create a history and identity that was purely their own and thereby value the cultural icons of most importance to its gay creators. Of theatrical ghosting, Marvin Carlson writes:

> Among all literary forms it is the drama preeminently that has always been centrally concerned not simply with the telling of stories but with the retelling of stories already known to its public. This process naturally involves but goes far beyond the recycling of references, tropes, even structural elements and patterns that intertextuality considers. It involves the dramatist in the presentation of a narrative that is

haunted in almost every aspect—its names, its character relationships, the structure of its action, even small physical or linguistic details—by a specific previous narrative.[32]

Here, Carlson is interested in drama as the main mode for this retelling and recycling to occur. Artists like Smith took this practice a step further, finding ways to evoke ghosts via the mediated, through his practices of "extended cinema," which allowed the recorded to become part of the live performance experience. In addition, Smith was addicted to editing his filmed works time after time. Because of this, the ghosting that Carlson describes as happening during live performance is heightened; the literal ghosts of a past performance, one that was recorded, are able to exist side-by-side with the living, breathing performers. The use of media in pop performance highlights the subtle ghosting that always occurs during a live theatrical presentation.

For these artists, the nature of the ghosting was incredibly significant; the choices of references delineated the framework for this community. These people shared certain interests, worshipped certain icons—such as the great Ms. Montez—and avoided other tropes more commonly associated with mainstream theatrical production. In this way, the Ridiculous act of storytelling through performance could be seen as being akin to the storytelling around the campfires of an ancient tribe; it reinforced shared cultural interests and strengthened community bonds and membership.

Indeed, this non-normative brand of theatre-making continues to have this connection to community identification. Taylor Mac, a later inheritor of the Ridiculous tradition, is, according to Sean Edgecomb, "the gay youth rejected by a normative culture and given up to the wilds of New York City, where he finds respite from homophobia through opportunities for the formation of community. In this context, Mac as fool found the opportunity to establish his own fool society, inviting audiences into his own queer space rather than entering the mainstream."[33] Like Mac, his Ridiculous predecessors created their own theatrical wonderlands—in some very non-traditional theatrical spaces—and allowed audiences to join in their spectacles. They created their own subculture as a safe space to make art—and live life—however they saw fit to do so.

This practice of building an insular audience community is very pronounced in the works of Jack Smith; he saw his late-night performances as only being for an elite audience who were both willing to wait as long as necessary to bear witness to the performance and who would understand the variety of references included in the production. Smith's performances tapped into a shared experience, building a concept of a cultural memory and, ultimately, a community of sorts who, if they did not understand the work entirely, could at least appreciate it. Carlson elucidates shared memory as an important aspect of theatrical production; making a play is never just creating an ephemeral performance. Rather, it is a way to archive a particular group's identity at a particular historical moment. Carlson states:

> Theatre, as a simulacrum of the cultural and historical process itself, seeking to depict the full range of human actions within their physical context, has always provided society with the most tangible records of its attempts to understand its own operations. It is the repository of cultural memory, but, like the memory of each individual, it is also subject to continual adjustment and modifications as the memory is recalled in new circumstances and contexts.[34]

In its own bizarre way, these Ridiculous performances acted as a queer archive of the cultural references that mattered to their participants and spectators, both in their incorporation of popular culture into the dramatic text and their use of filmed and recorded images and sounds. In highlighting shared interests, Ridiculous theatre participated in early acts of community building, especially among gay males living in downtown New York City in the 1960s and 70s.

Obviously, Maria Montez was key to this community that Ridiculous artists were constructing. Indeed, her influence cannot be underestimated when discussing the Ridiculous. Smith would take whatever items were at his disposal and attempt to recreate the worlds of his favorite actress's films. This meant that he refashioned his loft space into a kind of shrine to Montez, built of everyday, disposable objects transformed into icons of the exotic and the glamorous. Smith not only idolized Ms. Montez; he went so far as to attempt to evoke her in the realm of his own performances. Ghosting takes a somewhat literal form in the case of Smith; his ritualistic late-night loft performances attempted to raise the spirit of Montez into his experimental theatrical landscape. In so doing, albeit perhaps unintentionally, Smith gave birth to the entirety of the Pop Art and therefore Ridiculous Theatre scene.

THREE

The "Daddy" of the Ridiculous
Jack Smith, Pop Art and Proto-Ridiculous Performance

Despite his singular importance in expanding the influence of Theatre of the Ridiculous, Charles Ludlam was not alone in its creation. Rather, even Ludlam once admitted, "Jack is the daddy of us all."[1] The Jack of whom he speaks, experimental artist and filmmaker Jack Smith, never explicitly used the term Ridiculous to categorize his own theatrical contributions. And yet, his "ghost" infuses the entirety of the Ridiculous landscape—many of the other artists associated with the style worked with Smith and nearly all of them credit Smith as an influence on their art work. According to Uzi Parnes, recalling a conversation with performer Mario Montez, "Jack actually came up with the name for Ludlam, because…. Vaccaro's group was called the 'Theatre of the Ridiculous,' and so Jack suggested they call themselves the 'Ridiculous Theatrical Company.'"[2] Ludlam may never have created the Ridiculous work that he did without the contributions made by Smith.

Indeed, scholars of the "Downtown Scene" believe Smith to be an important source for the experimental work that exploded there, beginning in the 1960s. Gary Indiana, for one, suggests, "One explanation of Pop's earliest influences can be found in scattered writings of the artist and filmmaker Jack Smith, whose almost secret public performances and pioneering film *Flaming Creatures* had a powerful influence on Robert Wilson, Andy Warhol, the Theater of the Ridiculous, and other theatrical and visual innovators."[3] Indiana is correct, at least insofar as Smith's work was influential on the development of the Ridiculous. Although not Ridiculous Theatre *per se*, Smith's plays were "proto-Ridiculous" creations that went on to inspire the trajectory of the particular aesthetic associated with "Ridiculous-ness." Smith's performance works were unique; his work bridged what was happening in experimental photography and cinema with theatrical experimentation. For his theatre, he often used his home as the site for performance and dictated both the start time and the duration of the piece per his own artistic whims.

The backbone of Smith's style was a worship of the Hollywood films of his youth; the impact of his art-making was building a community surrounding this shared popular culture admiration. This love of pop culture icons takes the form of "ghosting," as Marvin Carlson discusses the term in *The Haunted Stage*. Meaning is made through the evocation of something from the past; watching these performances, then, was a shared cultural experience. Ridiculous Theatre evokes the presence of many of its creators' childhood movie idols. It is therefore impossible to fully understand their works without being aware of the popular culture from which it was born. Because of the presence of these popular culture ghosts—and the audience's communal worship of them at Smith's performances—a community of the Ridiculous began to take shape. Within this community, there was also continual "ghosting": artists borrowing or stealing ideas from one another.

A discussion of Smith is ghosted, too; it is impossible to ignore the link between Jack Smith and Andy Warhol—that is, the bridge between the Ridiculous and the greater cultural movement into which it is often placed, Pop Art. To a large degree, Ridiculous theatre was born of the Pop Art scene— Factory performers appeared in early Play-House of the Ridiculous works, such as *Conquest of the Universe*, under John Vaccaro's direction (1967). Additionally, Warhol credits Smith's films as a major influence on his own works. Much of the style of filmmaking that we have come to associate with Warhol actually was pioneered in the underground films of Smith. In general, scholars of Pop Art agree with this trajectory; many cite the connection between Warhol and Smith as crucial to Warhol's artistic development. Some artistic contemporaries and collaborators of Warhol and Smith sometimes go even further, suggesting, "Jack Smith was the real Warhol."[4]

Like Warhol, Ludlam and the other Ridiculous artists certainly learned from the artistic experiments that Smith began conducting in the 1960s. The significance of Smith's "ghost" in the Ridiculous scene goes beyond mere artistic influence, however. Smith not only quoted and sampled from outside works. Rather, Smith attempted to bring to life a forgotten past, a fantasy world built from the remnants of Hollywood films of his youth and his own imagination. The ghosts of Smith's cultural past are brought to life in his performances, particularly the spirit of his preeminent icon, the B-movie starlet Maria Montez.

Ghosting infused even Smith's style of on-stage myth-making. Unlike either the early chaotic romps or the later tightly drawn farces of Charles Ludlam, Smith created sprawling, epic ceremonies, often in his loft apartment, meant only for the "initiated," those willing to wait until the middle of the night for anything to begin. Smith did not create plays; rather, he performed rituals, a practice always preoccupied with the presence of, if not ghosts, then certainly some spiritual aspect or quality of human existence. The link between ritual and experimental performance is a key way to understand what makes such live art avant-garde. The structure of this ritual of avant-garde theatre, according to C. D. Innes, "is characterized by merging of audience and action, by a rejection of language or verbal logic as a primary means of communication; and where the aim is to induce trance states these are active and tend toward convulsion."[5] Unlike Ludlam, who saw himself decidedly in opposition to the avant-garde, Smith was working within that vein, experimenting and exploring the theatrical act so as to engage a deeper, more spiritual understanding of reality.

To create this ritualistic landscape, Smith reconfigured the concept of "performance space"; the location for many of Smith's shows was his loft, located at 36 Greene Street and renamed the "The Plaster Foundation" for purposes of his performances. By placing his spectators in his living quarters to witness his performance, Smith evoked the presence of his own self as a person, in place of the fiction of a character in a fictional stage setting, as one would find in more traditional performance. He also transformed the notion of "home"; his loft was no ordinary living space. Rather, it was a fantasyland where anything he could dream up might occur.

The works of Jack Smith, then, because of their physical setting, suggest a type of theatre creation that is not only a remaking of the artistic process but a reimagining of the audience experience as well. In addition to this phantasmagoric quality for the performance's site, Smith's spectacles took a great deal of time to start in the first place and then, even once they had begun, sprawled on for many hours. This extreme duration was necessary to complete the ritual that Smith was performing: the play needed to last a long time in order to ensure that all aspects were performed correctly, precisely per Smith's vision.[6] These ritualistic epics necessitate a style of performance that dictates its own duration.

By looking at these two elements—theatrical space and time—together, it becomes clear that Smith was remaking not only the process of theatre creation, but the role of the spectator in such artistic magic-making as well. Rather than sitting by and observing what was happening, Smith often asked audience members to take a participatory role, a practice much in line with what other Downtown Scene companies were doing during the same period. For many of these other companies, such as the Living Theatre or the Performance Group, this audience interaction had political implications. What makes Smith's version of this practice particularly "Ridiculous" is precisely that this audience interaction was not explicitly political, yet still had a radical quality to it. Instead of political didacticism or relevance to current events, the notion in Smith's performances is that the audience is always included as members of the community of performance; the Ridiculous community is not built around shared politics, but around shared popular culture. One came to the temple at The Plaster Foundation not to engage in political debate or to receive political instruction, nor to worship gods, but to bow down at the altar of pop culture icons such as Maria Montez and, by extension, Jack Smith, whose art had brought them to life.

Indeed, ghosting is perhaps the main way through which Smith endures in the memory of the theatrical Downtown Scene. His influence on others is often discussed, while his own theatrical works remain largely unstudied. Yet, as Sally Banes recognizes, "so much of what is central to current performance art—allusions to Hollywood, TV, and other aspects of mass culture; fusions of the home-made and the esoteric; funky, deliberately amateurish acting styles—stems from a set of fascinations and obsessions that can be traced back to Smith's sensibility."[7] Indeed, Smith's influence can be found throughout Ridiculous work; he not only influenced Warhol but the entirety of the Ridiculous. Rachel Joseph also recognizes that it is possible to "categorize" Smith among these artists, but that doing so limits the narrative that can be told about Smith's work.[8] Although I agree that Smith can be discussed without needing to connect him to the larger Ridiculous scene, I do not believe that the Ridiculous, as either an aesthetic or a theatrical movement, can be discussed in full without recognizing the incredible influence that Smith's live performance art pieces had on the form.

Despite this incredible impact, Smith was never satisfied with how his aesthetic concepts were changed by those who borrowed them. Ghosting as a tool for building cultural heritage can, therefore, be a fraught process. Though Ludlam once celebrated the inheritance that he received from Smith, citing him as a progenitor and father figure, Smith bemoaned the development of the Ridiculous aesthetic that Ludlam would later accomplish. As Joe Pogostin recollects, during a performance in which an actress was not taking her role seriously, "Jack shouted, 'If you can't be serious while saying your lines get off the stage. Lest we all end up like poor Charles Ludlam!' a damning epitaph on the corruption of the camp aesthetic into farce."[9] These Ridiculous artists may all have been citing one another—mixing the styles of those working around them into their own artistic creations—but it was not always a happy blend. A Ridiculous text is certainly marked by a combining of elements and the ghosts of many other cultural icons, but the process of remixing is sometimes burdened with very personal tension. These artists borrowed heavily from one another—Andy Warhol, for one, basically usurped cinematic techniques from Smith—which created a community that is forever ghosted. These gay male artists built an aesthetic around their shared cultural interests, creating a sense of community, but also disrupted that community by stealing from one another.

The Life and Times of Jack Smith

For Jack Smith, as well as for many of the other artists associated with the Ridiculous, films of the 1940s were the most important components of their cultural heritage. Uzi Parnes notes of Smith, "[his] favorite pastime while growing up was going to the movies, and he spent most of his Saturdays at the matinee where he often sat through the film several times. He particularly savored the lush exotic Technicolor productions that starred the likes of Maria Montez and Yvonne De Carlo."[10] As children and adolescents, these future artists delighted in seeing these full-color spectacles on screen and would keep these images in their minds, attempting to recreate them in their own on-stage endeavors. Smith's sister, Sue Slater, mentions putting on shows with her brother in their garage, with him as director-playwright. In addition, she reiterates his love of going to the cinema; she remembers, "Every Saturday we'd go to the movies. That was our treat. That's where he fell in love with Maria Montez."[11]

Smith's upbringing, according to his sister, was a bit unconventional, with her mother remarrying more than once and the family moving a number of times.[12] Jack Smith was born in Columbus, Ohio, in 1932, but moved first to Texas and then to Wisconsin at the age of thirteen. After graduating high school, he moved on his own to Chicago in 1951, then to Los Angeles in 1952, and finally to New York in 1953. Smith made his first film, *Buzzards Over Baghdad*, in the same year and studied film at the City College of New York. Smith was not only a filmmaker, however; he was also a photographer, publishing *The Beautiful Book* in 1962.[13]

In 1963, in addition to solidifying his connection to Andy Warhol and the Factory scene through various trips to Coney Island,[14] Smith would also release his most significant film, *Flaming Creatures*, which, thanks to a combination of the fortitude of Jonas Mekas and the influence of scandal on popularity, would go on to be a commonly screened, and commonly raided, cinematic presentation. Smith would combine filmed works with live performance, a practice known as "expanded cinema," and, by 1968, had transitioned to creating live performances in his loft apartment, "The Plaster Foundation."

His theatrical works connected him with a larger Downtown Scene of experimentation in live performance, such as productions by Robert Wilson. By the 1970s, Smith had created some of his most frequently used artistic images, such as the lobster and "a toy penguin as a 'surrogate for himself and Maria Montez'... named Yolanda La Pinguina or Inez the Penguin."[15] Smith continued performing in clubs throughout downtown New York into the 1980s.[16] He passed away in 1989 from pneumonia due to AIDS. His work was always interested in mixing popular culture—like references to movie star

Maria Montez—with more formal aesthetic experimentation, much like the many Ridiculous artists that he would go on to inspire.

Jack Smith's Rituals and Rehearsal for the Destruction of Atlantis

One way in which Smith attempted to engage the ghost of his (pop) cultural past was through the initiation of an on-stage ritual. Upon arriving at The Plaster Foundation for a performance, Stefan Brecht, a critic and frequenter of Ridiculous plays, found that there was no set starting time for the performance—nor was there any guarantee of a performance at all. Rather, people were simply milling about and Smith offered the option to "just listen to some records."[17] There is none of the formality that usually accompanies attending a theatrical production; the show would start whenever Smith decided it should begin, or never, if that's what the company assembled decided was best.

Additionally, once begun, a Jack Smith performance could go on for any unspecified length of time. From Brecht's description, it is clear that the lack of structure for the evening allowed the performance to meander on for many hours. Of a particular performance experience, Brecht relates, "It is very late.... Almost everybody has left."[18] These performances would sprawl on well into the wee hours of the morning. In this way, the art existed outside of or even beyond the normal time constraints for performance. Although transcripts from Smith performances cannot give a complete sense of what these works were like when performed live—the scenarios are more fragments than play texts—they do expose certain recurring Smith iconography and display the unrealistic nature of his performance works.

Smith recognized that his works were perhaps more ritual than play. His expanded cinema piece, *Rehearsal for the Destruction of Atlantis* (1965), presented at Film-Makers' Cinematheque and including such auspicious Ridiculous names as Mario Montez and John Vaccaro in its cast list, is subtitled "A Dream Weapon Ritual." The play text itself is more scenario than script; it describes what would happen in the performance and dictates actions, for performers and spectators alike. After setting the time and place for the performance, the text directs, "The audience files in blindfolded. Their files are taken from them and the usherettes (very tough Lesbians) (in matron uniforms) see that all the blindfolds are in place. A man in the audience objects to his blindfold. He is roughly cuffed and manhandled by the usherettes into submission to the bandage. Chloroform could be used."[19] Three things are apparent from this description: (1) Smith is imagining a theatrical world in which the audience takes on an active role; (2) Smith would need to instruct his audience members on what to do (he could not expect these actions to happen spontaneously on their own); and (3) the audience can be treated with cruelty if they do not follow the instructions correctly.

Rehearsal for the Destruction of Atlantis continues much in this manner, describing what is expected of the spectators with as much if not more precision than the performers' actions are inscribed. This direction was to be provided directly to the audience in attendance by a PA system. The announcements begin, "You are to imagine that you are a wino. This afternoon you were overcome by a fit of drowsiness and you slumped to the sidewalk. You lay there in the sun—baking and half asleep."[20] This use of the second person address lasts until the curtain rises, about a half a page later. Clearly, much of this performance was designed to situate the audience into a particular context, a place that Smith labeled as "Atlantis," before the actual action of the drama could begin.

The play fragment that remains suggests a bizarre fantasy world being evoked on stage, one in which marijuana is lauded, lobsters are anthropomorphized, and Mario Montez dances Swan Lake. Plot is not critical here, nor is it easy to surmise exactly what the narrative might mean or even *be*. Rather, the piece reads as a kind of spectacular pageant, one that keeps marijuana at the forefront of its celebratory exercises. The world of this play is all illusion; at one point, a character "returns with the moon held as a platter & goes past twins to hang it up. As she passes them—they pick up a paper off the moon."[21] Indeed, Smith's work is preoccupied with dreams and the subconscious, both in terms of fantastic splendor and nightmarish cruelty. Smith would need a setting for his productions that could capture this imagined fantasy world, one that reflected both his worship of Maria Montez and his own subconscious simultaneously.

If Maria Montez's main influence on the Ridiculous was the link the artists made between her and their own fantasies of escape and pleasure, then the setting for Smith's rituals, the titular "Atlantis," would have to be constructed to honor her image. Although *Rehearsal for the Destruction of Atlantis* was not presented at Smith's "Plaster Foundation" loft, it is clear that he is interested in fantasy settings, such as his commonly used "Atlantis" reference, for this piece. Tavel argues that it was through stage space, above all else, in which Maria Montez's ghost made her presence known in Smith's work: "But her more ultimate influence on him [Smith], and his ultimate tribute to her was the rebuilding of Baghdad/Babylonia into his apartments, a city, a world, a wall, a building. He had duplex lofts in Soho and removed the floor between them to construct, virtually by himself, and ostensibly for a projected picture called *Sinbad*, a cathedralling set that remind of Fairbanks, Sr.'s silent, *Thief of Bagdad*: but which got its seed from Maria's *Raiders of the*

Desert, Arabian Nights, Ali Baba and the Forty Thieves, and *Tangier.*"[22] The setting of Smith's loft suggested the exotic settings of Montez's films. The site of performance was always an unrealistic, exoticized fantasy-land.

Brassieres of Atlantis *and* Secrets of the Brassiere Mus

Besides the overall "Maria Montez motif" embedded in the setting, certain visual icons appear over and over in Smith's work, emphasizing that these performances are not designed to be Realist portraits of daily life. The presence of lobsters, for example, was a common image, as were references to brassieres and the setting of Atlantis. Another extant fragment of play text is Smith's *Brassieres of Atlantis* (no copyright), subtitled "A Lobster Sunset Pageant." This piece is noted on the front cover of Smith's handwritten document as being presented by The Reptilian Theatrical Company.[23] This name is particularly interesting, as it gives Smith's company (whoever they might be) the same initials as Charles Ludlam's more famous theatrical troupe, The Ridiculous Theatrical Company.

On this detailed title page, as with *Rehearsal for the Destruction of Atlantis,* there is no mention of this being a play or a drama; it is a pageant meant to occur in this fantastical setting. Once again, the audience finds themselves confronted with Smith's imagined Atlantis, though this is "10 million B.C. in the Prehistoric Brassiere Atlantis of the Future."[24] Brassieres, it is clear, are another common image in Smith's plays, suggesting both hidden glamour or femininity as well as something constricting or binding. Here the audience will see "the secret horrors of the Brassiere World!!!"[25] as though this were some bizarre carnival attraction in this seemingly impossible place and time. As this setting is an imagined impossibility, it has room within it for anything and everything, much like the more formal dramatic texts of the other Ridiculous writers.

This "Sunset Pageant," perhaps meant to be performed in the evening, much like the previously discussed "Atlantis" play, has little in the way of plot. What it does include are, once again, references to lobsters and another common Smith trope, the use of "Noxzema" as a character name. Here, we have "LITTLE NOXZEMA—Cylindrical Brassiere Girl of the Future." Most of the performance seems to center around a strange dance that Noxzema performs, known as the "FORBIDDEN DANCE of the Lost Continent of Farblonjet!" This one strange bit of wordsmithing appears in two places in the Ridiculous scene; Charles Ludlam, too, had a play that referenced such a fictional place, entitled *Der Ring Gott Farblonjet* (1977). Smith created a forbidden dance of Farblonjet that ends in both a mess of milk and foam on stage, followed by a procession featuring "A huge lobster." There are subtle references to capitalism, a favorite target of Smith's, in the mention of "CRAB OGRESS of Claptalism!!"[26] This use of commercial iconography as a route to provide commentary on the middlebrow fascination with commodity culture would become a feature of Ridiculous plays in the Play-House of the Ridiculous as well.

Despite Smith's distaste for the capitalistic, the accumulation of items is key to his visual aesthetic. If, as Jack Halberstam argues, "queer studies offer us one method for imagining, not some fantasy of an elsewhere, but existing alternatives to hegemonic systems,"[27] then Smith's work certainly belongs within a queer theoretical framework. His scenic and costume designs privileged all manner of items, especially those devoid of traditional value, like trash but also toys and toiletries, in such a way as to challenge the whole valuation system in American culture. Failure, as Halberstam theorizes it, allows for this sort of playful behavior on the part of the adult, while going "hand in hand with capitalism. A market economy must have winners and losers, gamblers and risk takers, con men and dupes."[28] Smith defies this entire system in his productions, allowing culture's usual losers—its disposable or valueless items—to be reimagined in his fantasy landscapes as magical relics with transformative powers.

Indeed, physical objects are important to Smith's performances, but the nature of these items is tied to Halberstam's theorization of failure: they are often disposable items, somehow refashioned into something remarkable on stage. For example, on the front page of *Brassieres of Atlantis*, Smith calls for "a volcano-pyramid, in front of which there is a pile of garbage and to the right of which there is a clump of cornstalks growing, forms the background of the pageant."[29] Indeed, the presence of stage properties, which Smith makes a point of mentioning outright, is another marker of Smith's work, though these items might more precisely be considered clutter or junk. In general, there was a proliferation of objects on stage in these productions. This interest in the artistic value of physical things links Smith with other avant-garde work of the 20th century. In Laurence Senelick's estimation, "in pictorial and graphic arts, the artist channeled and manipulated the object to create an entity ... that thwarted expectations of functionality or aesthetics. In the performing arts, a more common or literal practice was to show the performer at loggerheads with the physical object."[30] The arrangement of things could either be to question the meaning of art in light of the usefulness of an object or to question the meaning of reality in light of the act of performance. As the Ridiculous is preoccupied with both consumable and disposable items in their work, it is no wonder that physical objects play such a critical role. Their proliferation is iconic of the consumerist culture in which these artists were creating their work.

Secrets of the Brassiere Mus, an even odder fragment with an even more fragmented title, also welcomes its audience to Atlantis, but it is now The Plaster Foundation incarnation. Dancing once again breaks out and references once again are made to breasts, milk, and Atlantis. Noxzema returns as a character, as does a character called Steve Adore. Yet, here, Atlantis is a place that needs to be rented; Steve Adore implores: "Pardon Me/Forgetting to pay the rental/Of Atlantis!!!"[31] Here the commentary on capitalism is not even shaded in the text, it is stated outright. It is hard to make much of these pages as they seem incomplete and somewhat disconnected, though they do appear together in the Museum of Modern Art archive of Jack Smith materials. What is clear from studying both is that Smith maintained a commitment to certain ideas and particular images across his varied performance art works. It could be that these are versions of the same play in different stages of Smith's performance repertoire. To some extent, all of his plays are "rehearsals" of the same thematic and iconic elements over and over again. Smith ghosts all of his own works, even as he evokes other provocative pop cultural ghosts. He made artistic meaning out of everything around him, even his own negative experiences with the artistic scene. This is particularly clear in his taped work, *What's Underground About Marshmallows.*

What's Underground About Marshmallows?

Smith's 1981 recorded work, *What's Underground About Marshmallows?*, acts as an interesting summation of his previous two decades of work. Although the piece is once again non-linear, there is a sense in which it is a musing over the work that he has done. He speaks in the first person and makes references to the fact that "I have to live in squalor" and encounters with "Uncle Art Krust" and "Uncle Roachcrust." These could be seen as autobiographical references; Smith never made a great sum of money for his works and felt as though his art, especially *Flaming Creatures*, had been stolen from him by art distributors and displayers. In particular, the "Uncle" of which he speaks is likely Jonas Mekas; according to the documentary *Jack Smith and the Destruction of Atlantis*, even Mekas recognized that Smith had all sorts of nasty names like these for him, which became another common reference in Smith's plays.

Much of *Marshmallows* describes how "Uncle Pawnshop" stole his film, while still including the metatheatrical elements that one would come to expect from Smith's performance art. The narrator tells when it is intermission and later calls out for coffee, never giving the illusion that this tape is recording a scripted drama. Rather, this is realistic in the sense of actually being "real"; this is Smith telling his own story as he wishes to tell it. The second side of the tape once again brings Maria Montez to life, getting caught up in her films.[32] *What's Underground About Marshmallows?* sums up many of the key elements that Smith engages in his performance work.

The rituals that Smith created certainly attempted to engage icons and imagery with which he felt a personal connection. Maria Montezian style served as the basis for the design aesthetic while the rest of the production was sprinkled with objects and ideas that Smith found provocative. Yet, for a ritual to work, the audience must have some important role to play; Smith's theatre is no exception. His rituals were particularly provocative because of the performance language they employed; the repeated images (such as Atlantis or the lobster) would have become familiar to his spectators. Every Smith production was, to some degree, ghosted by those that had preceded it. In these works, meaning was best made by individuals who were already aware of Smith's work and what it entailed. Ghosting was used to create an audience of aficionados who could truly appreciate these late-night, sprawling, at-home productions.

Indeed, these performances were designed to operate on the mental and emotional level, as much of ancient ritual might have. In his discussion of experimental work like Smith's, Richard Foreman attests, "I believe that a good number of the theatrical events presented at Mekas's Cinemathèque pointed the way to a theater that can only marginally be realized at any historical time, a theater that functions as art functions, directly on the consciousness, and the way that consciousness operates, rather than a theater as illustrative psychology, mythology, or sociology."[33] The plays Smith presented were open for interpretation, not linear, narrative dramas. Their manifestation in performance was meant as a kind of ritual; in order for the ritual to be performed appropriately, the audience, like a congregation of worshippers, would need to take on roles and fulfill them per their leader's wishes. The performance would not be a polished finished product. Rather, it would be *play*, literally: human beings playing at particular roles in the performance. They would be learning as they were doing; the performance would remain incomplete without their interaction.

The Ghost of Jack Smith: Ron Vawter in What's Underground About Marshmallows?

Jack Smith, it seems, would be evoked as a ghost in later performances as well, most notably in the 1992 rendering of *What's Underground About Marshmallows?* performed by Ron Vawter as part of *Jack Smith/Roy Cohn*. As the DVD for the film of *What's Underground About Marshmallows?* displays, "Quoting Ron Vawter, 'A lot of people say that Jack only had about 12 ideas, but that they were the 12 most important ideas of the last 25 years."[34] If this statement is even remotely true, then the importance of Jack Smith lies not only in the works of art that he created but also in the legacy of his art works—what artists they inspired and what works were created based on them. Nowhere is the legacy of Smith more celebrated than in Vawter's *What's Underground About Marshmallows?*, a filmed restaging of a Jack Smith piece. This was a version of a radio show, which in itself was based on the radio shows of Smith's youth. There is a complexity of representational layers here, one of which is the blending of two of Smith's artistic output media: performance art and film.

In this piece, performed live between 1986 and 1994, and then released as a home video in 1996, Vawter took on the role of Smith, both mimicking Smith in this role and trying to evoke him, without actually pretending to be him. The notes on the DVD attest that Vawter "was not interested in impersonation."[35] In this performance, we find no attempt at realism: Vawter puts on a fake voice and employs stylized movements. Despite this, the overall effect of the piece is, somehow, seemingly "real." Although there is no attempt at theatrical reality, this comes across as a real fake performance (as opposed to a theatrical fake reality): an embodiment of the Reptilian acting technique.

Consider this moment from Smith's performance, as interpreted by Vawter. Vawter/Smith instructs the audience about acting; he declares, "'one of the secrets of great acting is always to contrive to be chopping onions in some dramatic moment' (PAUSE) then 'I think I'll start the onion soup now' (pulls out onions) 'now you can tell that this is one of the big moments of the play.'" Ostensibly, this chopping of onions is to assist the actor in being able to cry on stage. And yet, this technique is at odds with any realist attempt at making an actor cry. In place of calling up a sad memory and letting that inspire tears or allowing the events of the drama to inspire those tears on their own, Vawter/Smith uses neither the actor's "real" emotions derived from the self nor the "fictional" emotions of the character in the circumstances. Rather, Vawter/Smith allows for an entirely external piece of business to inspire this moment of great emotional depth.

Everything presented in a Smith work is a theatrical illusion, but that theatrical trick has been laid bare for the audience, so that they may see its machinations for what they are. The "real" that is happening is the act of acting, not the illusion of a fictional reality. Smith's performances were the manifestations of a "sometimes raving, sometimes broken, paranoid, cross-dressing queer."[36] Smith is never not himself in these performances; in the Vawter interpretation, there is the sense that the personality of this new performer is present right alongside his evocation of the personage of Smith. A great deal of the action on stage involves Vawter/Smith interacting with bizarre stage properties while storytelling—there is no actual narrative drama being enacted on stage.

Rather, what is present is the representation of a type—not a specific character, per se, but a construct of Smith's imagination. This personality is then filtered a second time through the lens of Vawter's performance of Smith in the role. Because he was not interested in impersonation of Smith, Vawter's character both is and is not Smith at the same time. The character being presented is styled in such a manner as to hearken back to Maria Montez's Cobra Woman, without impersonating the femininity of that particular persona. Makeup is worn, but it is neither glamorous nor beautifying. Vawter appears semi-Egyptian in style of dress, but the person being represented defies easy categorization, operating on as many varied levels as forms of media enveloped in this presentation.

In addition to the fact that the character is not a recognizable figure, the actor is going against the traditional styles of acting expected of a performer. Vawter/Smith laments, "worst of all, nobody thinks I'm acting, nobody thinks I'm a great actor or an actor at all, that this isn't even acting."[37] The liner notes explaining this piece seem to echo this cry; Smith was "perform[ing] himself *as himself*"[38] rather than embodying and presenting the personality of another, fictional human being. Who is this person on stage? It is hard to say. In both cases, the personality of the performer comes through as strongly, if not more strongly, than that of the character he is representing. The ghost of Jack Smith is everywhere in this production, as the ghost of Maria Montez was present in Smith's productions.

Ridiculous as Ritual

For Jack Smith, these performances mattered, in the same manner in which a ritual might matter to its participants. These are not just plays or works of dramatic literature; rather, they were rites through which he could bring "ghosts," like that of Maria Montez, to life. Therefore, Smith wanted to go beyond speaking a shared cultural language in his interactions with his audiences; he actually wanted to bring his audience members into his performances in a direct and participatory way. His work creates a distinct bridge between what we might consider a Ridiculous aesthetic and the larger avant-garde and/or experimental scene within the theatre. In speaking generally of radical performance companies of the 1960s, James Harding and Cindy Rosenthal argue in *Restaging the Sixties* that part of the radical quality of performance from this period is a "rejection of theater's traditional deference to the authority of the literary text and a rejection of the traditional boundaries separating performers and spectators."[39] In the works of Smith, this is as much the case as in any of the more obvious examples, like the performances of Richard Schechner or the Living Theatre. Smith's performances were not designed in order to manifest a production of a written play text (as may be the case for Tavel or Ludlam). Rather, they were experiences meant to occur in the present tense for whoever decided to bear witness.

For those who stayed for the duration of the rites presented, a role might become available, as was the case for Stefan Brecht in the performance he describes in *Queer Theatre*. The audience member then had to become active performer, subjecting himself to direction from the artist in charge in order to make sure that the details were all precise so that the ritual was completed correctly. According to Brecht, Smith would often berate his participants until they got the actions right. The assertion of power on the part of the director was an integral part of Smith's "make-it-as-you-go" aesthetic, and of the Ridiculous aesthetic more broadly. Brecht describes:

> Much of his [Smith's] time is spent directing his assistants who in fact tend to be the major performers. He is apt to get seriously irritated—is said sometimes to resort to physical violence (no act): people don't seem to be able to follow the simplest instructions.... Also they have no (adequate) sense of responsibility—their responsibility being considerable because of the importance of the whole thing. They think it can be done any old way. Also his cooperants tend to confer with him about the proper next step.[40]

It is Smith's concept for the production that must be fulfilled and done so correctly, per Smith's vision alone. As Brecht notes, "All of Smith's gestures are hesitant.... He is figuring out how to do it while doing it."[41] Smith's style of play-making is indicative of artistic practices found throughout the Ridiculous scene: an artistic genius pulling the strings of the night's events, both inside the frame of performance and among the spectators.

The most compelling aspect of Smith's performances—which do not quite stand up as dramatic literary texts nor seem simple to reconstruct on a modern-day stage—is the role that he prescribed to his audiences, implemented by breaking with the conventions of theatrical place and time. Clearly, as both Jonas Mekas and Richard Foreman will contend, an individual could be greatly changed by witnessing Smith's works. Yet, despite the importance I am giving to the role of the audience for one of Smith's loft extravaganzas, becoming such an audience member in the first place was a difficult endeavor, not because of a lack of economic capital, as is the case for many large-scale "uptown" productions, but simply from a lack of knowledge that a play was happening in the first place: "The audiences for these shows varied in quantity; they were mostly, but not all, aficionados. You almost had to be in order to know that a show was taking place every Saturday night in a Greene Street loft.... Advertising was sparse and not straightforward or necessarily truthful."[42] One had to know how to navigate the few listings that did exist for these shows in order to attend them at all. Smith's work was not affecting a great many of the "uninitiated"; rather, his productions principally were performed for an audience already well-versed in the nature of what they were about to see.

In Judith Jerome's estimation, lack of information about performances was not the only source for the complicated actor-audience relationship created by these sprawling midnight performances. Jerome lists some "tactics for ... destruction/construction of his [Smith's] audience"; these include "delay and slowness requiring endurance of tedium; demands for participation; and direct abuse."[43] These productions were not for the casual theatergoer. Rather, they were for a particular community member, one who was willing to engage with the production: to tolerate its length and lack of focus, be willing to take part in the action, and possess an acceptance of potentially being insulted by its creator. Yet, Parnes remembers the audience participation as being a less "cruel" practice; "it wasn't the kind of audience participation where you're dragged on stage against your will." He suggests that only "people who wanted to be in the show" actually performed.[44]

Many of these spectator-performers were fellow artists, working on their own experimental theatre pieces. One such aficionado of the work of Smith, Richard Foreman, recalls, "It is a theater that nurtures, at all times, the dreams of those few young theater artists who are most insightful and exact in the ability to dredge up from the mind what the social beast has not found useful in its struggle to suppress the real evolution of consciousness and the spirit."[45] An artist like Foreman might have special insight into understanding the plays that Smith put on, as he, too, would go on to construct non-traditional, non-linear experimental theatre pieces.

And yet, for those willing to push through the tedium and possible cruelty of a Smith production, there was the possibility of the magic associated with great performance. Mekas gives a sense of how the ritual worked and what it left in the spectator afterwards, summing up the valence of Smith's non-traditional theatrical productions:

> I began getting a feeling, it resembled more and more the final burial ceremonies, the final burial rites of the capitalist civilization, competitive civilization, these were the magic burial grounds and the burial rites of all the corruption, comfort and money and good living, and free gifts of the world that was now asleep, at 2 a.m., and Jack Smith was still alive, a madman, the high priest of the ironical burial grounds, administering last services here alone and by himself, because really the seven or eight people who were now his audience (the other three were on the set) were really no audience at all, Jack didn't need an audience, he would do it anyway, and I had a feeling that he did it anyway, many nights like this, many Saturdays, by himself, audience or no audience, actors or no actors, he reenacted this ceremony, the last man who was still around and above it all and not part of it but at the same time conscious of it all, very painfully conscious of it all, the sadness himself, the essence of sadness itself.[46]

Anyone who was willing to sustain interest until the wee hours of the morning of a Smith production was rewarded with having seen something uniquely meaningful. Somehow, the nine-to-five commercial world was superseded for these few hours with something magical that only Smith could create for you (if, indeed, you were one of his worshippers). Smith and his work intentionally stood outside of the system of theatrical production because the intent behind the works was to be separated from the larger commercial system of production at work in the United States. Smith was, to use Stephen J. Bottoms's classification, truly "underground"[47]: he dismissed traditional agendas in order to explore his own existential questions.

Smith as Political Artist

Due to its stylistic complexity, the political aspect of Smith's work may not always be readily apparent. Yet, for Parnes, "there was always a political content to his work for me."[48] Unlike many of his downtown contemporaries, Smith was not creating didactic political theatre. Rather, he was experimenting with form and style, allowing this reimagining of theatre-making to be his radical stance, and using key symbolic icons, such as his various incarnations of Mekas, throughout his oeuvre to stand in for his commentary. As Pogostin notes of Smith, "While Jack was an extremely political artist, the areas he dealt in were the 'politics of art' his endless struggle against the curatorial class that sought to mediate him and act as middleman between him and the general public."[49] Smith tried to find his own methods with which to create art so as to differentiate himself from the mainstream; this act, above all others, was his main political action. This experimentation is evident in his usage of unconventional setting (a basic living space turned into a theatrical salon) and his emphasis on audience participation (i.e., that anyone who attended a production could be and probably needed to be a performer in his plays).

Because of his interest in audience engagement, Smith was an innovator in types of artistic presentation. He found ways to bridge the gap between filmed and live performance, as well as between fantasy and reality in his loft performances. As the introduction to *Flaming Creature* notes:

> He did, however, go on to develop an innovative technique called "expanded cinema," which merged film and slide projection with live performance…. Spectators often had the feeling that what they saw enacted there was no more or less than Smith's daily existence, framed by an audience's presence. As with Smith's films, his performances demanded that the audience allow itself to be severed from the passive mode of observation to enter a performance that challenged its reactions to, and assumptions about, art and theater.[50]

The radical quality of Smith's productions was embedded in their ability

to challenge preexisting notions about the medium of art that he was employing and therefore about culture and even life more broadly. Even though
Smith did not use his productions to enter into political debate with his audiences—or to instruct them about particular political ideologies—Smith did
challenge their notion about how art was supposed to be made and presented.
He questioned the idea that one's home and one's performance space must
be separate locations and he confronted his audiences with the possibility
that fantasy and reality can be two sides of the same coin through the act of
performance. In this way, Smith's performances could have been as edifying
for his audiences as their more politicized contemporaries in the experimental
Downtown Scene and as provocative, in terms of form, as their historical
predecessors in the interwar avant-gardes.

Artists such as Smith were so far removed from mainstream culture that
their creations did not take the same explicit activist stance as some of their
more outspoken contemporaries. However, consider Naomi Fiegelson's comments on the subject, as she was investigating this "revolutionary" work as
it was occurring and her notion of "underground" art pairs well with Bottoms's classification of the term. In *Underground Revolution*, Fiegelson maintains that the "underground revolution is an *avant-garde*" because "in trying
to create a new culture, they are at least setting new styles."[51] In this way, as
Fiegelson suggests, "the Underground revolution is a cultural rather than
political one. While white revolutionaries have been criticized for not developing a political critique of the society, what they have developed is an alternative lifestyle. In the long term, this could be more significant."[52] This
"alternative lifestyle" is inherently underground; it is entirely separate from
mainstream society.

In addition, according to Fiegelson, within this Underground, there is
an interest in participatory performance; she relates: "The Underground revolution has popularized the idea of participation, mostly through guerilla
theatre, the Underground theater, where the reaction is part of the play."[53]
How these artists chose to live their lives—and the constructs that they used
for making their performances—were what was revolutionary about them,
even if they were not didactically political.

In this manner, Smith's use of non-traditional setting and duration for
his performances could be considered his activist stance. As Elizabeth Freeman argues, "Queer temporalities … are points of resistance to this temporal
order that, in turn, propose other possibilities for living in relation to inde-
terminately past, present, and future others: that is, of living historically."[54]
Freeman's notion that a refiguring of time can be a "point of resistance" creates
a theoretical lens through which to view the bizarre all-night rituals that took
place in Smith's loft. Perhaps, then, a loft is not an odd site for performances
but a "queer spatiality." And perhaps these productions were not just bizarre

exercises, but a new model for how a queer identity might be performed. These spaces became community sites for "raising the dead," a place where the particular, if at times peculiar, revered cultural ghosts could be brought to life, not just to be mourned, but also to invigorate the audience. These individuals shared similar cultural interests and understood how to use art as a tool for constructing worlds in which their preoccupations were central. Ridiculous artists staged their version of what a performance could be, which reflected a new aesthetic perspective, one that had implications for new ways of viewing the world as well.

What Smith was attempting was, if not political, then at least radical in terms of aesthetics. He was willing to abandon previously held norms for play duration or setting and disavow any sort of actor-audience divide in order to worship artists and objects that so many others would have rejected or disposed of. Andy Warhol, too, can be said to have engaged in similar practices in his Pop Art painting; he chose subject matter that many critics would not have considered "high culture" at the time and used techniques that broke with earlier models for "great art." Therefore, these Pop Art works were not merely "art for art's sake"; rather, they were productions that took up the task of remaking the cultural hierarchy per their own standards. Things usually considered insignificant or "low" could be valued as highly if not more so than icons traditionally held up as being of worth.

Smith did not enjoy such comparisons to Warhol as the one I made above. He saw his own work as the direct antithesis to what Warhol was doing, precisely because Warhol had given in to commercial pressures. As Pogostin remembers:

> He saw Warhol another artist from the working classes as one who had succumbed to "landlordism" as a user and was appalled. He hated the idea that Warhol had "borrowed" Jack's idea of flaming creatures as the model for warhol's [sic] "superstars." When I tried to comfort Jack with the idea that he had influenced Warhol and others he replied, "I didn't want to influence them, it's not a good thing that I influenced them. I never intended to create a race of prostitute drag queens." and "Warhol makes objects of people that have no way of using that objectification." He believed that it was he who had been used, his work and ideas stolen.[55]

Smith's ghosting of Warhol therefore also runs reciprocally; Warhol may have learned a great deal from Smith, but Smith would forever be ghosted by the impact of Warhol on the artistic scene of the 20th century. In the process, Smith believed that he saw his ideas put into a context that was directly opposed to the one that he proffered; instead of being part of an underground, anti-commercial artistic scene, Warhol would use these techniques as commodities to be bought and sold, in exchange for fame and fortune.

The Ridiculous and Pop Art shared both a literal, geographic scene and certain aesthetic elements. However, works by Warhol and those by artists who surrounded him, indeed even those associated with him, were often created with different motivations than his own. Clearly, Warhol was interested in becoming a commercial success and he fashioned himself into a celebrity. To Smith, Warhol's work lacked the kind of depth necessary to be meaningful. Smith saw Warhol's work as too disengaged, due to its interest in consumerism:

> They're all hypnotized by the blandness ... the smoothness of the finish. Critically you can't deal with Warhol any more than you can deal with the plaster.... What Warhol uses is icing instead of plaster ... and the sparkle on top of the icing is amphetamine. There's nothing underneath. He himself has been terribly bruised by commercialism. He's the product of unarrested commercial intrusion into our daily lives. His films are not much different from all the plaster that's showing on 42nd Street. His main contribution lies in the truth of his sound track which underlies the phony nature of the commercial movie. But there's still nothing underneath. And yet, in the long run he may be doing something good for the medium.[56]

Smith recognizes that the issue with Warhol and his artistic creations, no matter how popular or significant they may have become, is that they are too tainted by commercial culture.

Ridiculous Theatre and Pop Art

Indeed, much of what has contemporarily come to be understood as Pop Art has its genesis in Smith's works—and Smith knew he was making an important contribution. Pogostin recalls, "Very competitive, often mean spirited, Jack Smith was very aware of his place in the history of art and his contributions. He hated comparisons to other living artists seeing himself instead as their source."[57] On the one hand, this exposes Smith's own egotism; he believed that the artistic contributions of others were derivative of his own work. In addition, though, it exposes just how dangerous inspiring a movement can be. Often one can see one's best ideas co-opted—or even improved—and thus a fellow artist can overtake one on an idea that was not his or hers to begin with. For Smith, this usurpation was precisely what happened. Warhol took many ideas from Smith's work and then went on to become more famous for them.

Smith, like Ludlam, did not work in a vacuum, nor was he the only artist at this time to do the kind of experimenting that he was doing, particularly with film, nor the only one to worship Maria Montez. For Jack Smith, ghosting runs two ways: his performances were ghosted by Montez, but the larger Pop Art scene, even its most famous practitioner, Andy Warhol, were ghosted by Smith. For example, Bottoms states, "Both ... directors [Warhol and Jack

Smith] sought, in different ways, to make film more 'real' precisely by making it more obviously 'fake'—believing that the distinct personal qualities of their performers would become more immediately apparent if they were engaged in the construction of blatantly tacky, artificial 'illusions.'"[58] These filmmakers were more interested in presenting the personalities of their performers than in studying particular characters or character types. Reality, in these works, is achieved through a precise fiction; there is no conceit that the world of the performance is a slice of life. Instead, these productions were self-consciously performed, as much to bring attention to the personality of the performer as to the character he or she was portraying.

To some degree, Pop Art, as an aesthetic, achieves the same result as the Ridiculous: an abandonment of traditionally held norms of "high" and "low" or "good" and "bad." As Susan Sontag argues, "The best works among those that are called pop art intend, precisely, that we abandon the old task of always approving or disapproving of what is depicted in art—or, by extension, experienced in life."[59] In this sense, the Ridiculous is a form of Pop Art because its practitioners consistently rejected the notion that some content is worthy of being celebrated while other work should be scorned. Although this is not the only way to understand Pop Art as a form of artistic creation, it does serve to link what the Ridiculous artists were doing with the larger Pop Art scene from which it was born.

This sort of work demands a new theoretical framework if one wishes to study it; the former standards of "high" and "low" art, such as those that might have been useful for someone like Clement Greenberg in the 1930s, could no longer apply in the Downtown Scene, which came to life in the 1960s. This is due to the unique nature of art production in this historical period. Mark C. Carnes suggests, "The 1960s, then, did not entail the demise of criticism; rather, the decade ushered in a new group of critics and focused their attention on a new set of artistic problems."[60] The debate now, in Carnes's view, was not whether a particular work should be considered high or low. Rather, "the arrival on the scene of pop art, as well as the success of avant-garde experimental films such as Jack Smith's *Flaming Creatures*, blurred the lines between elite and popular culture. At the same time, pop art questioned the very status and function of the trained eye of the critic in determining truth in representation, thus opening the door to a theoretical flowering."[61] Even though, as Arnold Aronson claims, East Village theatre of the period may not have been "theoretically based nor intended to transform the idea of theatre,"[62] these Pop Art works made great strides in undoing previously held notions of high and low in art.

Because of its disinterest in traditionally held norms of high and low culture, the Ridiculous can be viewed as having been a logical outgrowth of Pop Art artistic production. For many critics, the connection between the

Pop Art coming out of the Factory and the Theatre of the Ridiculous is a linear, cause-to-effect one. Especially significant to the development of the Ridiculous, as a style of theatre-making, was Pop Art cinema, at least according to Bottoms: "Although firmly rooted in the make-it-up-as-you-go trash aesthetic that had been a feature of the off-off-Broadway movement from its inception, the Ridiculous owed its genesis to New York's underground film community, and particularly to the work of Jack Smith and Andy Warhol."[63] Their emphasis on popular culture as the subject for art as well as their preoccupation with elevating the everyday—such as Warhol's soup cans or Smith's naming a character "Noxzema," a popular skin cleanser brand name[64]—were at the heart of what made both Pop Art and the Ridiculous distinct from other experimental art forms. Like some avant-garde theatrical experimentation of the past, the interest here was in "art-for-art's-sake," creating a performance, no matter how amateurish, for the sake of performing.

In this instance, Bottoms is including Smith among the Pop artists, not the Ridiculous artists, and highlighting him, along with Warhol, as a key influence on the Ridiculous. Director Robert Wilson goes so far as to suggest, "Warhol couldn't have made the films that he did without having known Jack."[65] In the case of Andy Warhol, then, ghosting is clearly present; his work was always marked by what he borrowed from the artists with whom he collaborated[66]; this ghosting is nowhere more pronounced than it is in Warhol's connection to Smith.

Warhol would credit Smith as an influence on his own way of dealing with "actors." Warhol writes, "I picked something up from him for my own movies—the way he used anyone who happened to be around that day, and also how he just kept shooting until the actors got bored."[67] Smith was not bound by a traditional filming schedule, nor did he care if his performers were "actors" or not; Warhol used this technique and became famous for turning no-names into superstars.[68] This practice, of course, was its own sort of Ridiculous remix: individuals who would not have otherwise been considered "talented" or "artists" were given the opportunity to participate in and contribute to artistic production. Standards for artistic ability are unnecessary when anything can be art and anyone can be an artist.

Thus, it is significant that Warhol's claim to fame—Pop Art—was heavily derived from practices Warhol witnessed Smith engaging in before he began his most prolific Factory production. In 1964, Warhol filmed Smith filming "Normal Love," a meta action that now seems a metaphor for how Warhol took from Smith's art work to create the style of filmmaking that would later be associated almost exclusively with Warhol alone. By becoming much more famous than Smith, Warhol erased almost all "traces" of Smith, except through his ghosted presence in Warhol's own works.

Quotation in Pop Art Theatre

Pop Art may have borrowed a great deal from the Ridiculous; ghosting seems to run both ways between these two forms. As Carlson describes it, textual ghosting or "this 'intertextual' attitude, approaching the text not as a unique and essentially self-contained structure but as an open-ended 'tissue of quotations,' has become now quite familiar."[69] And yet, it is still striking in its Ridiculous incarnation. Consider the works of Factory Superstar Jackie Curtis; the ghosting in these pieces, as in many Play-House productions or Jack Smith presentations, is always of the icons of popular culture, engaging the audience in a game of "name that reference" from one line to the next.

Curtis is an interesting figure to consider because she, too, straddles the line between Pop Art and the Ridiculous, as Smith does. The nature of the works by both artists implies a gray, overlapping area between the two movements. One clear similarity is the interest in popular culture—and its mixing with higher forms of art—as well as celebrity worship. Curtis certainly occupied a similar space in terms of aesthetic choices to the one employed by the Ridiculous artists; she, too, created plays constructed from elements of all aspects of culture, with a particular emphasis on a worship of movie icons.

One Curtis play that achieves the goal of rousing the ghosts of the glamour of old Hollywood is *Glamour, Glory, and Gold* (1967). I am singling out this play in particular because of its central storyline: a starlet's preoccupation with Hollywood glamour and fame. In terms of nostalgia for 20th-century popular culture, this play exhibits its own special brand of that middlebrow phenomenon. According to Craig Highberger, "The play is very derivative of old movies, but is at times both a satire and a tribute."[70] Curtis's representation of the mythologized "Golden Age of Hollywood" both reveres and pokes fun at it. In classic Ridiculous fashion, Curtis explores the tension between making art and being a star.

Curtis engages in the same practice of quoting from other sources and referencing the mainstream culture that both Ludlam and Smith did. Consider this anecdote from Andrew Amic-Angelo: "In those days, they broadcast two episodes of *I Love Lucy* every afternoon, and this was Jackie's favorite show, so the rehearsals would be set according to the schedule of the *I Love Lucy* show. And during my key scene as Arnie, we actually wrote a line into the script: 'Look at you. You are such a pig! All you do all day long is sit around on your ass watching *I Love Lucy*.'"[71] Like other plays of the Ridiculous, Curtis's plays include elements that betray a love, bordering on obsession, with popular culture from the creator. In this anecdote, two layers of ghosting become evident: the text is ghosted by both the cultural reference *and* the "inside joke" about the rehearsal process. A Ridiculous play is always somehow more complex than merely a sum of its component parts.

Curtis's play is entirely ghosted by its creator's interest in the Hollywood culture of her youth. However, in a play like *Glamour, Glory, and Gold*, the interest in popular culture goes beyond merely trying to reference it or quote from it. Rather, these Pop Art plays attempt to bring to life the old Hollywood starlets on stage. Again, nowhere was this fixation on popular culture more evident than in the Ridiculous theatre artists' preoccupation with B-movie starlet Maria Montez. Vaccaro saw the connection between the work his company was doing and the plays of Curtis in terms of this star worship: "Jackie Curtis was completely in tune with what we were doing at the Play-House of the Ridiculous. We were really into the movies of the thirties and forties. That's where our sensibility came from. We were especially crazy about the terrible old films of Maria Montez."[72] Again, Montez was perhaps the deepest influence on the aesthetic of the Ridiculous, more so than any other artifact of 20th-century culture. Her "ghost" is always present on stage, sometimes literally, as Ridiculous performers were regularly preoccupied with evoking the spirit of Montez in all of the art that they created. Here, she is present in a work by a Pop Artist, suggesting again that the line between these two forms is inherently blurry.

In the next chapter, I look specifically at Vaccaro's company, as much of its aesthetic style was born directly from the Factory and many of its participants worked with both Warhol and the Play-House. Ronald Tavel, who was an associate of Jack Smith, got his start writing scenarios for Warhol, some of which Vaccaro directed. From the practice of writing and performing scenarios for Warhol, Ridiculous Theatre, as an actual named practice, genre, and company would literally come to life. Therefore, without Warhol's Pop Art scene, there might not have been a specific Theatre of the Ridiculous at all. The link is not only through ghosting, but a literal, tangible one between and among gay male artists who were interested in performance and a particular mode of expression. These individuals did not accept the status quo; rather, they used their art to revalue all aspects of culture. Through Vaccaro's company, that will come to be known as the Play-House of the Ridiculous, ghosting is taken one step further to the level of remix, where anything and everything that is said and done could be seen to evoke something else.

FOUR

"Ridiculous Remix"
Playing at Power at the
Play-House of the Ridiculous

One thing that made the performance art pieces of Jack Smith so remarkable was the blending of ideas and iconography from all strata of culture. Yes, Smith made many references to B-movies and the like, but he also had intellectual concerns, which he explored in his productions. Indeed, works like those by Smith and other artists of his ilk "occupied the boundaries between popular entertainment and intellectual inquiry."[1] The crossroads between that which is consumed for pleasure and that which is presented for intellectual debate is a key element of the Ridiculous landscape.

Despite the presence of key Ridiculous aesthetic elements, the works of Jack Smith were never called Ridiculous by their creator or by their spectators. Smith's connection with Andy Warhol and Pop Art, however, is necessary for understanding the Ridiculous, as its threads have their genesis in the realm of Pop Art. This is quite literal in the case of the development of John Vaccaro's Play-House of the Ridiculous. Vaccaro, born in 1929 in Steubenville, Ohio, might never have made Ridiculous Theatre if working for Warhol had not brought him and playwright Ronald Tavel, born in Brooklyn, New York in 1936, together to stage Warhol's at times esoteric, or even incomprehensible, film scenarios. I concentrate on the Play-House as a focal point for the birth of the Ridiculous because it was here that the word "Ridiculous" was first applied to any production by artists in the Downtown Scene.

Throughout the productions of the Play-House, there is an emphasis on citationality, or what I would like to brand "Ridiculous remix." Remix, as it has been theorized since the 1990s by individuals such as Lawrence Lessig and Lev Manovich, includes practices of borrowing or quoting from, alluding to, and sampling from works from the surrounding culture. In our era, "remix culture" allows "any grade-school kid [who] has a copy of Photoshop ... [to] download a picture of George Bush and manipulate his face how they want and send it to their friends," according to Lessig.[2] But the Ridiculous artists engaged in similar practices decades prior, mixing their pop cultural interests with their knowledge of erudite material. The difference was that the products of Ridiculous remixers were live performances as opposed to mediatized Internet properties.

Despite the prevalence of media remixing, especially on the web, the musical application of remix is closest to the Ridiculous practice of it. As DJ Spooky puts it, "This is a world where all meaning has been untethered from the ground of its origins and all signposts point to a road that you make up as you travel through the text."[3] In order to make sense of a Ridiculous play, one needs to trace the various threads present in the text, adding them together to get the complete picture.

Ridiculous remix can take three forms. The first emphasizes a renegotiation of cultural power, where low cultural artifacts are valued equal to or even more than those from the highbrow or elite strata of cultural production. Ronald Tavel's play *The Life of Lady Godiva* exhibits this remix style of cultural blending. Kenneth Bernard's *The Magic Show of Dr. Ma-Gico* displays a second strand of Ridiculous remix; in this play, remix techniques are used in order to blur the lines between reality and fiction within the stage world. This creates a complex metatheatricality, a performance self-aware of its own status as performance. This metatheatrical move is a postmodern one, as it "takes the form of self-conscious, self-contradictory, self-undermining statement. It is rather like saying something whilst at the same time putting inverted commas around what is being said."[4] In this sense, a metatheatrical play consistently draws attention to itself in order to comment on it itself. The apotheosis of Ridiculous remix is Charles Ludlam's *Conquest of the Universe or When Queens Collide*, which is simultaneously a pastiche of cultural materials, both of the highbrow and lowbrow variety, as well as an exercise in extreme metatheatricality. Remix may have taken different forms, but it was always a part of Ridiculous play-making.

In each of these plays, a cultural mixing in the dramaturgical structure highlights a subtle thematic motif: that of power. In the Ridiculous, remix is used in order to undo existing power structures as they relate to culture; the low can now be seen as high and vice versa. Form in the Ridiculous is able to throw into relief content, and a political undercurrent emerges. These seemingly apolitical plays—as they address no particular social or political issues nor serve any didactic or activist purpose—actually engage large questions about the possession of power: who has it, why do they have it, and how might it be taken away. One way in which power may be asserted, from the Ridiculous perspective, is through an undoing of the cultural hierarchy, both that which asserts high culture over low as well as that which privileges the educated over the uneducated. Even the hierarchy of wealthy over poor is undone in a Ridiculous production; these plays are not commodities to be sold for profit but experiences that cannot be quantified in dollars and cents. The Ridiculous undermines such hierarchies through its use of remix techniques in its dramaturgy.

Playing at the Play-House

To give a brief overview of the Play-House's history would be impossible without first recognizing the larger scene of experimental theatrical production in which the company was formed. Stephen J. Bottoms and others have labeled this scene "off-off-Broadway," both because of its geographical distance from the Great White Way and its disavowal of the sorts of commercial productions being mounted on Broadway. Bottoms reminds that "the term *off-off-Broadway* needs to be considered skeptically," especially in discussions that attempt to suggest it was a cohesive movement. Bottoms is sure, however, that among these companies, of which he considers the Play-House a key example, "there was ... a very clear sense of shared community, and a shared resistance to the economic imperatives of mainstream American culture."[5]

Zeroing in, then, on the Play-House specifically, this so-called repertory company principally consisted of director John Vaccaro and whatever playwright and actors he was working with at a particular time. Although much has been made about the overlap between the Ridiculous and Pop Art, aesthetically, "Vaccaro points back to the Caffe Cino as the inspirational starting point for such queer performance work."[6] The inception of the Play-House began in the collaboration of Vaccaro with playwright Ronald Tavel, producing plays that often featured other "Downtown superstars," particularly those from Andy Warhol's Factory. Tavel initially wrote scenarios for Warhol and "some writers attribute the beginning of the Theatre (or Play-House) of the Ridiculous to the staging of Tavel's second production, *The Life of Lady Godiva* in April 1966."[7]

In order to address the question of when the Ridiculous was founded, much of my concern must be semantic. In his article written exclusively about Ronald Tavel, Dan Isaac claims that "at the Coda Galleries, on June 29, 1965," due to a meeting between Tavel and director John Vaccaro, "the theatre of the ridiculous was born."[8] It was for this first collaboration between Vaccaro and Tavel that Tavel penned the "one-line manifesto" for his works: "We have passed beyond the absurd: our position is absolutely preposterous."[9] However, the ad for 1965's *Shower* and *The Life of Juanita Castro* does not include any mention of the word Ridiculous, neither in the company's name nor in any descriptive passage. The program for *The Life of Lady Godiva*, on the other hand, includes the title of the company, the Play-House of the Ridiculous

Repertory Club. With this 1966 production, the company was setting out Ridiculous as both their label and style while Tavel continued to define how he intended to apply the term "Ridiculous" to his work.

What's in a name, one might ask? If a connection is to be drawn between the Ridiculous and other 20th-century avant-garde movements, then titling a movement is critical to its formation. Many movements of the avant-garde proclaimed their objectives in manifestos, even before any works of art had been created. These manifestos, thereby, operated as declarations of what their movements' titles meant. This act of declaring was, in and of itself, the birth of these artistic styles and associations. Mary Ann Caws suggests, "The manifest proclamation itself marks a moment, whose trace it leaves as a post-event commemoration. Often the event is exactly its own announcement and nothing more, in this Modernist/Postmodernist genre. *What it announces is itself.*"[10] The existence of a particular artistic community, then, can be created in the moment the group declares that it exists. Declaring one's existence can be the entirety of the movement; as Caws reminds, "the artistic manifesto, whose work will be carried on in another world altogether—aesthetic battles having different consequences [from theological or political ones]—depends on its context as well as its cleverness, and on the talents of its producer."[11] Calling the movement Ridiculous was a critical step in bringing the movement into being; actually having a movement would be entirely dependent on what sort of work these artists would go on to create.

In terms of the avant-garde, then, the project of the Ridiculous, as Ronald Tavel conceived it, is most closely in dialogue with the Theatre of the Absurd. Tavel envisioned that the Ridiculous that he was creating was a direct reaction—or indeed counterargument—to the Absurd. To take Tavel's opinion of the genesis of the Ridiculous, "[he himself] invented the designation Theatre of The Ridiculous to identify the vision and styles of what would be … his more than forty produced stage plays."[12] Tavel's intention was to create something beyond what the Absurd had been able to accomplish in their theatre; "[Tavel] asked himself, 'What could come next? A theatre of The Ridiculous?'"[13] Supposedly, Tavel was consciously writing a style of play that was meant to react to, and perhaps even commentate on, the genre of the Absurd.

Yet, the Absurd was never a conscious movement in its own right, unlike the avant-gardes who had declared their existence via manifesto. Several playwrights, including Samuel Beckett, Jean Genet, and Eugene Ionesco, wrote plays independently of one another, yet have been forever linked by the analytical work of critic Martin Esslin. By grouping these plays together and *calling* them Absurdist, Esslin created a theatrical movement that had not been there before. So, too, did Vaccaro and Tavel's flyer indicating that a Ridiculous production by a Play-House of the Ridiculous company declare that now a new movement was about to begin: one that was no longer absurd, but now ridiculous.

If Tavel's story is not the complete account of how all of the artists came to refer to their work as Ridiculous, then how did this title come in to common usage? Bottoms relates the following anecdote in *Playing Underground*; as legend would have it, the term "Ridiculous" was created entirely inadvertently. "Though Tavel claims that he originated the company name, Vaccaro insists the label ridiculous was coined by his friend, actress Yvette Hawkins, in describing a rehearsal of *Shower*."[14] If this explanation is correct, then the Ridiculous, as a theatrical movement, was not only *not* a specific reaction to the Absurd; it was not even a conscious construct. The Ridiculous was, in appropriately ridiculous fashion, created by accident. The style developed from the theatrical practices being employed at the Play-House, not from academic debate about the meaning of theatrical practices.

In response to claims like this one, the Tavel archive announces, "Other accounts of the coining of the phrase, Theatre of the Ridiculous, appear on the Internet and in various publications. But any account differing from the above is patently false."[15] While I tend to agree with this latter designation of the naming of the Ridiculous—both Tavel's and Ludlam's plays do, in fact, contain elements that seem intentionally designed to "get beyond the Absurd"—in either of the cases, the Ridiculous, as a signifier of genre, was first applied to productions from this particular company.

These two figures—Tavel and Vaccaro—are theatrical giants when it comes to discussing Theatre of the Ridiculous. In addition to the supposed appellation of Ridiculous to the form, Tavel wrote "more than forty stage plays" in this style, many of which, including Tavel's "only formal tragedy" *Bigfoot* (1972) earned Obie awards and very successful theatrical runs. In terms of his elision from theatre histories, the 2015 online archive of his works may describe the situation best:

> Ronald Tavel never registered the label, Theatre of the Ridiculous, at City Hall, believing that if he alone use it, it might well be forgotten. But he did not anticipate that the three or more companies (including one in Paris), which subsequently adopted the label, would merely imitate some of the stylistic, surface qualities of his early stage work: and never probe their, or his, later themes mythic, religious, political, or otherwise.[16]

Tavel was creating not just a style of play-making, from this point-of-view; rather he was investigating complex themes and ideas in his play texts.

Consider Tavel's 1967 *Gorilla Queen*, a strange but sophisticated example of the Ridiculous genre. In the play script uploaded to the archive, a preface by M. S. is included, which perhaps best sums up the experience of reading—and, I can assume, watching—this wildly anarchic play:

> *Gorilla Queen* is one of the most insane plays I've ever seen, even counting other works by Ronald Tavel. Crammed into the camp form of a movie musical is a farcical

treatment of ultraserious themes. Two whole civilizations, the scum of the jungle and the cream of Hollywood, are tossed about in a whirlpool of philosophy. Beast and movie star couple in grubby lust. Purity is despoiled by a mad male nun. Transformation leads to transformation with vertiginous extravagance. All the climaxes are in the wrong places, and dualisms multiply until the tragic ending is only a pretext for another happy, or at least manic, beginning. Meanwhile the language never ceases its headlong punning, beyond vulgarity, beyond criticism, beyond belief.[17]

I quote this epitaph at length because we find here mention of our key Ridiculous markers: a camp aesthetic, chock full of jokes and puns; references to Hollywood glamour; cross-gendered performance and sexuality represented on stage; and an emphasis on defying traditional dramaturgical structures. Indeed, Tavel was a master of the Ridiculous form and, with the archiving of his materials online, there is strong hope that in this moment of Ridiculous Renaissance the plays of Ronald Tavel will find new life.

Vaccaro, too, benefited from the recent renewed interest in the Ridiculous, at least in terms of the cultural recognition of the significance of his death. Indeed, as Lee Black Childers claims in *Please Kill Me*, "John Vaccaro was more important than Charles Ludlam because Ludlam followed theatrical traditions and used a lot of drag. People felt very comfortable with Charles Ludlam. Everyone's attitude going to see Charles's plays was that they were going to see a really funny, irreverent, slapstick drag show. They never felt embarrassed. But John Vaccaro was way past that. Way, way past that. John Vaccaro was dangerous."[18] To a large extent, especially by the final years of his career, Ludlam was creating farces, albeit with some camp elements, that were ultimately tightly scripted plays.

Vaccaro, on the other hand, was doing something revolutionary in his theatre: challenging his performers and audiences alike in such a way as to provide a commentary on his contemporary America. Of his own work, Vaccaro states in *Please Kill Me*, "I really wasn't interested in campy things. I wasn't interested in promoting homosexuality. My sensibility is different from camp.... I used glitter as a way of presentation. Nothing more. Glitter was the gaudiness of America, that's what I interpreted it as.... I used it because it was shoving America back into the American faces. It was the gaudiness of Times Square. You know, take away the lights and what do you have in Times Square? Nothing."[19] Discussing Theatre of the Ridiculous, at least as it was practiced at the Play-House by Vaccaro and his contemporaries, is more complex than just stating that this was a "campy gay" theatre aesthetic. Vaccaro saw himself as a critic of the American values of his time, which were interested in glitz and glamour, on the surface, with little concern for what is underneath. His theatre worked to expose those realities. Thus, Vaccaro, like Ludlam and Tavel, saw himself as a theatrical and artistic innovator of a far more complex ilk than others of his time.

Indeed, Vaccaro was an incredibly significant theatre practitioner in his own right. Upon Vaccaro's death in August 2016, all major theatre outlets, including *Playbill*, ran an obituary on Vaccaro, as did the *New York Times*. While each of these articles did mention the significance of his connection with Ludlam, they also highlighted his unique contributions to the theatrical scene. the *New York Times* credits Vaccaro and the Play-House with "help[ing] establish Off Off Broadway [*sic*] as a source of antic creativity and thumb-in-the-eye subversion of social and artistic conventions" and creating performances that were "heavy on the glitter and makeup, broadly comic and shamelessly vulgar, sexually confrontational and terribly, terribly impolite,"[20] a fairly thorough explication of the Ridiculous genre more broadly.

For Vaccaro, the Ridiculous was a reflection of his lifestyle; Vaccaro was quoted in an interview with *Cue Magazine*, saying, "I'm very free. And that's the theme in all our plays: Freedom. Total freedom."[21] This notion of being free to be oneself on stage is precisely at the heart of the Ridiculous project. Much of what Stefan Brecht saw as progressive within the Ridiculous is due to its lifestyle production, not its artistic work. Brecht describes, "Essentially I think this theatre proposes a certain ideal life-style or attitude, doing theatre as part of living that way, which it conveys by its style on stage and which it defends in its plays by ridiculing its opposite and *in no other way* because that life-style is rigorously indefensible."[22] The nature of Ridiculous work, in Brecht's understanding of it, came from a larger concept of how to live one's life, and from building a larger society in which this art form is a vital component. In addition, Brecht emphasizes the sense of a family structure inherent in the manner in which the company worked. Brecht notes how this is a family of individuals who have chosen to be members of the group and who therefore play their roles (both on stage and off) as a part of their larger identity as members of the community.[23] Ridiculous participants are free to be who they are, both on and off stage.

Indeed, the dramatic and theatrical style of early Ridiculous works penned by Tavel and directed by Vaccaro at the Play-House were marked by this sense of freedom, as much about anti-art as they were about making art. For example, for the scenario *The Life of Juanita Castro*, penned by Tavel for Andy Warhol's Factory players, the stage direction appears: "This play should never be rehearsed."[24] The emphasis here was on the act of performing, not a polished finished product; the actors are fed their lines during the performance itself by an on-stage director, a clear marker of the work as queer in its rebranding and acceptance of failure at performative perfection as a key aesthetic element, as discussed in this book's preface. Because of this, the audience is "seeing an activity as such—a doing, perhaps a making—rather than the doing or making of something. We are not so much seeing a play as the making of a play."[25] The potential amateurish quality that this would lend to the production would become a stylistic marker throughout many of the works associated with the Ridiculous.

Therefore, in addition to borrowing material from a large-scale cultural reserve of ideas, Ridiculous plays also indulge an interest in spontaneity in performance. In no Ridiculous theatre is this more prevalent than in productions at director John Vaccaro's Play-House of the Ridiculous. An interest in improvisation and the fluidity of theatrical presentation became a quintessential aspect of Vaccaro's directing style:

> Vaccaro began to see the potential in treating theatre not as a tightly rehearsed edifice, but as an opportunity for "live" improvisation around certain structural parameters (i.e., the script). The Ridiculous subsequently developed as a kind of latter-day commedia dell'arte company, whose rehearsal process was directed not toward arriving at a single, ideal performance to be consistently reproduced, but toward drilling performers in a scenario's improvisational possibilities. The challenge for performers was to find a way to spark off each other's individual styles and personalities, so that the show could evolve spontaneously—moment by moment and night after night.[26]

These plays were meant to be new and unique at each performance, never the same twice. There was no final, definitive production; the work was always in flux.

The plays, therefore, exhibited an anarchic, free form approach to artistic creation.[27] Artists associated with the Play-House were interested in discovering new ways to make theatre while, at the same time, altering conceptions of the divide between low and high in the arts. Bottoms writes, "By the early 1960s, moreover, the need to throw off traditional conceptions of high and low art, respectable and despised, was being felt even by those with more self-conscious artistic agendas."[28] The Ridiculous, like other companies operating in the Downtown Scene at the time, was interested in undoing the outdated categories of high and low in their theatre. Ridiculous artists took their own personal interest in things like 20th-century cinema and mixed it with more traditionally canonic material, such as works of classical literature and myth.

Before lumping the Play-House and other Ridiculous sites in with any and all other companies that mix various cultural elements, however, it is worthwhile to highlight what makes it unique. As Arnold Aronson suggests in *American Avant-Garde Theatre*, "one branch" of avant-garde theatre of the 1960s "was the formalist work to be found in performance art and the creations of Jack Smith, Richard Foreman, Robert Wilson, and others that was informed by Happenings, Cagean aesthetics and influences from other arts."[29] On the one hand, the Ridiculous was participating in this gesture toward art for arts' sake—a return to an almost Dadaist performance sensibility. Yet, on the other, Ridiculous plays were neither "abstract," which George Rickey considers "abstracted from nature" nor "non-objective," in Rickey's terms "subjectless art."[30] Rather, they appropriated from the culture around them, shook up the various pieces, and poured them out into their own particular production. The final product that emerged was a mixture of American culture, which in itself is a mixture; these productions were unique because of their blended form, Ridiculous remix.

Middlebrow America: Setting the Stage for Ridiculous Remix

The elements being remixed, in the case of the Ridiculous, were borrowed from all aspects of culture. It was precisely an interest in popular culture that made the Ridiculous so pertinent to its historical place and time. As Bonnie Marranca suggests, "Its [Ridiculous theatre's] dependency on the icons, artifacts, and entertainments of mass culture in America—the 'stars,' old movies, popular songs, television and advertising—makes the Ridiculous a truly indigenous American approach to making theatre."[31] Branding the Ridiculous as American sheds light on its preoccupation with commercial advertising, consumer products, and popular culture elements. David Savran notes in *A Queer Sort of Materialism*, "By February 1949, middlebrow's moment had arrived"[32] in the United States, heralding in an age that included such varied cultural creations, "from teen movies to abstract expressionism, from bebop to *Queen for a Day*, from 'Hound Dog' to *The Sound of Music*."[33] Therefore, the world of many of the Ridiculous artists' adolescence, as most were born in the 1930s and 40s, would have been the world of "the post–World War II boom years … [which were] filled with institutionalized bowling leagues and paid vacations and brought television, long-playing records, and paperback books into almost every American home."[34]

Savran labels this explosion of popular culture "middlebrow," theorizing about the contentious space between "highbrow" art that "refus[ed] commodity status and [functioned] as a signifier of cultural purity, consecration, and asceticism during a period marked by the widespread and unprecedented availability of luxury goods, both utilitarian and decorative"[35] and the "lowbrow," "whose taste was almost always associated with a fraction—or perhaps I should say a fantasy—of the working class, the primitivized 'masses' who were usually seen as dupes, or potential dupes, for those most un–American of ideologies, communism and fascism."[36] From the elitist highbrow standpoint, the lowbrow was considered too common, designed for too uneducated a strata of the populace, to be worthy of the consideration of cultural critics. The lowbrow was also in conflict with the "American way" of capitalism, yet the highbrow was often celebrated for its distance from the commercial concerns of marketability and profitability. The complex and contentious crossroads between commercialism and aesthetics would remain at the heart of debates over cultural hierarchy throughout the 20th century.

Indeed, cultural critics of the mid–20th century were interested in differentiating between what was considered high and what low. For example, Clement Greenberg positioned the avant-garde against the kitsch, discussing the avant-garde as a movement outside of mainstream culture in which "'art for art's sake' and 'pure poetry' appear, and the subject matter or content becomes something to be avoided like a plague."[37] Form is valued above all else in the avant-garde, yet it is being invaded by "academicism and commercialism" which "can mean only one thing: that the avant-garde is becoming unsure of the audience it depends on—the rich and the cultivated."[38] This has lead the avant-garde to become less confrontational and therefore to lose some of its important cultural status. That status is entirely dependent upon its separatist position, yet that outsider status is reliant on financial support from the upper class.

Kitsch, on the other hand, "is a product of the industrial revolution which urbanized the masses of Western Europe and America and established what is called universal literacy,"[39] according to Greenberg. Kitsch is built on "debased and academicized simulacra of genuine culture"[40] and is principally preoccupied with being bought and sold. There is nothing genuine about kitsch; it is the lowest of the low, a terrible byproduct of the capitalist system.

Kitsch also serves a function in memory-making, both melancholic and nostalgic, per Celeste Olalquiaga's categories. She notes that an item may not have intrinsic value, but it can be imbued with value by its owner. In this way, "melancholic kitsch revels in memories because their feeling of loss nurtures its underlying rootlessness." Because kitsch has no value, it can intensify feelings of sadness and longing. On the other hand, "nostalgic kitsch evokes memories in order to dispel any such feelings, stubbornly hanging on to any inkling of the past that may provide it with a sense of continuity and belonging—that is, with a tradition."[41] Here, the value of kitsch is its ability to evoke the past, a clear preoccupation for these very nostalgic Ridiculous remixers.

Certainly, the Ridiculous could be called kitsch because of its preoccupation with nostalgia. And yet, the Ridiculous cannot be said to fit easily into either one of Greenberg's categories. On the one hand, the Ridiculous *is* kitschy, as it is preoccupied with some of the most disposable elements of American culture and intended for a commercial audience. It is also "low" in terms of content, often relying on crude humor or sexual situations for a laugh. On the other, the Ridiculous could be said to be an "art-for-art's-sake" movement and thereby potentially avant-garde and highbrow. *Shower*, Tavel's early scenario for Warhol, is an example of this blending of the seemingly dichotomous high and low. Tavel observes, "[*Shower*] was dirty like the Mae

West I had loved for so many years, it was action-packed and streamlined for movement, yet totally devoid of character or identity, direction, plot, or subject matter."[42] *Shower*, then, could be said to be both a product of the highbrow, avant-garde project of valuing form above content while at the same time being manifested from the bawdy, popular forms of kitschy low culture that Tavel had come to admire.

Because of this integration of high and low into a single finished product, as in the case of *Shower*, the term "middlebrow" is apt for discussing Ridiculous work, especially because of its ties to commercial commodity culture. Savran distinguishes the middlebrow from its upper and lower companions, stating, "the middlebrow is the unapologetic consumer and cultural middleman."[43] The Ridiculous, despite an ostensible aestheticist mentality of artistic creation, cannot be said entirely to eschew an interest in the commercial; these artists were obsessed with the icons of the cinema and cited quotations from commercial advertising. The Ridiculous, certainly, was willing to consume anything and everything from the surrounding culture, repurposing all of that material into its finished products. References to the popular were no less employable than citations from the elite.

The valence of this culture blending suggests an undoing of the cultural hierarchies, which had been so popular in the preceding decades of the 20th century. The high and low, in the Ridiculous, have equal usefulness in terms of being used as the material from which to make art. In this way, even if the Ridiculous artists were not the authorities on culture—indeed much of their work went unnoticed—they enacted *power* over the culture around them within the plays that they created. As Michael Kammen mentions, "Cultural authority may also embody or manifest cultural power; but authority and power are not exactly the same, and it has not been commonplace for the two qualities to be combined. Cultural power involves the production, promotion, and dissemination of cultural artifacts."[44] The Ridiculous artists set their own standards for what was "valuable" and what worthy of being discarded. In this manner, the Ridiculous, as a movement, was preoccupied with power—power over the culture in which they worked and the power to highlight to their audiences what was worthy of being mocked (which, ultimately, turned out to be everything).

This undoing of preconceived notions about cultural hierarchies was not unique to the Ridiculous alone. In this particular period, throughout the Downtown Scene—the larger landscape of artistic production in New York City in which the Ridiculous found itself situated, usually considered to be concentrated below Fourteenth Street—"a distinctly new attitude toward artistic production surfaced."[45] This new attitude was particularly preoccupied with "undermin[ing] from within the traditional structures of artistic media and the culture that had grown up around them."[46] Rather than overturning the system that was in place, these artists were interested in working from inside of that system, destroying it from its interior with its own elements of production. There is no clear manifesto for the Downtown Scene; as Brandon Stosuy rightly recognizes, mapping this scene "prove[s] only so helpful."[47] Rather, what connects these works together is that they "not only served as an alternative to mainstream publishing." Rather, the Downtown Scene "presented writers with a shadowy shifting, often ad hoc blueprint of how to create works that breathed freely and remained connected significantly to the everyday."[48] There was no single way to create a so-called "Downtown work of art." These artists positioned themselves outside of mainstream culture and thus the power to create rested in the hands of the artist, who reflected on the everyday world in which he or she lived.

This landscape of artistic experimentation questioned the status quo of the surrounding culture. In order to do so, the artists associated with the movement employed many of the same artistic concepts and ideas. The Downtown Scene, and, by extension, the Ridiculous, can be analyzed based on certain key elements that run throughout the artwork produced. Marvin J. Taylor sets out four themes as well as a "tendency" that appear to be present across all of the works in the Downtown Scene—and indeed, their traces are evident in the works of the Ridiculous as well. These are "authenticity," which addresses questions regarding originals and their reproduction(s); "performativity," a preoccupation with the meanings and boundaries of performance; "politics," particularly those of an activist quality; "accreditation," which "investigates the processes by which cultural power is created, maintained, and distributed"; and the "tendency," which Taylor labels "subversion."[49] Building on Robert Siegle's argument in *Suburban Ambush: Downtown Writing and the Fiction of Insurgency* (1989), Taylor explains this tendency through an example: "As Siegle notes, Downtown artists appropriated existing cultural models, such as business structures, only to use those models to disrupt the hegemony of business, for example."[50] Mainstream structures were employed so that these artists could undermine them from within.

If we link the Ridiculous to the surrounding community of experimental artistic practice, then these discussions of subversion, and by extension, of power—or even politics—become essential to the conversation. It is easy to call the Ridiculous, particularly its Play-House incarnation, an apolitical art movement; Vaccaro was preoccupied with exploring art and experimentation, specifically improvisation, in theatre, not with presenting didactic political lessons. Tavel, however, was interested in moving beyond the Absurd, a nihilistic, fatalistic, minimalist movement at heart. Could his gesture toward this more baroque, over-the-top, anarchic dramaturgy have been a reaction to the resignation of Absurdism? Could that have been, in and of itself, if not an activist stance, then perhaps a politicized gesture?

Should the Ridiculous be considered an avant-garde movement to any degree, then discussions of politics are critical to understanding the meaning of the movement. The debate over whether or not the avant-garde was principally aesthetic or actually political in nature has been bandied about in avant-garde studies for years. In *Anarchist Modernism*, for example, Allan Antliff dismisses the apoliticaliticization of the avant-garde in America, debunking "three pervasive myths codified by Barbara Haskell in the Whitney Museum's benchmark end-of-the-century exhibition catalog, *The American Century: Art and Culture, 1900–1950*."[51] These so-called myths seem oddly apropos to this discussion of the Ridiculous: (1) "early American modernism is best defined stylistically, according to degrees of abstraction"; (2) "early American modernism was an exercise in formalist innovation"; and (3) "American modernists were quietist and apolitical."[52] Antliff puts re-politicizing the first wave of the American avant-garde at the base of his discussion of their artwork. No longer are these formalist movements, principally preoccupied with changing the nature of artistic expression. Rather, they are the products of artists deeply engaged with the issues of their time.

I, too, "debunk" these myths, insofar as they apply to the plays of the Ridiculous. In terms of Ridiculous plays, then, I suggest that they were not principally apolitical plays, nor was their form meant to be more significant than their content. Rather, the form was used precisely to mirror the content: the practice of Ridiculous remixing allows these plays to tackle the concept of power. This meant the blending of high culture and low culture was a politicized action—the form of these plays, as Taylor and others have suggested was the heart of the "Downtown Scene project," subverted the already existing systems of cultural power. In the Theatre of the Ridiculous, complex middlebrow tension is derived from the blending of interests in both commerce and art. Artistic power is not clearly situated with either the elite aestheticians or the commercial sell-outs. Rather, in the Ridiculous, those who are able to wield power seem to be those who operate from somewhere in between these two poles.

Ridiculous Remix I: Blending the High with the Low (The Life of Lady Godiva)

Before discussing the use of remixed elements, it is worth remembering that *The Life of Lady Godiva* was part of the bill that first employed the term Ridiculous to advertise what audiences were about see. The style of this production would be the first practical evidence of what was meant by a Ridiculous production. Of this play, Bottoms writes, "Premiering in April 1966, this was the first presentation at the new Play-House of the Ridiculous—a large, rectangular loft at 12 West Seventeenth Street."[53] The space, a "former parlor room" had a limit on audience capacity, as it was on the second-floor; yet, legal constraints hardly stopped the Play-House from its work. Bottoms relates that "Tavel claims that the designation 'Play-House,' with its disarming hyphen, was chosen as a means to sidestep the licensing implications of having a 'theater' or 'playhouse.'"[54]

The play, famous for including Charles Ludlam's first role, was also recognized as a triumph in its own right. Michael Smith notes that "this is a real play, solidly constructed and intelligently written."[55] In addition, later Ridiculous Theatrical Company contributor Everett Quinton suggests that this play was a subtle commentary on the preceding decade and the House Un-American Activities Committee. He sees in this play, as well as the Ridiculous more broadly, "a reaction to the oppression of the 1950s."[56] Although these plays may seem like humorous romps, there may be a much more meaningful theme hidden behind the laugh-out-loud façade.

Despite the fact that this company may have been "'playing' at theatre" (as Bottoms suggests), the play that they presented, even if under the title of Ridiculous, was coherent. Of the three plays that I discuss here, *Lady Godiva* is the most tightly plotted. Yet, even though Tavel wrote a clear and specific story, this production was still subject to Vaccaro's interest in improvisation; by playing one of the roles and therefore always being on stage, Vaccaro provided "himself the opportunity to bark commands and improvise on the spot."[57]

The Life of Lady Godiva uses a classic style of remixing, taking an old idea or theme and adding new material to it in order to create an original finished product. Commonly, remixing is thought of as practices of taking preexisting songs and altering them in some way: for example, taking the lyrics from a song and setting it to a different melody or backbeat. According to Simon Langford, remix is only one style of musical montage; to distinguish a remix from a mashup, for example, "a mashup is a mix or edit of two (sometimes more) other songs to create a new one. Most often mashups contain little or no actual music added by whoever created them."[58] So Ridiculous plays cannot be considered to be mashups in their quotational style, as they do contain some (at times, a great deal of) original content.

In the case of music, in contemporary remix, the trend is to move away from just reorganizing or reorchestrating elements from the original piece of music. Instead, "the remixers of the late 1980s and early 1990s were using less and less of the original instrumentation in their remixes and using more newly created musical parts."[59] This style of remix—according to Langford, the type of remix most commonly used in music today[60]—lines up with the style of play-making the Ridiculous artists used. They took elements of existing work, the plot line from a classical story or drama, perhaps, and dropped in brand new artistic elements.

In so doing, remix practices create a subculture, as has been the case in hip-hop music for decades. If indeed Ridiculous remix is a practice employed by these artists, it was not just an aesthetic one; rather, it was a method for building a community identity. As Michael B. MacDonald discusses in *Remix and Life Hack in Hip Hop*, "In *The Gospel of Hip Hop*, the production of Hip Hop collective subjectivities is articulated in the oft-repeated phrase: I am Hip Hop."[61] There is no distinction between the art one is making and one's own identity, much like the lifestyle claims that Stefan Brecht made of the Play-House of the Ridiculous. Thus, as we read through three key examples of Ridiculous remix structure in practice, it is worth remembering the musical context of this style of art-making: it is a way to speak within and amongst a group of people who recognize and comprehend its structural and lexical contours.

The Life of Lady Godiva uses this basic remix structure: it takes as its basis a classic story and adds original content to it. The play operates as a loose, metatheatrical adaptation of the story of Lady Godiva; from the show's first line, the players make it known that they are aware that they are performing for an audience. Mother Superviva (John Vaccaro in drag as a nun) opens the play by stating, "You will discover that from this point on, every line is better than the next."[62]

Most of the play then adheres to this arrangement of quotational one-upsmanship. As opposed to advancing a plot, each line seems to build on the last as though in a comedy routine. There are puns, jokes, and witticisms from all of the characters and very little of the dialogue acts to further the simplistic plot, a dramaturgical structure common among plays of the Ridiculous. The familiar story of Lady Godiva is being created anew by the addition of all of these linguistic elements; the remix occurs when these plays on words are layered into the already existing narrative structure of the story. In this version, everyone knows what Godiva's fate will be: to ride naked through the town. The only action, then, is to get her to fulfill this destiny.

In the original Godiva story, as, according to Robert Lacey, it was written down in the early 13th century by Roger of Wendover,[63] Lady Godiva performs this sensational task out of charity. The chronicler writes:

> Longing to free the town of Coventry from the oppression of a heavy tax, Lady Godiva begged her husband with urgent prayers, for the sake of Jesus and his mother Mary, that he would free the town from the toll, and from all other heavy burdens....
> She would not stop pestering her husband, until he finally gave her this reply. "Mount your horse, and ride naked before all the people, through the market of the town, from one end to the other, and on your return you shall have your request."[64]

It is then that she disrobes, cloaks herself with her hair, and completes the mission. Consequently, the taxes were lifted.

In Tavel's version, too, Godiva wishes to free the town from financial burden. Godiva cries out, "O, beneficent Leofric, good and rich, Earl of Mercia and most merciful, movable Master of Castle Coventry and O worshipful Ward of Warwickshire, O remit the heavy duty that thou hast laid upon the peasantrie [*sic*] in the hereabouts, that thereby relieved they might come hither to this house and further relieve themselves. Do thou this in remembrance of thine own lecheries. We four supplicate thee, then, for this" (30). This line brilliantly manifests Ridiculous remix; it is at once both a highbrow construction and a lowbrow dirty joke. The heightened language suggests a highbrow work of theatre, like Shakespeare, in which the poetry of the language is as valued as the plot itself. Yet, the double entendre of "relieve themselves," which can imply both rest and using a restroom or seeking sexual pleasure, suggests a simple-minded entertainment for the uneducated masses, a lowbrow phenomenon. The fact that these two elements are combined together in order to create the text of the play is exactly how the Ridiculous works; the low and the high are blended together to create a comic effect. This comic effect—laughing at the incongruity—gives the audience an opportunity to question exactly what is so incongruous in the construction.

Levity, of course, is what wins out in this version of the tale, not sincerity. When Godiva makes this plea, the others realize in what story they have found themselves and explain to Godiva what her sacrifice must be in order to free the town:

> LEOFRIC: Ah, Godiva. Lady Godiva. Then it is clear, my child, what you must do. And my duty is clear too, the demand I must make is clear. For all this was written in the mind of God and thereafter inscribed in the history books long before either of us was born. And all these things I re-rehearse in you that that which happens in the future may be closer to you.
> TOM: Go on and tell her already.
> LEOFRIC: Lady Godiva:—you must
> THOROLD: Ride through the market place of Coventry
> VERONICAS: At high noon
> TOM: On the back of this old horse
> SUPERVIVA: Stark naked! [31].

In this version, the narrative has already been written; now that the characters have discovered themselves within this particular tale, their main mission is to play out the story's key events as they have always happened.

In this light, Tavel's play could be seen as a parody; as Eva Gruber notes, "[parody] does not necessarily concern itself with the extratextual reality [of the story]; and ... it proceeds by transforming rather than just exposing its subject matter."[65] Tavel is not only recounting the legend of Lady Godiva; he is reimagining that tale through his use of remix. What is created from his careful blending of silly puns and pop culture references into this classic tale—the outcome of this Ridiculous remixing—has the capacity of parody to "involve imitation plus humor or mockery."[66] Ridiculous remixing exposes what is laughable not only in the added quips and cultural sampling, but also in the original source material.

Therefore, once the characters recognize their own status as characters in the Lady Godiva fable, the gravitas of the tale is lifted. Godiva is not fearful of being nude in public. Rather, her reason for not wishing to fulfill her fate is a fairly preposterous one; Godiva states, "But, good Earl, how can I possibly ride through the marketplace of Coventry at high noon on the bare back of that old horse when I'm stark naked? I have hemorrhoids." Leofric then asks, "Do they hurt?" to which Godiva replies, in true Ridiculous fashion, "No; but they photograph dreadfully" (31). In this play, we find a classic story being travestied—a bawdy version of an otherwise respected cultural tale of a woman doing whatever it takes to help her fellow citizens. Every moment is played for laughs.

By making this story into a joke, Tavel subtly implies that the power of the story is being undone, particularly its moral component. The audience is forced to recognize their own role as spectators; as Bottoms argues, "it is the audience's voyeurism that is manipulated, as the implied promise of Godiva's nudity is used to taunt the salaciousness of anyone expecting a rerun of *Shower*."[67] By contrast, the original legend celebrates the goodness of Lady Godiva, and by the 17th century, the story invoked the morality of the citizenry as well. Lacey describes, "According to the seventeenth-century version, the medieval villagers had shown their solidarity with Godiva's protest by staying indoors on the day of her ride, with their shutters decently closed so that she could pass by unobserved."[68] This story became so popular by this period that "an account of 1678 describes a Godiva procession that attracted tens of thousands of visitors."[69] Tavel's version would only be the most recent of many retellings and even reenactments of this mythic event, an event that historically had allowed an entire community to celebrate its own strong moral fiber. This time, however, the audience might be forced to confront quite the opposite: its own lecherous desire and potential immorality.

Because of this Ridiculous remixing, this tale of morality, in Tavel's reimagining, turns into a playground for lewd jokes and obscene gestures. All of the anachronistic references being made—the 20th-century popular culture allusions thrown in—undo the moral imperative of the original story. In its place, we find characters that engage in grotesque acts, but only do so for the audience's pleasure. We find a Godiva who "wanted to be a Playboy bunny" (24) and a Mother Superior who claims, "We was having Oedipus sex, sonny and me was" (32). The most notable, and classically Ridiculous, stage business is the action of this version's Peeping Tom (portrayed by soon-to-be Ridiculous superstar, Charles Ludlam). Tom is guilty of looking upon

Godiva's nakedness, but only because it was his fate as the "peeping" character in this tale. He proclaims, "I am Tom, the Peeping Tom. *The* Peeping Tom of history, if you please. A voyeur, to you" (48). Watching Godiva is merely his role in the drama; he has no choice in the matter and therefore cannot be held accountable for his actions.

Yet Tom is no innocent in this tale. In fact, his activity is lewd before he ever even encounters Miss Godiva. The stage directions describe that when something goes "*wrong with the mechanism of the horse.* TOM *has trouble with the brake and pedal. He dismounts and examines for the trouble in the horse's mouth, in its rear end, and notably its pendant sex which he cranks like a jack*" (20). Indeed, it is Tom's relationship with the horse that is his most physical; later "TOM *writhes on the floor by the horse as if being ravished*" (40). Secretly staring at Godvia will be one of the least scandalous things this Tom has done in this play. The whole idea of virtue that is celebrated in the original is thrown into question in this version.

In terms of the idea of the Ridiculous as a style of theatrical remix, it is also important to pinpoint the references used in this play. I would like to highlight two key references: a riff on a popular advertising slogan on page 28 and a reference to Shakespeare on page 40. After a self-referential jab at the possibility of "bearded ladies" among the group, Superviva is handed a phial from Thorold, who tells her, "Here, have some Ban, Mother, it takes the worry out of being so close" (28). This phrase, which references a popular deodorant brand, includes a slogan that had been a part of the advertising campaign for that product since 1960.[70] Consider this against the mention of Shakespeare. Unlike the importance that seems to come through from the advertisement tagline, Shakespeare comes across as being useless in the world of this play. Leofric dismisses the Bard, crying, "Shakespeare?!—he belongs to the ages" (40). Shakespeare is no longer relevant to the world of this play; he is dated, out-of-touch with the times.

What might be the valence of a play that chooses to mix a reference to a television commercial with an allusion to the oft-considered greatest English-language playwright who ever lived, especially when it appears to put more value on the former than the latter? In my estimation, Ridiculous remix, in Tavel's play, is precisely the kind of subversive undoing of pre-existing structures that Taylor and others have celebrated as being iconic of the countercultural Downtown Scene. The low is being valued and the elite is being devalued; at the same time, in this play, the norms of traditional morality are being mocked and turned on their head. Certainly, these elements suggest a subversive quality within the play, one designed to throw into question and even contradict contemporary standards for cultural power.

The Life of Lady Godiva, subtitled "an hysterical drama," is an example of the middlebrow remix of elements that I described as being a key marker of a Ridiculous work. As Marranca states, "The play takes as its starting point the eleventh-century legendary figure, and in a structure that parodies Medieval and Elizabethan literary convention, cowboy and B-movies, Tavel brings together references to television, the *New York Post*, the Rockettes, Franz Liszt and Art Nouveau in one campy, anachronistic whole."[71] This play is orchestrated chaos, a display of the controlled anarchy that can emerge when you mix unlike materials together into the same dramatic structure.

The source of meaning in this play, then, is not the story itself, but how the story is presented. And this is a presentation totally preoccupied with itself—it demands its viewer be a "peeping Tom" on all of its preposterous behavior. In so doing, it shines a light on a very particular aspect of cultural production in this period: a complex blurring of the lines between moral and immoral and between high and low art, a confusion between what is meant to be culturally meaningful and what is meant to be avoided or discarded.

As Marranca states in the introduction to *Theatre of the Ridiculous*, *The Life of Lady Godiva* is a key example of one style of Ridiculous plays. She writes, "*Lady Godiva* is the campy, kitsch side of the Ridiculous. Not only does it illustrate the Ridiculous's grounding in popular culture ... but even more important, its dependence on performance to realize itself. *The Life of Lady Godiva* is art about artifice."[72] Despite the fact that Marranca uses "campy" and "kitsch" almost as synonyms here, there is an important distinction between the two terms. For Matei Calinescu, "Lovers of kitsch may look for prestige—or the enjoyable illusion of prestige—but their pleasure does not stop there. What constitutes the essence of kitsch is probably its open-ended indeterminacy, its vague 'hallucinatory' power, its spurious dreaminess, its promise of an easy 'catharsis.'"[73] In a sense, kitsch aspires to be valuable, while lacking any actual value; it indulges in the pleasures of achieving something of worth without actually having done so. "Camp," on the other hand, "cultivates bad taste—usually the bad taste of yesterday—as a form of superior refinement."[74] Even in her theorizing about the Ridiculous, Marranca finds herself trapped within a Ridiculous remix: a blend of a disavowal of real value for the escapism of illusory value with an absolute indulgence in that which is known to have no value.

Indeed, Tavel's Ridiculous play remixes a classic legend, imbuing it with iconic Ridiculous content, like cross-dressing, quotation from all aspects of popular culture, and a great deal of commedia-style *lazzi* on stage. *Lady Godiva* is a play about its own status as a performance; Kenneth Bernard's *The Magic Show of Dr. Ma-Gico* takes this metatheatrical quality of the Ridiculous to an even deeper, more troubling, level.

Ridiculous Remix II: Blending the Real World with the Fictional World on Stage (The Magic Show of Dr. Ma-Gico)

The Magic Show of Dr. Ma-Gico considerably post-dates the other two plays discussed in this chapter. Whereas both *The Life of Lady Godiva* and *Conquest of the Universe* were both produced in the tumultuous late 1960s, *The Magic Show* came later, in the equally complex early 1970s. In terms of the development of the Play-House of the Ridiculous, this was also a new time; no longer was the company situated in an apartment on the second floor of a building on Seventeenth Street. Now it was performing at Ellen Stewart's iconic La MaMa Repertory Theatre, as a resident company, no less.[75]

This move further downtown is worth noting. Originally, as Bottoms describes, the Downtown Scene favored playwrights; it gave writers a chance to get their plays seen and heard, with little or no preoccupation about success or fame. However, by the end of the 1960s, "the delicate balance of power of writers and directors had shifted to the point where the latter tended to enjoy more creative autonomy."[76] Issues of power were negotiated even among the companies and their associated artists; now the Downtown Scene and even the Ridiculous began to have artistic power hierarchies of their own that needed to be contended with in order to get work produced. Playwright Bernard was only able to have his plays produced at La MaMa because of his "collaborative partnership" with director Vaccaro.[77]

The addition of Kenneth Bernard to the Play-House family allowed Vaccaro to take Play-House productions in a new, previously unexplored, direction. Like some of Jack Smith's Ridiculous performance art pieces, Bernard's plays explore the nightmarish quality embedded in fantasies of pleasure. The two both "shared … a similarly dark, apocalyptic worldview" which is perhaps best explored in Bernard's 1973 play *The Magic Show of Dr. Ma-Gico*. Like other plays by Bernard, such as *The Moke Eater* (1968) and *Night Club* (1970), *The Magic Show* "demanded an overtly theatrical treatment in production."[78] Bottoms is isolating what I call the "metatheatrical" quality of remix in this play. Not only is Bernard mixing elements of the surrounding culture into his drama; in addition, he is blurring the lines between the real world and the staged fiction. The play is always a performance within a performance, one that may have strong implications for the audience's perception of what is meant by reality outside of the theatrical frame.

Remix takes a different form in Bernard's play from how it was used in Tavel's; Bernard is less interested in mixing high and low culture in order to expose the ways in which the high is as open to being mocked as the low is. Rather, *The Magic Show* mixes various narrative threads into the fictional realm of the magic show. The performers for these scenes appear to emerge from the audience, with the scenes they must perform seemingly conjured "by magic." If this is the case, it is up to the spectator to establish what is real within the fictional world (i.e., what is happening for the characters portrayed) versus what is an illusion meant to trick the participants and spectators alike.

Remix in Bernard's play not only pokes fun at its source material; it also muddies the distinctions between the performative and the real. Bernard "blends not only cultural styles but also cultural judgments" as Chris Barker argues was the intention of "'Raging Fred,' a mashup of the highly esteemed Scorcese film *Raging Bull* with the pop culture TV show *The Flintstones*."[79] Barker links this "blurring of boundaries" with postmodernism, which "is marked by a self-conscious intertextuality."[80] So, too, is Bernard's play—except in *The Magic Show*, the texts being woven together are not merely disparate source material; rather they are the reality of violence and the seeming safety of the fiction of the stage world. A very disturbing aspect of real world human nature is thrown into relief through its representation via multiple performative layers (for example, a scene within the scene of the magic show narrated by Dr. Ma-Gico).

Indeed, this reflection of the problems of the real world through the ugliness of the staged one is something *Village Voice* critic Michael Smith celebrated about this bizarre play. Smith contemplates, "Kenneth Bernard's new play 'The Magic Show of Dr. Ma-Gico' is a shocking vision of evil.... Yet it's no grosser than reality, we are meant to see, for the play and the production have a malicious elegance and cold-blooded viciousness that must be taken as passionately moral in order to be tolerated."[81] Again, we see the theme of morality being bandied about in the so-called Ridiculous world; the concepts of morality are viewed from a skewed perspective in these Ridiculous plays— in this case, through the kaleidoscope lens of a metatheatrically remixed dramaturgy—so that the audience might reconsider what is meant by morals in the first place.

Telling the plot of *The Magic Show* would be a difficult task. Rather than advancing a particular narrative thread, the play is more a study of a particular dark psyche, exploring the violent visions conjured by its narrator. Bernard's plays expose and explore the darker side of the Ridiculous, not only reveling in the surreal but also pushing the limits of how much violence can be represented on stage. In this play, we witness both magic and murder, seeing what dangers can lurk behind the curtains of a Ridiculous performance. Marranca describes, "The grotesque side of the Ridiculous is reflected in Kenneth Bernard's *The Magic Show of Dr. Ma-Gico*. Set in a seventeenth-century drawing room bordered by mirrors, the play is a series of episodes orchestrated by the magician Ma-Gico for the 'enlightenment' of his audience (in the play and in the theatre)."[82] In the case of Bernard, our Ridiculous entertainment is meant to expose some more sinister, obscured truth.

Since the tone of this play is so different from that of other Ridiculous works, the remixing in Bernard's play must take a different form than in Tavel's. In *The Magic Show*, culture is being recycled (which happens to a lesser degree here than in *Lady Godiva*), but, more importantly, two levels of performance are being interwoven in this play. Tavel's characters were aware they were in a play and playing for an audience, committed to seeing their tale's action played out to its completion. Bernard's magician-narrator, on the other hand, views himself as the manipulator of the night's events and can therefore both direct the action happening around him and interact with it. In this way, something unique is created from the material being used; this is no ordinary magic show. The magic here is not that of illusion; rather, it is the power to control what happens and by whom. Magic is a dangerous tool, used for asserting one's own authority and, in a world in which the lines between the real and the fictional are blurred, a reminder that anyone can succumb to its power. The theatre is no longer a safe space for audiences to delight in violence while protected by the darkened house lights; they have now become complicit in the magician's actions.

In terms of remix, then, a cultural artifact is created that is unstable; it is more than just a play made up of bits and pieces of other aspects of culture. It is something new entirely: a performance of a performance meant to have implications for the audience's understanding of reality. Eduardo Navas contends, "Remix affects culture in ways that go beyond the basic understanding of recombining material to create something different. For this reason, my concern is with Remix as a *cultural variable* that is able to move and inform art, music, and media in ways not always obvious as discussed in remix culture."[83] By remixing metatheatrically, Bernard exposes the ways in which the real world could be a performative fiction and how fiction is no stranger than real life. *The Magic Show* created from this remix is very discomfiting, even in its ridiculousness.

As a cultural variable, here remix is able to allow performance to question reality and vice versa. Dr. Ma-Gico instructs, "Ladies and gentleman, we come now to the first sequence. Or episode. There will be several of these, and you must look for a theme, continuity. But not too hard or you might miss it entirely. For example, we have a lot of kings. Perhaps you should make something of that."[84] By recognizing that this is a performance for spectators, Dr. Ma-Gico is able to give the audience a task to complete. He highlights the presence of rulers throughout the play, noting that they may be important to the audience's understanding of the meaning of the play, which, of course, they are.

This performance does not exist only for its own sake; rather, its use of remix allows it to force its spectators to grapple with important themes, in this case, ones related to the wielding of power. As the show's grand finale, the king, "as every night … will be assassinated" (131). Yet, despite having his throat cut, the king will regain his throne at the next performance; the things that happen on stage are not real and therefore have no consequences. These fictions reflect a hidden truth about the loss and gain of power in the real world; for every ruler who is unseated, another will come to take his place. There is no escaping from power; someone will always rise to wield power over others.

Like Tavel's play, the dramaturgy of *The Magic Show* includes a blending of elements, but Bernard's style takes a different form from Tavel's earlier work. In this play, the references remain elevated and highbrow (at one point a Verlaine poem is included in the original French), as opposed to being placed alongside low cultural references. Instead of being mixed with commonplace references, these elite cultural citations are paired with reenactments of scenes of extreme violence, which are all masked in a form of popular entertainment: that of the magic show. On one level, all of the severity and seriousness of this production is undercut by the fact that the audience knows that they are watching "a magician" (114), albeit one who claims he is "not a prestidigitator" and does "*not* deal in tricks" (115). By calling this a magic show, Bernard is pointing to the fact that this is an act of illusion meant to entertain its spectators.

As in *Lady Godiva*, we find the presentation of a type of *lazzi*, but the onstage clowning takes on a more threatening guise in this performance. Most notable are Ma-Gico's instructions to the King, directing him to perform a nearly impossible task in which "he must rise, and as he rises transfer both symbols of his power to one arm, so that with the other he may sweep up his robe, step forward, and, without stopping, bend and pick up the book. He must do this in a continuous, graceful, kinglike motion, without losing his crown, tripping, or dropping anything" (110). Because this is a live performance, it is up to the actor to try to accomplish this physicality in real time. Ma-Gico forces him to do the task over and over and, should he fail too many times, "*An assassin steps forward as the* KING *stands trapped and trembling with his robe and symbols, a shambles of kingliness, and sticks a knife in his belly*" (111). All of this playacting has dire consequences, at least within the performance. A real performance failure leads to a theatrical death; the King is murdered on stage, all because he could not complete his performance correctly.

It is also worth noting that the items that this King is meant to negotiate are his "symbols of power." These objects are clearly nothing more than symbolic, as Dr. Ma-Gico is able to declare his usurpation of power and make it so. An old ruler dies and a new one replaces him immediately, prepared to perform his role. Implicitly, then, this play takes as its subversive stance the fact that an old generation, one no longer able to perform, is being supplanted by a new one. Once the King is dead, our magician-narrator is happy to assume his role: "I myself shall be king" (111). Unlike Mother Superviva who can do nothing to change Godiva's fate—the Lady must play out her story as she always has for centuries—Dr. Ma-Gico can make whatever he wants happen at will. The power to rule resides within the power of performance within a Ridiculous play. Dr. Ma-Gico, a lowly performer, can perform the role of King, just as in Tavel's play a line of advertising can supersede the writing of Shakespeare. The hierarchies of the past have come undone in the world of the Ridiculous. The play thematically hearkens back to the themes that Marvin J. Taylor highlighted as being key to the Downtown Scene. Bernard's play is renegotiating power through the performative and, by extension, is a subversive critique of the power structures already in place.

What, then, is the effect of this dark and violent Ridiculous theatricality? Marranca explains, "Through a succession of 'turns' on the themes of evil, justice and betrayal, *Dr. Ma-Gico* invites the spectator—or is he a voyeur?— into a reflecting world of violent images, peopled by royalty, courtiers, and commoners. Ma-Gico himself is the narrator and actor in his theatre; the grand illusionist, he teaches by negative example. But what is the lesson to be learned?"[85] In the same way that Peeping Tom must look upon Lady Godiva's nakedness, the audience of *The Magic Show* is forced to witness Dr. Ma-Gico's violent deeds on stage. Through this study of the act of "looking upon," these plays throw into relief the notion that the theatre is a site in which outsiders are always looking at the actions of others; an inherent aspect of being spectators is being powerless to act.

The question Marranca raises of what "lesson is to be learned" is also important in light of the travesty of a tale of morality that Tavel created in *Lady Godiva*. Morality disappears in the landscape of these Ridiculous theatricals; they are not "immoral" but "amoral" in theme. In the case of Tavel's play, morality falls away because these characters are only playing at events that were predestined for them. The sense of moral imperative is thereby lost from the Godiva story. In Bernard's play, on the other hand, morality vanishes because we find ourselves entrapped within a nightmare, governed by the violent and the grotesque. In Tavel's play, the characters are entirely powerless to change their fates; in Bernard's, power is unstable, easily able to be lost or usurped, and is only executed in the most gruesome manner possible.

The use of Ridiculous remix undercuts traditional notions of power; the characters in these plays have no power over their own fates. With the exception of Dr. Ma-Gico, these personages are merely performers in someone else's drama, with no agency of their own. Dr. Ma-Gico only asserts power through his performance, because, as he contends, "*I*, you will note, am very kinglike. Observe my walk, my grace, how the very air around me is scented with power and authority" (111). Dr. Ma-Gico is a king because he acts like one. The metatheatrical variety of Ridiculous remix privileges performance as a mode of enacting power.

The violent deeds of *The Magic Show* can be presented on stage because they are couched as performance. We are not literally witnessing a murder occurring—we are consistently reminded that we are watching the performance of such a deed, which, for the audience, creates a double-layered effect, the experience of watching a play within the play they have come to see. The theatre is no longer a space in which the audience can be safe from the horrors of reality; it is a site in which to be confronted with them. Because of the multiple layers of performance, it is hard to know where performance ends and reality begins—is the theatre, where anything can happen, really a dangerous place, one where someone can meet a grisly and untimely end? Or is it all make-believe, a sleight of hand, an act of misdirection, and, if so, might things that appear to be real also be similar fictions? The metatheatrical quality and the mixing of elements in *The Magic Show of Dr. Ma-Gico* highlight large philosophical questions about the nature of reality, suggesting that the Ridiculous may not be so preposterous a form after all.

Ultimately, in this performance, power is exposed as a tool—one that can easily be taken by anyone who wishes to perform the role of the person who holds such power. There is no safe fiction into which one can escape. The metatheatricality here suggests, through its remixing of layers of performance, that anything that happens in a stage world could have repercussions on the real one. It is never certain that performing is always associated with that which is not real. Through performing one could, as if by magic, enact power over others.

Ridiculous Remix III: The Queen of Mixing (Conquest of the Universe *or* When Queens Collide)

Although "*Conquest* does not fall high on the list of more successful works by Ludlam,"[86] the play is perhaps the most significant in terms of Ridiculous space formation; because of differences between Vaccaro and Ludlam, the Ridiculous Theatrical Company would be born. Bottoms relates, "The fundamental differences between Ludlam's and Vaccaro's conceptions of *Conquest* resulted in a permanent parting of the ways, during rehearsals for the play's November premiere.... Vaccaro felt that Ludlam was interfering too much with his directing; Ludlam that Vaccaro was ignoring the conception of the play."[87] Like much of the mystique associated with Ridiculous Theatre, there is no definitive account of how this split actually occurred. In his biography of the late Ludlam, David Kaufman states, "No one can say with certainty what precipitated the permanent falling out between Ludlam and Vaccaro.... According to Vaccaro, Ludlam just stormed out in the midst of an argument, which was unusual only in terms of his departure, as arguments between them had become standard operating procedure. According to many others, Vaccaro banished Ludlam."[88] However the actual break between the two may have played out, it was this production that forced the community of the Ridiculous to expand.

Upon his exit from the Play-House, however it actually occurred, Ludlam convened his own troupe of actors, made up of many of the original cast who had left Vaccaro along with him. In light of this grand exodus of performers, Vaccaro called upon contacts of his own, especially from "the underground film community" and staged the play without Ludlam under the play's original title. Vaccaro owned only the rights to the play's title, so Ludlam could mount his own production but was forced to produce his version under the name *When Queens Collide*. As Gary Garrison narrates, "Ludlam's new company found its first home at Tambellini's Gate (a movie theatre) on the lower east side of Manhattan, but like so many fledgling theatre companies, the troupe continually traveled from venue to venue seeking a permanent home."[89] Ludlam had the distinction of two productions of his play occurring simultaneously; I will only focus on Vaccaro's production, as my interest in this chapter is the Play-House.

Vaccaro took a dark perspective on the events of the drama, which is built of the framework of an Elizabethan drama and contains references from every angle of culture, while the characters are continually self-aware of their presence within a play. In this, *Conquest* is the clearest example of Ridiculous remix. As a practice of artistic construction, remix employs the concept of "cultural recyclability."[90] According to Navas, "Remix culture, as a movement, is mainly preoccupied with the free exchange of ideas and their manifestation as specific products."[91] This comment takes a seemingly positive approach to remixing: it is a culture in which ideas are shared as a common good in order to create new products. Indeed, Ludlam's play may be the apotheosis of all Ridiculous remix practices because of its immense reliance on the practice of recycling elements from the surrounding culture. The play, at its root, is a series of quotations, lifted from anywhere and everywhere, ranging in source from Shakespeare's *Hamlet* to a speech by Goering to the Prussian police to the line "Goodnight, Mrs. Calabash" lifted from Jimmy Durante routines.

This collage-style of play-making was not entirely successful when it was presented on stage by Vaccaro and his troupe. Stefan Brecht, in his reflections at the time of the original production, notes, "How much of the credit is due Vaccaro as a director, I am not sure.... The spirit of reckless gaiety may even be largely his. Ludlam's script seems less terrible than the production, more inclined to fun and games, not as black as the production."[92]

Indeed, the play text does betray a sense that this play is perhaps more pleasurable than gloomy in tone, though it is concerned with dark subject matter, similar to that of Bernard's play: a despotic ruler is willing to commit murder, simply because he possesses the power to do so, in order to conquer the universe.

One element of the production that Brecht is able to celebrate are the performances, particularly that of Factory star Mary Woronov, who took on the lead role of Tamburlaine. Brecht refers to her as a "superb actress" and remarks how "with hysteria, paranoia, she plays a bare core of sadist energy."[93] In terms of how these actors were directed to perform, this play is an example of the Play-House's exploration of the portrayal of personalities on stage, as opposed to the creation of specific and repeatable characters. Bottoms notes, "Vaccaro's emphasis in *Conquest* was, as ever, on personality rather than text: 'Our actors are acting themselves as well as their roles,' read the Play-House's press release; 'the real person [is] more interesting than the plot.'"[94] In terms of this play, this is perhaps as much because of the strength of the performers associated with the production as the thinness of the plot itself.

Although the production might not have been remarkable, as Brecht's analysis implies, what is noteworthy about *Conquest* is how expertly Ludlam is able to use quotations, plot devices, and references lifted from many other works, both popular and obscure, highbrow and lowbrow alike. Brecht highlights this remixed quality in the play:

> Charles Ludlam's *Conquest of the Universe*: some great little monologues, replicas, cameos from the great dramatists: a firesale of theatrical properties.... It's crude entertainment: the stuff that in the good old days of the republic crafty semites democratically cooked up alike for the robber barons and the ethnic hordes is here served with the same broad gesture. Nowadays this fake glass glitters like diamonds. But, more particularly: a slaughter of the theatre, not a nostalgic gloss on mass culture.[95]

Elements from all aspects of culture are being rescued and repurposed in this play. Unfortunately, Brecht sees this reappropriation as a failure; these references are simply made, these quotations merely restated, without providing the necessary commentary underneath in order to be as incisive as much other Ridiculous remix is.

As much as one might be following the thread of the plot in *Conquest*, one could also find himself preoccupied with trying to trace and place all of the references therein. Indeed, such a task would prove time-consuming, as the play is overflowing with borrowed content. Elizabeth Freeman reminds, "Deleuze and Guattari write that one form of minor literature dislodges referentiality by overloading the dominant language to the point of explosion via neologism, hypotaxis, or semantic overpacking.... This is a kind of 'fat' aesthetic that rebinds fixed meanings and allows new associative chains to form."[96] A similar "overweight" quality is found in this play, through an almost excessive use of quotation. The meaning of the narrative of the play—a ruler's attempted violent conquests—is potentially undermined by all of the plays on words and cultural allusions included in the text. And yet, through undermining the play's surface-level meaning, another source of meaning may emerge, one that is only clear when both form and content are taken into consideration. *Conquest* is a play about possessing power, but the source of that power is not solely political rule. Rather, it is also cultural: it is based on how many references one has on hand and how many jokes one is able to tell.

This work's originality is not found in the lines themselves but rather how they are being arranged, deconstructed and reconstructed into the framework of Christopher Marlowe's *Tamburlaine the Great*. Both the Elizabethan source material and the Ridiculous play being scrutinized here tell the story of a tyrant's rise to power and his subsequent fall. In Ludlam's version, however, the telling of the narrative is only a part of the drama; the consistent quoting and misquoting provides a kind of game for anyone watching or reading the play. The winner, it would seem, would be the person who could identify the source for the most quotations.

As in Tavel's *The Life of Lady Godiva*, there are poetic-sounding sections interspersed with the quick wit associated with the Ridiculous. For example, Bajazeth and Zabina wax poetic about their love:

> BAJAZETH: Within this restless, modern, hurried world,/We took our hearts' full pleasure, you and I,/And now the white sails of our rocket ship are furled/And spent the lading of our argosy.
>
> ZABINA: Wherefore my cheeks before their time are wan,/For very weeping is my gladness fled./Sorrow has paled my lips vermilion/And ruin draws the curtain of my bed.[97]

Yet the conclusion of this scene breaks the highbrow conceit that this is verse drama. Zabina cries out, "I say to you and to Jove, my will be done.... No more nuggie till Tamburlaine be slain or overcome" (34). The heightened language is undercut by the silly slang for having sex; the use of remix undoes the power of the language.

Indeed, whenever anything appears to take a serious turn in *Conquest*, some popular cultural element is thrown in to offset its effect. When Hunger laments that "every night a million Americans go to bed without supper" he finishes by saying, "Twiggy, what hast thou wrought?" (37). The issue is no longer the lack of enough food to feed the entire populace; rather, the concern is the modern preoccupation with being thin. Despite its use of a hundreds-year-old play as a narrative framework, Ludlam's *Conquest* is always specifically of its historical moment in time. Even though the setting is meant to span the lengths of the galaxy, the dialogue always returns to references that are distinctly 20th-century American.

In this way, cultural power is always first and foremost in the hands of contemporary culture: this is what is most valued in the dramaturgical form of *Conquest*. In terms of power within the plot, as in the final episode of *The Magic Show of Dr. Ma-Gico*, the characters are forced to recognize that for every tyrant you unseat, another waits in the wings to take his or her place. Bajazeth contemplates assassinating the King; taking Cosroe aside, he whispers, "Suppose we kill a king ... and then a king..." However, Cosroe already realizes, "Princes are waiting everywhere." "Suppose by water or with poison kill a queen," Cosroe suggests instead. But, again, Bajazeth knows what would occur: "Her daughter waits upon the stair" (43). Power cannot be undone in this society; like Dr. Ma-Gico who can instruct the King to his own demise and then usurp his throne, these characters seem entrapped by the power structures at work in their world.

Power is once again present as a major theme in this work, yet, in this case, that discussion does go beyond the historical or imaginative framework of the drama. Of the three Ridiculous plays looked at in this chapter, this is the only one with an explicit reference to world events. Tamburlaine goes off to conquer the universe, as the title suggests, ending his run by overtaking "Neptune—Uranus—Pluto—Cambodia—Laos—North Vietnam—South Vietnam—West Hempstead" (34). Pairing the conquest of planets with the part of the world in which America was engaged in military action could suggest a political statement; the juxtaposition of the Southeast Asian nations with a town on Long Island could be meant to expose the absurdity of such military conquest. This suggests a slight political undercurrent to the work.

On the other hand, however, such a reference could have been a mockery of the practice of trying to reflect world events in drama, common at this historical moment. As Kaufman reminds, "*Conquest* was not as aggressively political as a number of other works that had recently opened Off Broadway and fueled the protests to America's role in Southeast Asia, including Megan Terry's *Viet Rock*, Jean-Claude van Itallie's *America Hurrah*, and Barbara Garson's even more incendiary *MacBird!*"[98] Even in this play, so explicitly about conquest and abuse of power, there is not any direct or specific political engagement as might be found in other theatrical works of the period.

Despite this interest in questions of power that serves as a theme in these Ridiculous plays, the Ridiculous cannot be called political in the same right as many of its contemporary theatre companies. James Harding and Cindy Rosenthal note that "the blurring of performance and politics ... was not only the defining gesture of group theatres that emerged in the tumultuous social context of the 1960s but continue to inform and shape activist theatre today."[99] The Ridiculous would not have fit within the confines of Harding and Rosenthal's collection, nor within any discussion of so-called "activist theatre"; their works were not explicitly engaging in political debates.

Any political gesture on the part of the Ridiculous was implicit in their aesthetics, particularly the negotiation of icons of 20th-century American culture.

Unlike their more overtly political and/or activist contemporaries, such as companies like The Living Theatre, the Ridiculous artists were reveling in the excesses of mid–20th-century consumer culture. Like consumers on Long Island's North Shore buying up new appliances and furnishings with which to fill their brand-new ranch houses, the Ridiculous theatre-makers were accumulating cultural material from all over the cultural spectrum, using the particularity of their social position to their advantage. These individuals had access to both the low and the high because of their middlebrow status.

Conclusion

But what does this middlebrow status mean in terms of our understanding of the significance of the Ridiculous? On the one hand, it suggests the kind of progressive gesture that Bottoms mentioned many underground companies were working towards in the 1960s—the undoing of preexisting cultural hierarchies. Simultaneously, however, this interest in a middlebrow identity suggests something much more problematic: a practiced *disinterest* in fundamentally altering the system in any way.

In fact, many of the artists associated with the Ridiculous, including some of those discussed already in this chapter, had aspirations beyond the underground Downtown Scene. Vaccaro's company took up residence at La MaMa, which although still part of the Downtown Scene, gave the Play-House access to more mainstream audiences and theatre critics alike. Even working with Bernard was a move away from the so-called "queer" aesthetic of the early Ridiculous; "Bernard, a college professor with a wife and family, had little of the queer flamboyance of Tavel or Ludlam."[100] With the expansion of the Ridiculous into more mainstream theatrical spaces, and with the passage of time, from the radical late-1960s into the perhaps less revolutionary 1970s, the Ridiculous found itself more in a struggle for a place in the mainstream than happily situated on the cultural margins.

Play-House productions ultimately are preoccupied with the crossroads between high and low culture, a stressful middlebrow position, linked with the particular cultural experience of the artists associated with the movement. Interestingly, the plays studied in this chapter—all by different playwrights and created at different moments during the company's development—all share an important thematic link. All three of these plays are concerned with the desire for and the dangers of power. They explore this issue through the aesthetic of theatrical remix—blending bawdy humor with classical allusions, juxtaposing one-liners from popular television and radio programs with quo-tations from the dramatic canon.

In addition, however, all of these productions "remix" something else: the construction of gender. In nearly every play created throughout the Ridiculous scene, there is at least one instance of cross-dressing or gender play of some sort on stage. This is its own sort of "remix"; elements of both genders are blended together to create a character on stage. This mixture is more stratified than that of the cultural references; genders seem layered on one another to create something unique in the person on stage. In the next chapter, I look at this practice of gender blending—and bending—on stage, particularly as it was manifested by one of its most innovative pioneers, some-time Ridiculous Theatrical Company collaborator and contributor, Ethyl Eichelberger.

FIVE

"Ridiculous Mashup"
Ethyl Eichelberger and the
Performance of Gender

As time passed, the main location for Ridiculous Theatre began to migrate: from the once countercultural SoHo section of Greenwich Village to the East Village. Jay Sanders writes, "SoHo's increasing gentrification and association with a newly defined, desirable lifestyle ... pushed its art activity elsewhere.... What had previously been loft performances migrated to bars and nightclub stages—the Pyramid Club, 8 BC, and many others—where forms of entertainment might actually entertain."[1] Over time, the sites appropriate for Ridiculous Theatre shifted; these works began in the loft of Jack Smith, then found a home in the theatres of the Play-House of the Ridiculous and the Ridiculous Theatrical Company, and now were settling in to the club scene of the East Village.

This geographic shift really made an impact on downtown performance of the early 1980s, creating a linear trajectory both of sites and of performance aesthetics. As performer and playwright Ethyl Eichelberger once said, "What's going on down here now is a steady progression from the sixties.... Charles Ludlam used to appear downtown a lot. I went to Jack Smith's house in the sixties to Flaming Creatures. All that's happening here now is a tie-in. I imagine if you were around earlier you could go back even further. The Lower East Side, there was Yiddish Broadway down here. The clubs just took advantage of what was already here."[2] Eichelberger's work was a product of the location in which it was created. In his estimation, this site, downtown New York City, had always been inspiring groundbreaking new work and his contribution was only the latest in a long history of such innovation.

In addition, in this quotation, Eichelberger sees the connection between what he was doing in his own work in the downtown club scene and what had preceded him in Ludlam's early performance days and Smith's all-night homespun extravaganzas. The club scene, in which Eichelberger often worked, spurred the careers of many important performance artists, particularly those associated with the development of drag. According to Uzi Parnes, Eichelberger is a link between what Ludlam was doing—creating plays—and what Jack Smith was doing in his more experiential performance art. Parnes states, "Ethyl bridged ... both doing stuff that was more like actual theatre and little vignettes that he would do in the clubs."[3] Eichelberger is a key Ridiculous figure, because he brings together these two important threads of Ridiculous performance types and Ridiculous performance spaces.

Indeed, Eichelberger worked within the Ridiculous performative vein, adopting a similar emphasis on the improvisational and spontaneous as John Vaccaro and Jack Smith had before him. Within a night's performance, Eichelberger allowed himself the freedom to adapt the performance to whatever ideas came to mind at the time; as Joe E. Jeffreys puts it, "I call those moments where he would start improving in the middle of a performance the 'Eichelberger etcetera' and they were often materialized from even more play text quotes in his actor's head, current events, gossip or who was in the audience that night that he wanted to acknowledge or tell a story about."[4] This openness to altering the performance might have been thrilling for audiences—guaranteeing that each night's performance was a unique, ephemeral experience—but much like Vaccaro's on-stage barking of orders or Smith's forced audience participation, this practice could be very stressful for anyone else on stage. Eichelberger worked with the artistic techniques of the earlier incarnations of the Ridiculous to create an original and provocative form of performance, one that was freeform enough to adapt to its surroundings and audiences.

Ethyl, born in Illinois in 1945 and named James Roy Eichelberger, was an important theatre-maker, one who created plays based on historical events and the great works of literature—often taking the great female lead within those tales—while employing some of the most extravagant as well as the tackiest of costume pieces. He would perform his works in all sorts of settings, from traditional theatre spaces to hole-in-the-wall clubs. Eichelberger was a part of an increasing trend in performance art—to perform anywhere and everywhere that there was a space suitable for performing; even Ludlam had begun his career this way before settling in to One Sheridan Square. Perhaps more so than any other Ridiculous artist, Eichelberger was a product of an artistic scene already in place when he began creating performance art. Unlike Jack Smith, who was attempting to be original, or Ronald Tavel and John Vaccaro who were trying to flesh out the contours of a new movement, or even Charles Ludlam who was honing his own unique playwriting and acting voice, Eichelberger was inserting himself into a scene that existed before he came to it.

If it is true, as Robert Mills contends, that "queer-history exhibitions will adopt a style of presentation partly modeled on scrapbooks and college;

in place of the representative 'object,' they will appropriate fragments, snippets of gossip, speculations, irreverent half-truths,"[5] then perhaps queer theatre, of the sort Eichelberger was creating, demanded non-traditional theatre spaces in the same way that these queer exhibitions would never make sense in traditional museums or galleries. Roselee Goldberg relates that in this period, beginning in the late 1960s, "artists stayed away from traditional galleries and museums on principle. They performed on rooftops, in vacant parking lots, or in warehouses turned studio-cum-rudimentary-habitat."[6] The dismissal of "Broadway-style" theatres went hand-in-hand with this avoidance of traditional museum display sites.

This interest in new types of art spaces was helped along by inexpensive rental prices for property, especially below Fourteenth Street, where the Downtown Scene took root. Goldberg states, "Cheap rent generated a particular aesthetic in the art of the 1970s, and the extraordinary spaces that it made available to a large and immensely talented community provided the model for exhibition spaces for years to come."[7] Performances such as those created by Eichelberger were a product of their particular historical moment—one in which artists were interested in experimenting with the form for their work—as well as the economics of the location in which the work occurred. Downtown rents were extremely cheap; Goldberg notes, "In 1974, a two-thousand-square-foot loft in the heart of SoHo cost just two hundred dollars a month."[8] Therefore, such a space might serve as well for a theatre as it did for a home; as is the case with Jack Smith's works, then, part of a performance's meaning might be embedded in its literal setting.

As theatrical productions moved into performance clubs, the artists adapted their style to the particular setting, creating a new form of performance. Goldberg mentions the role drugs and alcohol played in these settings as well as the desire for "larger-than-life performers such as Ethyl Eichelberger."[9] The raucous and exuberant setting in which many of his works were performed dictated an entirely new brand of performance art, one that, in the case of Eichelberger, displayed its originality most clearly in the ostentatious and extravagant on-stage representations of cross-gendered personages.

The bars and clubs in which Eichelberger performed were an integral part of his performance career. In his authoritative dissertation on Eichelberger, Joe E. Jeffreys quotes an "encore to *Minnie the Maid*" which "prais[ed] s.n.a.f.u.," a site that had served as a theatre space for Eichelberger's performances. Jeffreys notes that "its second verse paints a musical portrait of the cabaret":

> This is the house built by handsome Lou Tattoo
> It's perverse chic, don't you think
> Let Cliff serve you up a drink

Steve and Rick and John provide the view
They're young and lovely, Suzanne and Charlie too
(Don't forget Miss Kathy
she keeps everyone in line)...[10]

Here, the site is as important to the performance as the action itself is. In fact, that action is being shaped by the surroundings of the performance—the people who run the club and those in attendance—as much as it is by the artist performing. In a sense, this concept of interactive space builds upon the precedents set by Smith's loft shows and the Play-House of the Ridiculous; the audience and even the theatre itself have as much of a role to play in the work created as the artists doing the creating.

Indeed, Eichelberger is an artist who would be shaped by the scene in which he found himself as much as he would go on to influence the shape that scene would take after him. Eichelberger credited the already existing Ridiculous Theatre movement with helping to develop his particular brand of performance. Building on the concept of a Ridiculous remix, Eichelberger was able to take various aspects of male, female, and cross-gender performed identities and layer them into unique productions that still concerned themselves with the blending and blurring of high and low cultural artifacts. Eichelberger's works, like Smith's, were ghosted by popular culture icons, such as Maria Montez, while also standing on their own as profound statements about the performative nature of gender by maintaining the presence of the performer and layering the character identity(s) on top.

This complicated performance of gender identities on stage is a crucial aspect of the Ridiculous scene. I discuss the practice of building gender-blended characters in terms of the concept of "mashup," a contemporary practice of creating music and Internet content from the combining of two or more pieces of source material. In looking at Eichelberger as a case study of Ridiculous gender mashup, it becomes clear that gender, as a performed and performative construct, is constantly being "remixed," and is always ghosted by the popular culture that surrounds it. For the Ridiculous, this popular culture was defined by Hollywood feminine glamour, such as that embodied in Maria Montez. Therefore, it was essential for these male performers to perform in drag in their productions if they wanted to embody these film icons; there would be no other way to personally personify the ghost of Montez, or other starlets like her, without representing those individuals outright. Mashup techniques were necessary to maintain the "remix" approach insofar as it applied to gender; this was a way to use gender performance to quote from other sources while still avoiding taking too realistic or serious of an approach.

Connecting the Ridiculous fascination with Maria Montez, who has been widely considered a mediocre actress, to the idea of "failure," in Halberstam's construction of the term, a potential progressive value of the gender mashups done by Ridiculous performers, such as Eichelberger, emerges. I am particularly interested in the way "failure" can be used as a way to understand cultural "failings" as their own type of success, at least insofar as these failures consciously break with traditionally held cultural norms.

Queerness and the Ridiculous

Due to this "mashup" style of gender construction on stage, these performances indulged in the playfulness of play-acting, drawing attention to the fact that they were performed through the blending of the classic and the tacky, arts and crafts items paired with designer gowns. There is no illusion in an Eichelberger play that one is peering in on reality; Eichelberger wants his presence as the performer to be visible, with the character layered on to, but not obscuring, his self. Therefore, his works were almost always unrealistic and/or metatheatrical; that is, they drew attention to themselves as performances. Yet, for the Ridiculous, this often seemed to be the point of donning the opposite gender. The purpose was never to fool the audience into believing that the performer was something he or she was not; rather, it was to draw attention to the practice of performing, both because it is pleasurable and because it was relevant to their experience of the world. These individuals felt shaped by 20th-century America, which was filled with films and television advertising, the mixing of high and low culture on a regular basis. Ridiculous artists also noted the fluidity of gender identity as necessary to their aesthetic approach; in order to embody all of the characters they wished to play on stage, these artists had to envision new ways to cross gender in their performances. What they chose was a style that allowed them to layer a female character on top of their unique male frames: what I am labeling gender mashup.

This mashup technique for gender construction is a key aspect of what makes the Ridiculous a unique movement of theatre and sets it apart as a progressive type of artistic creation. The Ridiculous artists neither accepted the proffered models of gender presented in their youth nor the commonly exercised practices of cross-gendered performance. Rather, they found their own way to construct gendered identities on stage; by placing the female identities that they idolized on top of their own male bodies they threw into relief both the performed component of gender as well as their own progressive stance on gender. Predating Judith Butler and other groundbreaking gender theorists in some cases by decades, the Ridiculous performers, like Eichelberger, took an inherently "queer" approach to gender: they exposed it as performed, not as an innate part of the essence of identity. Additionally, these performances were "queer" in that, like the historical avant-gardes that preceded them, they broke with historical models for creating art, in this case cross-dressed or drag performance. Ridiculous artists, like Ethyl Eichelberger, proved that failing to be mistaken for the opposite gender can be a key component of, not a detriment to, drag performing.

Failure, as a theoretical concept is integral to understanding how cross-dressing functioned in the Ridiculous. Jack Smith, for example, did not idolize the great Oscar-winning actresses of his youth; rather, he mythologized a B-movie star, Maria Montez. Smith accepted that Montez was not great by traditional standards,[11] but she met Smith's demands, based on his own rubric, for what made someone a star. By idolizing a failure, Smith suggests a whole new standard for greatness, one based on his own qualifications, not those of mainstream society.

Like Smith, who would go on to create a temple to Montez in his apartment through the accumulation of seemingly disposable objects, Eichelberger created his "female" characters out of many non-feminine characteristics: his own height and build, a massive tattoo across his back, lots of junk and arts-and-crafts materials, and his consistent referencing of the larger drag scene of which his performances were a part. Once again, one could label this artistic practice a "failure" by traditional standards. In fact, one could go so far as to say neither Smith's nor Eichelberger's live works were "great plays," in terms of literary construction (though Eichelberger did write some rich play texts); rather, they were demonstrations of characters in front of a live audience, manifestations of the combination of various disparate elements combined into a whole.

For many critics of theatrical presentation, not having created a great body of dramatic literature would constitute an artistic failure. And yet, these artists created work based on their own standards, according to their own rules, not caring whether they failed the traditional system. With most Ridiculous drama (the obvious exception being Charles Ludlam), the idea was not to make a successful work of dramatic literature; on the contrary, it was to explore what could occur in the act of live performance for spectators: a failure for traditional drama-making, perhaps, but a success in terms of avant-garde art.

As in Smith's rituals, these experimental artists reconsidered the role of the audience, often making them an active part of the theatrical setting. Like the "Total Pandemonium"[12] one might have found in the Dadaist Cabaret Voltaire in Zurich, Switzerland, Smith created performances that demanded certain participatory roles from the spectators, though his were perhaps less raucous and more ritualistic. The Play-House of the Ridiculous, on the other hand, engaged the cultural icons most relevant to its spectators, daring them to recognize both the most obvious high culture allusions and the most obscure advertising slogans. In Ridiculous Theatre, the performances were for a particular community who wished to share in the live event, actively or intellectually.

For Eichelberger, this "active role" for the audience was often built right into the downtown clubs in which he often chose to perform. In these sites, Eichelberger needed to contend with his audience members, as the performers at the Cabaret Voltaire had, at least when he performed in a bar setting. These performance spaces would always have ambient noise interrupting or distracting from the performance. The Dadaists, as well as Eichelberger, embraced this new actor-audience arrangement. As Rudolf Kuenzli describes of the Cabaret Voltaire, "These nightly encounters with their audience, which was primarily male and composed of fellow dissidents, challenged the creativity and energy of the performers."[13] Eichelberger also performed for an audience of the "converted": fellow gay men who knew the drag scene and the sorts of performances associated with that aesthetic. This sort of "preaching to the converted," as Tim Miller and David Román would call it, is a key aspect of what makes the Ridiculous queer. Although their claims could be applicable across the Ridiculous landscape, Miller and Román single out the "Playhouse [*sic*] of the Ridiculous" as a site where "lesbian and gay men were able to begin offering alternative representations to the standard fare of mainstream representation," an act that ultimately led to "developing both lesbian and gay artists *and* audiences locally, regionally, and nationally ... [who] forged energies to simulate and enact a sense of queer history and community."[14] One progressive quality of Ridiculous Theatre was inherent in its applicability and appeal to lesbian and gay performers and spectators.

Eichelberger built on this "preaching to the converted" style of performance. Because of his audience's familiarity with the aesthetic that he was engaging, Eichelberger chose to innovate within its confines, "remix" the remix, in a way; he took the kind of cultural blending seen in other Ridiculous-style drag performance and mixed it a second time. He drew attention to the performative nature of both the "preacher" and his "converted congregants" in order to engage topics and issues relevant to his community scene. In this way, it is impossible to discuss the Ridiculous without also discussing queer theory, as a theoretical movement.[15]

Ridiculous performers took a queer approach to gender, seeing it not as an inherent characteristic but rather as another aspect to be performed for an audience. The idea was not to create a flawless portrait of a female heroine. Instead, it was to explore what might happen—what or how a character might mean—when it is built on multiple gender identities. The Ridiculous conception of queer, although predating *Gender Trouble* by decades, seems to exemplify Judith Butler's principles. According to Butler's psychoanalytic approach to gender identity formation in her groundbreaking 1990 work, "'becoming' a gender is a laborious process of becoming *naturalized*, which requires a differentiation of bodily pleasures and parts on the basis of gendered meanings."[16] One is not born a particular gender; rather, one becomes that gender through understanding the particular gendered associations of both physiology and desire.

In drag performance, as opposed to mere cross-dressing, the performer not only dons the apparel of the opposite gender but also takes on the physicalities and identity of the other sex. For Butler, therefore, drag becomes the key example of the instability of any sense of reality being born of one's apparent gender identity.[17] This concept, which reframes how we think and forces us to restructure how we understand the whole notion of "personal identity" is, if not revolutionary in and of itself, at least a first step on the road toward change, in Butler's estimation. Butler contends, "No political revolution is possible without a radical shift in one's notion of the possible and the real."[18] A queer approach to identity suggests something much larger than just an unstable sense of self; it is also a marker of potential radical change.

Other scholars agree with this broad approach to the concept of "queerness" and the applicability of that ideology to radical change. Jose Muñoz, for one, suggests hope as being part and parcel of the queer aesthetic, a concept that seems quite applicable to Theatre of the Ridiculous. Muñoz writes: "Queerness is not yet here. Queerness is an ideality.... Queerness is a longing that propels us onward, beyond romances of the negative and toiling in the present. Queerness is the thing that lets us feel that this world is not enough, that indeed something is missing. Often we can glimpse the worlds proposed and promised by queerness in the realm of the aesthetic."[19] Ridiculous Theatre, despite often being cruel or even malevolent, or so silly as to defy value judgments, actually does precisely what Muñoz describes here. In these plays, there is not only a longing for a world in which other ways of being are possible; there is the actual presentation of such worlds. Other models for existence are put forward, often for their own bout with mockery, but without any need for explanations or any grounding in so-called reality.

The profundity of this reading of Ridiculous queerness is that, of course, these on-stage realities were never manifested beyond the imaginative. In most cases, these artists were not political activists, per se,[20] and their plays did not lead to grand scale political or social change. Rather, the plays depict these strange universes on stage, only to allow them to disappear into the ephemera of performance; if it is true that "the art of losing [is] a particularly queer art"[21] then this is another way in which the Ridiculous embodies contemporary notions of queerness. Eichelberger's plays in particular are preoccupied with the fact that the world of these sorts of performances may be coming to an end.

Dasvedanya Mama, for example, looks back upon the great days of its protagonist's performance career, bemoaning the loss of those great times; indeed, if "losing … is a queer art," then no one knows it better than Olga. She has lost her career and all of the trappings of her lifestyle that went along with it. This character, played by Eichelberger himself, understands that there is so much more complexity to his/her queer positionality than just gender performance. Her position is queer because she still is performing herself, even after she has left the stage. For Olga, no matter how great things once were, all she can see at the play's end is failure.

And yet, as Jack Halberstam notes, "failing is something queers do and have always done exceptionally well."[22] Therefore, failure, in all its forms—failure to make an impact, failure to change the world, and most importantly, the failure to be great—are integral aspects of all of Eichelberger's plays. His work is not just queer because he often dons female attire, but because he accepts a different set of standards, ones in which failing to be great, based on mainstream norms, is actually a kind of success. The transformation into the onstage character is not meant to be a complete one; rather, it is meant to be a metatheatrical mashup, drawing as much attention to the performer as to the character being performed.

Therefore, these "female" performances may have failed at being "great" in a traditional understanding of theatrical performance, but they were groundbreaking works of art because they presented performance in a way that had never quite been done before. In their failure to make art the way others before them—and even their contemporaries—had, the Ridiculous created a style of performance that takes a radical stance on the issue of gender. Eve Shapiro asserts that "drag is not simply an expression of performers' preformed gender identities; rather, the process of participating in drag communities may also function as a form of consciousness raising and a site of identity transformation for performers."[23] Again, we see the emphasis on the concept of community: drag can be used by these groups as a politicized action in its ability to bring to light important issues and to present them to like-minded audiences.

Additionally, this type of performing can have an immense personal impact on the performer. In the case of Eichelberger, it marginalized his legacy to some degree; he is principally remembered for his cross-dressing as opposed to his playwriting or acting. Despite the fact that Eichelberger, if remembered at all, is recalled as a drag performer, Mel Gussow remarks, "With equal zest Ethyl Eichelberger played men and women."[24] Eichelberger had an illustrious career, playing many roles of his own creation as well as the classics, with "a rare and idiosyncratic comic spirit."[25]

Eichelberger's Background[26]

James Eichelberger came to New York to be an actor, first studying at the American Academy of Dramatic Arts and then becoming a member of the Trinity Repertory Company in Providence, Rhode Island.[27] Yet it was the Downtown Scene, the center for Ridiculous artistic creation, that would be his true theatrical education. Both Gussow and Jeffreys cite Ludlam as not only a source for Eichelberger's style of performance but also as a mentor. Eichelberger would perform with Ludlam's Ridiculous Theatrical Company, even starring in drag as Ludlam's mother in *The Artificial Jungle*, the play which would be Ludlam's last before succumbing to AIDS in 1987. Eichelberger, too, would be a victim of the AIDS virus, though he took his own life in 1992 before the disease could kill him.

Before his death, however, Eichelberger had an impressive career, performing various roles both in drag and out, with a cast of other downtown stars and on his own. He wrote 32 plays, though few, to date, have been published. Many of these are adaptations of famous works, such as *Medea* (1980) or *Hamlette* (1985). Others are original works; of such, many are solo performances in which Eichelberger presented a drag character of his own imagining, based on history, literature, or an original creation. These performances are particularly notable for their gender mashup aesthetic: they are as much presentations of Eichelberger's virtuosic talent as they are incarnations of the particular performed personages. Indeed, Eichelberger wanted to be visible to audiences beneath whichever character he found himself portraying that night. From the original category, Eichelberger's *Minnie the Maid* is one of his most notable solo performances, as his performance clearly presents the practice of Ridiculous gender mashup.

Minnie the Maid *(1981) as Mashup*

Eichelberger's "Minnie the Maid" is made up of various elements, despite being a "one-man show." This performance is a routine constructed of layers of popular culture, drag performance, accordion music, and tacky makeup. In it, Minnie, played by Eichelberger, sings, quotes from the surrounding popular culture, muses on life and love, and plays the accordion. Her look is constructed from Eichelberger's long lanky frame, bedecked in a maid's costume, and a great deal of flamboyant makeup. Eichelberger's identity is never lost in this performance; he can always be seen, just beneath Minnie's façade.

This piece, like the plays of Charles Ludlam or the Play-House of the Ridiculous, and even Jack Smith's late-night rituals, is a Ridiculous remix, a blend of elements from different aspects of the culture. Minnie is certainly a product of her contemporary popular culture—quoting from films and musicals—but she also hearkens back to popular culture of the turn-of-the-century, like vaudeville. Although this act is perhaps one of Eichelberger's that is least influenced by "high culture," in the rest of his oeuvre, there are many instances of classical works, such as *Medea*, which he reimagines in his remixed, gender-blending style. In this sense, Eichelberger's club acts were a continuation of the "Ridiculous remix" practices begun at the Play-House of the Ridiculous.

In addition, Eichelberger used a blended approach when it came to gender representation on stage. In his representation of "female" characters, Eichelberger's work highlights another key element of the Ridiculous landscape: gender mashup. I use the term "mashup" because of its contemporary usage in music studies, particularly its similarity to the concept of remix, but with an emphasis on self-created artistic work. Aram Sinnreich contends that the role of DJ and other remixers of music creates a "middleman position" between the artist and the audience, suggesting that an individual can take something that he or she likes and then transform it to even better suit his or her needs. Sinnreich writes, "While configurative music practitioners acknowledge a breakdown of the traditional artist/audience dichotomy and celebrate the communitarian values surrounding the emergence of liminal roles such as the DJ/active fan/curator/connoisseur, many are quick to emphasize that gradations of quality, professionalism, and artistry still do exist."[28] Through mashup, the audience can engage with musical content in new and exciting ways, though their creations may never live up to the quality of a studio-produced original. The original may seem to be of "higher quality," but the at-home artist has the option to make what he or she likes from the artistic material at hand, no matter the quality of the finished product.

To a large degree, this "middleman position" is the role of the Ridiculous artist, and a uniquely middlebrow cultural construct. Someone like Eichelberger borrowed from the cultural material present both in the surrounding popular culture, and in the canon of high art, in order to construct works of his own devising. Eichelberger and others like him, such as Smith and Ludlam, used a similar approach to that of musical mashup when designing gendered identities on stage. Their on-stage Ridiculous personas, especially when they were cross-dressed creations, were "constructed" from the surrounding culture, like a contemporary mashup would be. In the case of Minnie the Maid, for example, Eichelberger blended the traditional French maid outfit with his male frame and then with an over-the-top makeup and hair aesthetic.

This drag performance, of course, was not traditional cross-dressing, as has been present throughout the history of world drama. Rather, it was a kind of "cut-and-paste" approach to creating character identity, similar to the remixing of existing works that Tavel and others did in order to create play texts. Yet, for Eichelberger and other Ridiculous artists, construction of gender identity went beyond remixing, and it was more than mere borrowing and collaging. They layered these multiple identities, one atop another, so that the mixture was not seamless or perfectly blended. One could parse through the various elements and separate them out, categorizing which pieces might be cataloged as "male," which "female," which others "drag," and even to some degree the source of at least some of those references.

In this way, gender is not quite a remix—something original is created from outside source material but those sources are not obscured in the process of mixing; you can still find Eichelberger, for example, as a unique entity in each of his performative constructs. Instead, performances of artists such as Ethyl Eichelberger are more precisely a form of mashup, particularly in the manner in which the term has been defined in relationship to contemporary Internet productions. Internet mashups, like musical ones, involve constructing a work from the layering of two or more other products. For Stefan Sonvilla-Weiss, mashups are distinct from other forms of remix because "Mashups ... put together different information, media, or objects without changing their original source of information, i.e. the original format remains the same and can be retraced as the original form and content, although recombined in different new designs and contexts."[29] In a mashup, a new product is created, but the source material is always recognizable.

This is the case in Eichelberger's Minnie the Maid. Consider the opening to Eichelberger's sketch; this monologue suggests that he expects his audience to know the familiar tropes of gay male drag performances. Minnie begins:

> For those of you who wanted a classy drag act—I'm sorry. But I'll do a little something for you so you won't be disappointed. So here goes, classy drag act: Is that a gun in your pocket or are you just happy to see me what a dump blanche what a dump there's no business like show business the calla lilies are in bloom again falling in love again on the good ship lollipop stop in the name of love happy birthday mister president can we talk diamonds are a girls best friend of course I just farted darling do you think I always smell like this o Nanine I van to be alone. I will not do Judy. She's sacred. You can do Judy—and your little dog too![30]

This rant is an example of Ridiculous remix; it shuffles all of these references together, creating a pastiche both of the original works and of the numerous impersonations of them. Eichelberger is both evoking his own place within the drag tradition and setting aside what he is about to do as separate from it. Minnie the Maid, and, by extension, Ethyl Eichelberger, is simultaneously part of the classic drag tradition and a commentator on it. Within this speech, one can identify various famous quotations, such as Mae West's "Is that a gun in your pocket..." and Ethel Merman's classic "There's no business like show business" routine. The performance was fluid and the lines themselves could change a little bit from night to night.[31] Still, the same major drag tropes were employed in each, even if to some degree the text was created anew in each performance.

This performance displays Eichelberger's virtuosic talent. As was the case in many Play-House of the Ridiculous performances, this is also a performance clearly designed to draw attention to itself as a performance: Minnie knows that she is performing for an audience and recognizes what they expect to hear from her; Eichelberger is as much showing off his performance chops as he is creating a realistic on-stage persona. The speech quoted above is incredibly metatheatrical, aware of its own position as a work of theatre. Because of this, we cannot take everything that Minnie says as entirely sincere; as the audience, we recognize that she *knows* she is performing and therefore must always judge her as a performer first and a reliable narrator second.

In addition, the pace of this speech is particularly interesting. Unlike many of her drag contemporaries, Minnie resists being "classy," suggesting that doing one of these tried-and-true shticks would have been just that. Instead, she rushes through this text, trying to get on to both her own music and her own musings on life and love. One way to interpret what Eichelberger was doing in performing Minnie this way is to realize that his intention was *always* to draw attention to the larger drag scene, exploiting how most of these performances are not unique, but drawn and remixed from the same pool of characters and quotations.

Within this section, Eichelberger hits on many of the favorite routines for female impersonators; Eichelberger's act is clearly ghosted by all of the other similar performances that have come before it or are performed alongside it. Eichelberger understands what it is his audiences expect to see when attending a "drag show," and attempts to appease these desires in his rant early in the proceedings. As Marvin Carlson writes, "All reception is deeply involved with memory, because it is memory that supplies the codes and strategies that shape reception, and, as cultural and social memories change, so do the parameters within which reception operates."[32] The presence of this theatrical ghosting clearly links Eichelberger's work with that of Jack Smith; these are performances that are in tune with the cultural interests of the surrounding community. They may be performing for those who already appreciate these references, but in so doing, they are engaging in the queer practice of community building, perhaps the Ridiculous's most radical action. In addition, the *Minnie the Maid* routine is initially filtered through the audiences' expectations for such an act before it can be processed as an original work. Eichelberger was aware of this, and made it his business to draw attention to the spectators' expectations in order to move on to what he really wanted to do in the performance.

In this opening "bit," then, Minnie covers many drag icons—Marilyn Monroe, Ethel Merman, Mae West—while also making off-color jokes, like the oft-quoted "gun in your pocket" line. It is also hard to ignore the mention of "Nanine," as this was the name of the maid in Ludlam's famous cross-dressed *Camille*. Nanine the maid was one of few female roles in the play not usually played in drag. Eichelberger's performance is self-consciously ghosted by the presence of other iconic female and female impersonator routines, as well as by his own performance career and artistic lineage. The performer is as present as the character, again suggesting the layering of mashup as opposed to the blending of remix.

The setting, be it a downtown club or the more venerable Performance Space 122, as well as the larger New York City location that included each of these sites, also influence this ghosting. Carlson argues, "An audience not only goes to the theatre; it goes to the particular part of the city where the theatre is located, and the memories, and associations of that part of the city help to provide a reception context for any performance seen there."[33] Site is still critical for understanding these Ridiculous works, as it was for Smith's performances; Eichelberger recognized that because of the setting of his production, the audience would have expected a very particular sort of performance from him. His production was ghosted by the larger scene of which it was a part and on which it was commenting.

Despite being ghosted, the *Minnie the Maid* bit lacks the ritualistic feel of a Jack Smith production, both in duration and in treatment of subject matter. These images are not worked through slowly, in a ritualistic manner that is being carefully orchestrated to bring them to life; they are rushed through, mentioned rapid-fire, one right after the other: something to get out of the way as opposed to being something to be revered. Additionally, the setting is not a specific site for these rites to occur; it can be either a raucous club, where Minnie's performance must compete with the sounds of the bar, or a more controlled performance setting, like P.S. 122.

This drag act seems most at home in a club, however. This may be because this was the usual site for such performances during this time period. In *Mother Camp: Female Impersonators in America*, an anthropological study of drag performance of the 1970s, author Esther Newton narrates, "Female impersonators typically perform in bars and nightclubs. In most cases these are public places run by profit-seeking owners and managers who have no interest in impersonators other than as audience-attracting employees…. The bars are usually located in entertainment or gay areas of large cities such as New York, Chicago, and San Francisco, but sometimes in middle-sized cities, too, such as Toledo, Phoenix, and Indianapolis."[34] Eichelberger honed his own style of performance in precisely this sort of setting:

Eichelberger's theatrical sensibility developed in the club environment. At clubs like Freida's disco, the Paradise Garage, the Pyramid, King Tut's Wah Wah Hut, 8 B.C., and the Chandelier Club, his maximalist performance style took root. A style developed in conjunction with his Ridiculous experiences and in reaction to the rowdy club environment in which he found himself performing, it strove to steal focus away from the noisy, drunken chatter of late night bar patrons.[35]

In a similar manner to the way in which the location of Smith's performances dictated their non-traditional structuring, Eichelberger's works were very much shaped by his place of performance. The plays almost demanded a confrontational, direct-to-audience approach if they wanted to draw attention away from the social interactions of being in a bar.

Because of this need to draw an audience's attention, to a large degree, Eichelberger's characters needed to be painted with broad strokes, performed in such a way as to demand that attention. Additionally, they needed to tap into familiar and popular iconography to retain the spectators' focus. Therefore, Eichelberger's use of common drag tropes makes sense; these common quotations and routines would draw an audience in with their familiarity. He was tapping into the cultural consciousness of the larger drag scene of downtown New York in which he wished to intervene.

Community again emerges as an important aspect of Ridiculous artistic creation, which is linked to the practice of gender mashup. Indeed, "another distinguishing feature of mashup music is its underground, do-it-yourself nature that usually falls below the commercial radar."[36] Here, George Plasketes contends that mashups are more commonly shared between individuals as opposed to being sold across commercial platforms, like iTunes. In this sense, mashup distribution hearkens back to the kind of "connoisseurship" that led one to attend a Jack Smith performance: one had to know the work existed to want to access it and perhaps the only way to find out about such a performance was through interaction with another fan.

Indeed, these mashups of gender identities on stage were all about "insider knowledge." This insider information was built upon the notion of a shared cultural lexicon that brought these individuals together as a community. In the same way that most Ridiculous artists revered Maria Montez, they likely also would have been aware of the drag tropes to which Minnie is referring. Similarly, their audiences would probably have been privy to similar cultural material as that on which Minnie riffs. Therefore, what the Ridiculous provided this community of spectators was sites at which to witness works constructed from this shared cultural language. Miller and Román argue the value of the theatre as a site for sharing a common culture because that practice allows for "community-based, and often community-specific, lesbian and gay theatre and performance."[37] It was precisely through attending performances, which were created and then performed through their own language of cultural references, that these gay artists began building their own community within the Downtown Scene. For Smith, this took on a ritualistic aspect, complete with slow, meandering productions that needed to be performed with precision in the secluded site of his loft apartment. For the Ridiculous Theatrical Company and the Play-House of the Ridiculous, this involved writing plays that included references to all of the cultural material for which they felt some reverence, be those references classical or commercial. For Eichelberger, this could take place in the loud, social atmosphere of a club, mixing together all sorts of common drag routines.

All of these types of locations, from lofts to performance spaces to clubs, would come to be known as "theatres" of some sort during this era. In this period of immense artistic production, there was an explosion of "theatre spaces," places where performances could occur, even though they were not necessarily *theatres* in a traditional sense. The club 8BC, for example, located on 8th Street between Avenues B and C, although not a gay bar per se, would be the site of many important performance works of the period; many of Eichelberger's performances were held in this former farmhouse, made up of three levels. Such non-traditional theatre spaces almost demanded a new sort of theatre-making, one that made sense in these more interactive layouts.

These performance spaces, of which Eichelberger regularly took advantage, must not be underestimated in terms of their importance in creating a cohesive and coherent Ridiculous theatrical movement. They provided sites in which these gay artists could pay homage to the cultural icons that they preferred and create art in the manner in which they wanted. Brett Beemyn notes, "Whether in bigger cities like New York and Washington with a relatively large number of gay-dominated establishments or in smaller locales like Flint and Buffalo with only a handful, bars and cafeterias served as important sites for people interested in same-sex sexual relationships to meet and to develop a sense of shared experience."[38] Although not every site in which Eichelberger performed was a space for gay people only, his performances certainly indulge in the sense of "shared experience" of which Beemyn writes. Eichelberger highlights this in his presentation of the laundry list of common drag quotations. He also pokes fun at it in his refusal to "do Judy" and then adding a *Wizard of Oz* reference as his punch line. Eichelberger knows that his audience will recognize at least some—if not all—of his quotations and uses this to comic effect, as is often the case in Ridiculous remix.

Yet, Minnie also wishes to get these common drag routines out of the way early in her performance, so that she can get to other topics of more interest to her. In particular, she tells of her misfortunes regarding love and relationships. She is, as she puts it, "the upstairs maid though I'm familiar with the basement," who just cannot seem to get it right when it comes to romance. She also gives a subtle taste of what the "scene" was like, not from the artist's standpoint, but from the perspective of a patron in search of human interaction. Of "lover number five," Minnie notes, "[Harvey, lover number five] had intellect and a craving for L.S.D. Oh he was no damn good and I got bored and Harvey floated out the door. He stole my heart and most of my cash. But when I see him in the Village I remember the good times."[39] She mixes a raucous accordion tune with a heartfelt, almost sad, narrative of an inability to make lasting connections in the Village dating scene. In a sense, Minnie, and by extension, Eichelberger, is using this performance to paint a picture of a particular place and time, in which Minnie was searching for love and Eichelberger was making art. This performance layers the same kind of nostalgia that the Ridiculous artists often have for the icons of their youth onto the scene in which they performed that nostalgia for like-minded audiences. Minnie is a completely "meta" performance, consistently aware of its own cultural and historical positionality and drawing attention to that position through textual layering of references and commentary on those references.

In addition to textual layering, Minnie's gender is also similarly "layered." This character is neither distinctly male nor female, nor merely cross-dressed. Rather, this character is meant to refer to the entire canon of such gender-mixing performances; she is a mashup of many gender identities and also of other drag performances, layered on top of Eichelberger's ever-present performing self. *Minnie the Maid* throws into relief the form in which these characters are created. The references are all genre-specific and, because of this, are also directed at a particular community: those individuals who would regularly have attended drag shows and therefore known the routines associated with them.

In this manner, Eichelberger's performance draws attention to the existence of the genre in which it operates. Realism has no place in this sort of Ridiculous performance; there is no imaginary fourth-wall through which to peer. In addition, Minnie draws important attention to her position as neither male nor female, exposing that gender, as a marker of identity, is unreliable. This aspect of an individual is not only performed, but can be built from the mixing of elements of more than one gender identity. Minnie wears a classic maid's costume, accentuated with many jewels and gems. Alongside this, Eichelberger does not do anything to alter his tall, lanky frame; in addition, the makeup is so over-the-top as to suggest "performer" above and beyond any particular female character. His face is painted almost white and covered with lots of bright colors and glitter around the eyes, cheeks, and lips.[40] It is not a makeup design that an average woman—or even a female lounge singer—would wear regularly. Minnie is an original construction of character, in every sense of the concept of "original."

Nefert-iti *and Solo Performance of Historical Icons*

Yet, although iconic of both Eichelberger's performance career and what one might mean by "Ridiculous drag performance," *Minnie the Maid* is somewhat unique among Eichelberger's creations. In fact, Eichelberger more often played great literary and historical roles, as opposed to original creations. Like Charles Ludlam before him, Eichelberger was profoundly committed to casting himself in all of the roles that he believed he would never be able to attain in the mainstream theatre scene; Jeffreys quotes Eichelberger's lament: "I wanted to play the great roles but who would cast me as Medea?"[41] Therefore, many of Eichelberger's gender-bending performances were adaptations of stories of great figures from history and literature, like Egyptian queen Nefertiti.

In the piece *Nefert-iti* (here spelled with a dash), another one of Eichelberger's solo works, he layers the female character of Neferet-iti on top of his own gay male experience. Jeffreys accepts this interpretation; he writes, "As a gay man, Eichelberger personally identified with these brave, struggling women. His take on these figures is intensely personal and deeply intertwined with his day-to-day experience."[42] Again, we find the presence of Eichelberger the person meant to be accessible to audiences alongside of the persona being portrayed. Although this is never stated outright (Eichelberger plays the role as though he *were* the famous ancient queen), some subtle references within the text suggest this interpretation. Nefert-iti cries out, "It's true most people would rather queens should stay under wraps,/so to speak!/Hide!/Deny your feminine soul!"[43] One can see here how the mashup is functioning: the layer of the female character allows for the gay male person underneath to speak an important truth about how a gay male was treated by mainstream society. This line operates on both levels simultaneously: laying out Nefert-iti's plight in her tomb while at the same betraying the performer's (and his surrounding community's) predicament in his contemporary late 1970s New York world. Once again, here we find gender that is constructed through a layering of identities.

Building on this textual gender mashup, Eichelberger is also able to pronounce radical ideas through his performance as this noted queen. Nefert-iti states, "No one is turning my priceless uniqueness into worthless guilt" (74). If I continue to read Eichelberger's experience as a gay male through his performance of this female character, then a line such as this suggests a moment of activism. Through this role, Eichelberger is proclaiming a sense of pride in who he is: he may be different from others, as Nefert-iti was, but in no way should this be viewed as a negative. The former standards for ranking what should be appreciated and what devalued no longer apply. In the same way that the Ridiculous community of artists dared to hold Maria Montez up as the paragon of the fabulous aspects of acting, Eichelberger, through his portrayal of Nefert-iti, asserts his own prerogative to perform in the manner that he sees fit. No one can make him feel guilty for portraying characters in this "mashed up" way.

Finally, Eichelberger's mashed up performance of gender undoes any notion of the self as some kind of fixed truth. Nefert-iti asserts, "But if truth were beauty, more girls would get their hair done at the library!" (79). The appearance of beauty is no more real for an actual female body than it is for a cross-dressed performer; it is something to be put on at a beauty salon, not to be found proven in some scholarly text. Identity, particularly as it is tied up with gender, is always performed in a Ridiculous work. Eichelberger's solo works of the great women of the past are only the most obvious example of this practice. Gender, in this sense, is always a mashup; it always something that needs to be constructed from elements present in the surrounding culture, like remix.

Of course, also like remix, mashup is not a term generally applied to theatre. Plasketes introduces, "Mashup music, in its simplest definition, is a song or composition created from the master track and instrumental music of one song and the a cappella vocal master track from another." Plasketes sees this practice, often performed by DJs, as an extension of jazz musicians' interpretations of popular standards.[44] A work of mashup takes elements from one source (in his description, the lyrics or text of a song) and pairs this with the background information from another source (in his example, the instrumental track). Unlike the remix, which can have a multitude of sources being blended together, Plasketes is suggesting that the components of the mashup are usually far more limited: in this case, it only takes mixing two elements to construct a new musical creation.

For Eichelberger, this mashup construction is not done by separating out the aspects of musical construction, but rather by parsing out those of gender construction. Eichelberger would layer elements of the female characters he was portraying on top of his evidently male persona and, markedly in the case of Minnie the Maid, pepper this with elements from other drag routines. For *Nefert-iti*, however, Eichelberger "mashed up" his own male persona with a feminine costume as well as some homemade accessories; "Eichelberger wore an original, black, pleated, silk, Fortuny gown. He accessorized with a large jeweled collar and papier-mâché headdress of his own construction."[45] Elements of the female character were simply donned upon his male body; he never intended to confuse the audience into believing that he actually was a woman. Both identities were to be obvious in this layering; they both lent interpretative meaning to the piece being presented.

"Mashup," as a theory of artistic production has wider application than simply for musical composition or Internet memes. Plasketes continues, "The term 'mashup' can apply to any art form, not just music. The methodology itself is an extension of current society and the digital DIY culture. Mashups can be seen as content aggregation; they combine existing data from two or more sources in innovative ways. Mashups are not revolutionary, they are evolutionary."[46] Even though Eichelberger and the rest of the Ridiculous scene predate this "digital DIY culture," these artists engaged in many similar artistic endeavors.

Indeed, in their borrowing and usurping of fellow artists' styles, Ridiculous creators were certainly employing a collaborative, do-it-yourself approach. Each artist built upon the work of those who came before him: Warhol stole ideas from Smith, particularly those related to durationality and anti-acting practices; Smith based his work on Maria Montez; Ludlam contended that Smith was a key influence on his style of performance; Tavel and Vaccaro began their work under the umbrella of Warhol's Factory; Ludlam broke from Tavel and Vaccaro's company; Eichelberger cited Ludlam as a mentor; and so on. From the seed of Ridiculous performance, born in Smith's late-night loft shows, came the entire Ridiculous scene. The idea was not to change the entire theatrical landscape in New York (as might be the case if the work were "revolutionary"), but to develop their own unique voice and style for making art, sharing what they had created and building upon it when each new branch of the Ridiculous sprouted, an evolutionary gesture. The style of Ridiculous Theatre continued to develop as it moved from one artistic site to the next.

One trait that each of these branches had in common, however, was a reverence for aspects of the popular culture with which they had grown up, particularly those that they found represented their ideals of glamour or their preferred modes of presentational performance. They then chose to mix these aspects with cultural elements considered more sophisticated. These artists were committed to B-level stars, people like Maria Montez, whose greatness was as complicated to understand as was these artists' ability to turn trash into the treasure of theatrical properties. Eichelberger, for one, could find the perfect assonance in mixing a designer gown with an arts-and-crafts style headdress. The high and low are always being blended in one way or another in the Ridiculous because it is the aesthetic pleasure that can only be found in rubbish that these artists attempted to highlight, even in their Ridiculous performances of female identities.

Dasvedanya Mama: *Eichelberger's Brand of Ridiculous Remix*

This mixing of high and low culture is nowhere more pronounced than it is in Ridiculous travesties of great works of dramatic literature. Like his

Ridiculous contemporaries, Eichelberger's brand of gender mashup extended into his adaptations of so-called great literary works. Eichelberger was a versatile artist and playwright, and he designed works to be performed solo, as well as constructed ones for a larger cast of players. One such production, *Dasvedanya Mama* (1990), first performed at P.S. 122 in New York City and including in its cast Ridiculous Theatrical Company veteran Black-Eyed Susan, was a mashup of sorts of some of Anton Chekhov's most famous plays, including *The Three Sisters* (1901), combined with *The Seagull* (1895), and blended with some references to *The Cherry Orchard* (1903). This layering of Chekhov plays seems right in line with the stacking of gender identities so common in Eichelberger's plays. In this incarnation, cross-gendered performance was once again used, as Eichelberger himself took on the role of Olga.

This role seems particularly suited to Eichelberger's position, especially if we believe the claim that much of Eichelberger's casting of himself in female roles was used to speak toward particular aspects of his actual life. Olga is a former great actress, like Arkadina of *The Seagull*, and begins the play by reminiscing about her grand old days upon the stage. She tells Fierz (a name perhaps referring to Firs from *The Cherry Orchard*, who is the only character left behind at play's end), "I am Olga Pluchinskaya, who was the greatest actress of the '60s. And the '70s."[47] Although the character, as Chekhov would have imagined her, speaks of the century prior, this comment cannot help but hearken back to the heyday of the Ridiculous in the 20th century. Like Firs at the end of *The Cherry Orchard*, Eichelberger has been left behind by many of his artistic contemporaries; by 1990, many of the great artists associated with the Ridiculous had already passed away, most notably Eichelberger's mentor Charles Ludlam, or moved on to other projects. Like the characters of Chekhov's play, a Ridiculous artist like Eichelberger might have been very preoccupied with looking back to the past, to a moment of greatness that had already ceased to be. Olga says to Fierz, "Does it not matter to you that all your friends are gone, that you alone are still here rubbing the walls with patchouli oil on Sunday, and mopping the stairs? We are relics, Fierz, you and I" (268). By this point, Eichelberger and Black-Eyed Susan would have been considered "relics" as well, some of the last remaining stars associated with the original Ridiculous Theatre.

Despite Eichelberger's ingenious decision to put himself in the role of Olga to comment on his historical moment, what is most fascinating about the casting for this play is Eichelberger's use of Susan to play Masha, Irina, and Maude. Black-Eyed Susan played the parts all at once, wearing a costume piece that allowed her head to be situated between two puppet heads, for which she would provide distinct voices. Obviously, as in other Eichelberger Ridiculous productions, we are not in the realm of Realism here. The play consistently breaks the fourth-wall; Olga, for one, both engages the audience and, at one point, speaks directly to "Miss Black-Eyed Susan," the actress, as opposed to any of her three characters.

More tellingly, Olga actually morphs into Ethyl himself later in the proceedings, offering an "X-rated [piece]. I used to do it down at 8 B.C.... Ah, yes, those were the days" (287). Olga then begins to mime Eichelberger's *Catherine the Great* to a tape recording of his performance. Like Smith trying to evoke the ghost of Maria Montez, his popular culture icon of the past, or Vawter reliving Jack Smith during his recreation of *What's Underground About Marshmallows?*, Eichelberger attempts to ghost his performance with another of his performances, to bring the glory days of Ridiculous Theatre to life in his production, engaging both his own ghost and the ghosts of his contemporaries, and to wish them all once and for all, "*Dasvedanya.*" This is a mashup of Eichelberger's own work and performances, representing a farewell to a Ridiculous scene that had already begun to die, both figuratively and literally, with the loss of some of its greatest icons. The ghosting in this piece lends a profundity and an overarching sense of melancholy to the otherwise over-the-top and zany proceedings.

Indeed, this play is a climax for the Ridiculous Theatre, perhaps its final one. It invokes all of its key aspects—ghosting of and from the pop cultural past, blending of high and low cultural references, and mixing of gendered identities—while still seeing itself as a form of general entertainment, not a niche style for a particular group. Like Charles Ludlam and Jack Smith, who both disdained references to their work as "gay," Eichelberger similarly dismisses that categorization in this play. Olga identifies as a straight woman, "[not] lucky enough to be born a lesbian, like Holly Hughes." She reminds them, "You want to see gay art, go over to the Public Theatre. There you will see living, in the flesh heterosexual men playing faggots, and they'll make you cry and feel sorry for them" (289). These works even fail at being "gay plays"; they are something else entirely, something beyond representations of gay people or even people in drag. Olga claims, as Ludlam often claimed, that her goal is to "make ya laugh" (289). These plays are serious commentaries on art and performance that make those serious comments through silliness. Ridiculous Theatre succeeds specifically through failing.

Like many Ridiculous plays, the seriousness of each scene in *Dasvedanya Mama* is undercut by popular culture references; the play often intentionally fails to be the same kind of heart-wrenching story that its source material is. Or perhaps Eichelberger recognizes Chekhov's desire for his works to be seen as comedies and updates that idea for 20th-century audiences. For example, in wishing for beloved Vaslav's return, Olga must mention both that the "massive iron door [was] carved in the Biedermeyer style my mother loved" and that her son was sung "tales of the burnished woods of Stolichnaya" (273). Although both references fit the European setting for the play, the first reminds of the importance of consumer objects to the world of the Ridiculous and the second, of course, reminds one of vodka as much as it does the deep, dark woods. Additionally, by the end of the play, things have devolved into a flurry of quoting; references to Shakespeare's *Romeo and Juliet*, to *South Pacific* by Rodgers and Hammerstein, and to contemporary reviewers of Eichelberger's plays are used alongside the forward-moving dialogue. This play is as much a version of Chekhov as it is a remix of all sorts of other material.

It is precisely its failure to be a complete modern adaptation of any of Chekhov's works that allows the most meaning to come out of this play. The characters of this fictional world are not only experiencing the disappointments that Chekhov wrote about but also the ones against which the Ridiculous Theatre once fought. They contend with the prevalence of American popular culture and American dominance, bemoaning, "Oh, why, oh, why couldn't [Vaslav] have gone to the gold rush in America and been trampled by the greedy hordes" (276) while at the same time recognizing that the underground culture of which they were once a part is now potentially as commodified as more mainstream entertainment. Olga, the former performer, berates the contemporary experimental theatre scene, crying out, "Listen, just because you work with the Mabou Mines does not mean everything is avant-garde" (277). Masha then mentions both Robert Wilson and Anne Bogart, to which Olga responds by bringing up "H. M. Koutoukas.... An expert in the art of acting!" (277). Koutoukas was a playwright associated with the Caffe Cino, a direct predecessor of the Ridiculous Theatre, and a practitioner of a similar brand of pop culture-infused camp as the Ridiculous artists. By putting contemporary experimental theatre at odds with Koutoukas's style of play-making, *Dasvedanya Mama* throws into relief the ways in which the Downtown Scene had changed in the past few decades. In this sense, the debate in this late Ridiculous play is grounded as much in the 19th century of Chekhov's originals as it is in the 20th century of Eichelberger's artistic work, if not more so.

Ridiculous Theatre, even as a form, is forced to engage failure, because although its work with gender performance was groundbreaking, it clearly had difficulty maintaining prominence outside of its historical moment and without some of its greatest artists at the helm. Eichelberger, here, is exploiting that fact, showing that this sort of failure was *always* inherent to this type of artistic work. It is Ridiculous Theatre's failings to be great—both as art and as impersonation—that actually allowed Ridiculous artists to do and say something significant about American culture and identity politics.

Gender Performance and Failure

The negotiation of important female personas on stage is perhaps the most striking aspect of Eichelberger's work. Just mentioning Ethyl Eichelberger blurs the line between the masculine and the feminine. Consider Eichelberger's chosen stage name: saying the name "Ethyl" aloud suggests the female name "Ethel," while, on paper, the scientific spelling employed defies any easy gender categorization. Immediately, it becomes clear that traditional discussions of gender—in terms of a male/female dichotomy—are no longer appropriate to explicating Eichelberger's negotiation of gender both in performance and in life.

Eichelberger did not live his day-to-day life as a woman. Nor did he intend to fool the audiences of his drag performances with his own femininity. As Eichelberger himself once said of the impressive tattoo he had on his back: "I'd been playing a lot of female roles, but I'm not a female impersonator, and I figure this would get the message across. No serious drag queen would have a tattoo across his back."[48] Eichelberger was never trying to *be* a woman, nor even a drag queen; he simply wanted the opportunity to play the roles that he desired to play. By extension of this practice, he was also creating roles that broke with the norms of gender performance, and even those of cross-gendered performance. He was creating a brand-new style of gender representation on stage, one that forced the audience to recognize the persona of Ethyl Eichelberger—perhaps a performance in and of itself—beneath the layers of the character. This mashup is never a seamless blend; rather it is a way to draw attention to gender, and all aspects of identity, as performed.

To some degree, then, the Ridiculous is directly in line with later theories of gender, such as those of Judith Butler. In Butler's important *Gender Trouble*, she proclaims, "Drag is an example that is meant to establish that 'reality' is not as fixed as we generally assume it to be."[49] The so-called "reality" of a person's gender cannot be an unalterable factor if one can easily assume the markers of the opposite gender. The performances of gender in the Ridiculous make a similar claim; reality is always constituted through and by performance. Neither identity nor circumstance is fixed. The self is always being made and remade from moment to moment.

Therefore, the Ridiculous can be understood as being queer, at least insofar as that term was applied during the 1990s, when Butler was writing. Butler continues, "The contentious practices of 'queerness' might be understood not only as an example of citational politics, but as a specific reworking of abjection into political agency that might explain why 'citationality' has contemporary political promise."[50] These artists could use the image of the somewhat overlooked Maria Montez to their own radical ends; they fixated on Montez precisely because of her flaws. In this sense, she is, to quote Vaccaro, "the apotheosis of the drag queen,"⁵¹ both glamorous and grotesque simultaneously.

In their use of "gender mashup," the works of Eichelberger suggest a "queer" interpretation of the concept of gender. In this instance, I am continuing to look at queer in its 1990s incarnations, as these theoretical constructions of the term easily apply to Eichelberger's performance work. As Moe Meyer describes the term in *The Politics and Poetics of Camp*, "What 'queer' signals is an ontological challenge that displaces bourgeois notions of the Self as unique, abiding, and continuous while substituting instead a concept of the Self as performative, improvisational, discontinuous, and processually constituted by repetitive and stylized acts."⁵² Queer suggests a performative approach to identity; identity, and therefore, gender, are not fixed and can be assumed and discarded based on the circumstances in which one finds oneself. One is consistently making and remaking his or her identity.

This construct breaks with any sort of dichotomous construction of either gender or sexuality. Meyer continues:

> The use of the word "queer" to designate what is usually referred to as "gay and lesbian" marks a subtle, ongoing, and not yet stabilized renomination.... "Queer" does not indicate the biological sex or gender of the subject. More importantly, the term indicates an ontological challenge to dominant labeling philosophies ... as well as a challenge to discrete gender categories embedded in the divided phrase "gay and lesbian."⁵³

Queer does not allow for easy categorization or definition of an individual. Like a name that when said aloud suggests a female but when written down suggests a chemical compound, something queer cannot be easily explained as being one thing and not another.

To put it another way, consider David Halperin's discussion of queer, also from the 1990s. In *Saint Foucault*, Halperin contends, "Queer is by definition *whatever* is at odds with the normal, the legitimate, the dominant. *There is nothing in particular to which it necessarily refers.* It is an ideality without an essence. 'Queer' then, demarcates not a positivity but a positionality *vis-à-vis* the normative.... [Queer] describes a horizon of possibility whose precise extent and heterogeneous scope cannot in principle be delimited in advance."⁵⁴ For Halperin, queer is always associated with whatever is positioned against the mainstream; its meaning, therefore, is not fixed. It is defined through juxtaposition against normative culture. Again, Maria Montez is iconic of this: her greatness, for her devotees, is bound up with her performative failure, the fact that she was the opposite of what would traditionally have been seen as talent.

In addition, "Montez Worship" also creates an insider culture, separate from the mainstream. As filmmaker Nick Zedd says, "She seemed to be a mediocre actress, at best.... I think it was some kind of a [*sic*] inside joke to gay people. They seem to find her an object of adoration."[55] One either understood what it meant to be an admirer of Maria Montez (a non-normative behavior) or one was perplexed by the act of idol worship in her honor (a more mainstream belief).

In this way, queer, as it pertains to notions of reimagining the concept of failure alongside of the concept of performative self-formation, sheds light on the kind of theatre that the Ridiculous performers, such as Ethyl Eichelberger, created. These plays did not simply call for men to play women and vice versa; rather, they demanded an entirely new set of rules for gender performance and a unique set of standards for evaluating what is meant by artistic greatness. In the same way that Eichelberger "failed," intentionally, to become a woman in his *Minnie the Maid* routine, Maria Montez "failed" to rise above B-movie star status. And yet, it was precisely this "failure" that can allow us to see the Ridiculous as progressive: Eichelberger's performance method threw into relief the presence of the performer in performance, reminding us that all identity is unfixed and unstable.

This act of failing is critical to understanding how "queer," as a theoretical concept, can still shed new and interesting light on the Theatre of the Ridiculous. Consider Jack Halberstam's re-interpretation of the concept of failure: "We might read *failure*, for example, as a refusal of mastery, a critique of the intuitive connections within capitalism between success and profit, and as a counterhegemonic discourse of losing."[56] There is an implicit power in the act of failing: one is choosing to go against the standards set out by others, creating their own standards in place of the previous ones. According to mainstream principles, Montez may not have been a great actress. However, the Ridiculous is supplanting that rubric for greatness with one of its own. In this way, they are remaking the system at large. The original standards for quality have been thrown out; in their stead, the terrible is celebrated and the supposedly great, ignored. Montez can be championed as a "great" actress because the old standards for evaluating good and bad have been dismissed.

In order to explore this notion of "failure," the Ridiculous began their own process of character construction, born of a desire to embody the great icons, often female, of film and stage, such as Montez, and combined this with experimental artistic techniques, prevalent throughout the Downtown Scene where they chose to create their art work. Because of this "avant-garde" artistic community, the Ridiculous felt comfortable breaking with traditional aesthetic standards. Thus, in order to create their on-stage personas, the Ridiculous performers, at least those performing in drag, would often layer elements of the female characters right on to their male personas—without any attempt to "pass" at being a woman by physically altering their body or personality. By "failing" at becoming women, these performance artists would succeed at creating something entirely new in their character construction.

Eichelberger's *Catherine Was Great* (1982) certainly failed at being a realistic representation of the life of Catherine the Great, for example. This was "a show whose title was appropriated from a Mae West play"[57]; again, a reference within a reference, one that showcases popular culture as much as it does history. Rather than representing who this famous queen was, Eichelberger was more interested in "the rumor. So [he] played that as a sexual fantasy. That's like a comic sexual fantasy that has nothing to do with the real Catherine the Great. Whenever you think of Catherine the Great, you think of the horse. Everybody does."[58] The production was more about this "comic sexual fantasy" than it was about anything else. Eichelberger played Catherine and made the sexual act with the horse, played by a person with a "five-foot-long balloon as a dildo," a central comic set piece for the performance and reminiscent of Peeping Tom in Tavel's *The Life of Lady Godiva*. This is an example of how these studies of great women in literature and history, a major category of Eichelberger's plays, were as much deconstructions of these figures as they were portraits of them; they made the audience as aware of the Ridiculous scene and of Ethyl performing the role as they did of the particular historical figure being presented. Eichelberger used his cross-dressing to throw into relief the most extreme cultural associations that society has with them.

Even his well-researched *Lucrezia Borgia*, from the same year, allows Eichelberger to explore the contradictions built in to our understandings of historical figures. He notes, "She's not a nice woman" yet created the piece because "she was so maligned; there was this woman who everyone says was so beautiful and her father was the Pope…. And they say she was such a lovely woman, so nice, and yet she was just used by her family."[59] Based on Eichelberger's explanation of this historical person, any representation of Lucrezia Borgia would likely fail; it seems contradictory that she could be both a pawn and a person who did terrible things on her own behalf simultaneously. By exploring the contradiction—the failure—Eichelberger was able to show that even a historically accurate representation of a historical figure can be riddled with complexities not easily ironed out.

In this way, again, the Ridiculous took action in an aesthetic way—reimagining how to approach cross-gendered performance—even if they did not take particular social or political action. Their elevation of the low to the status of high, such as their emulation of Montez, an otherwise derided film siren, was a radical act. Eichelberger was a visionary in terms of drag; he found new and exciting ways to perform characters on stage, building on Smith's Montez spectacles but adding his own unique comic touch. He also showed how every day, commonplace items, as well as trash, could be elevated to be true theatrical objects, imbued with artistry and filled with theatrical magic. Eichelberger, like other Ridiculous artists, also performed in non-traditional sites, exploring what sorts of locations could be included in the category of "theatre." In addition, the Ridiculous artists re-imagined what makes a performance "great." With Maria Montez as their touchstone for exceptional performing, these artists explored the aesthetic possibilities of failure. Unlike many other Ridiculous performers, Eichelberger was formally trained, yet it was the anti-acting choices that he made, particularly in his female roles, which were groundbreaking.

The anti-realist preoccupation with the unfinished or the disjointed was part of the brilliance of these performances. These performances were not amateurish; on the contrary, it was only because of these artists' great intellect that they were able to undo the norms of performance in their presentations. Ann Cooper Albright reminisces about Eichelberger's *Klytemnestra*, another solo work, presented at P.S. 122 in the late 1980s:

> Put together on a shoestring budget, with some of the intentionally worst costuming ever seen (layers of cheap acrylic curtains from Goodwill together with fake boobs made from stuffed nylon stockings strung across Eichelberger's tall, bony frame), this was ancient Greek (melo)drama splayed out in all its twentieth-century vaudevillian glory. Nonetheless, the power of Eichelberger's dramatic pathos resounded, even in the midst of a campy, S & M-inflected pastiche of late-1980s performance art. A tour de force of solo acting, it was like seeing Aristotle duke it out with Andy Warhol.[60]

This battle between the pathos of the classics and the aesthetics of Pop Art plants Eichelberger's play precisely in the same complex crossroads between commerce and art as his compatriots in the Ridiculous scene. It also celebrates the performer as much as, if not more so, than the piece itself, reminding us that this mash-up style is meant to draw attention to the persona underneath the character. Additionally, however, Albright's recollection puts great emphasis on the significance of the faulty nature of the female imper-sonation, the "intentionally" bad costume choices, the "campy" style, and the sexual overtones. This performance of a female character was much more complicated than just a man playing against his biological sex. Rather, it was an individual laying bare both the importance and the preposterousness of our most canonical texts and throwing into relief the reality and fiction of stage performance.

Conclusion

Despite how provocative and compelling Eichelberger's performance pieces were for those who saw them, the works of Ethyl Eichelberger do not have the same acknowledged status of those of Charles Ludlam nor the more academic bent of the plays of Kenneth Bernard or Ronald Tavel. What Eichel-berger created on stage does not always translate to the small screen or to YouTube. As Michael Feingold asserts, "A printed text gives only the barest sense of a performance art like Ethyl Eichelberger's."[61] Much of what this actual performance is like cannot be conveyed in a play script or short video clip; the performance involved interaction with the audience and continued to evolve throughout its run of performances. Like Smith asking his viewers to take on roles in his midnight rituals, the affect of an Eichelberger performance was designed for live performance. For example, no play text could encapsulate what it felt like to attend "his Medea [(c. 1980) which] combined elements of Kabuki with old-fashioned hoofing and accordion-playing.... Medea bombarded her [rival in love] with small but deafening charges of live explosives (cherry bombs), sending patrons seated in the front half of the performance space scurrying for cover, hands over ears."[62] The works that Eichelberger was able to create needed the act of performing to be complete.

Therefore, having the text of one of Eichelberger's works may not mean that one actually has the blueprint for the production. Even of one of Eichelberger's plays (as opposed to his solo works), Feingold accepts, "*Dasvedanya Mama* may or may not be performable by others; it may or may not 'mean' something in the largest literary sense. It certainly does mean something in the context of our time, and the climate of disapproval that makes every step into the imagination a step toward danger. One we should all take bravely, as Ethyl did, head held mockingly high, to a tangy accordion tune."[63] Despite Feingold's concerns, *Dasvedanya Mama* has been remounted since Ethyl's death, notably by the California-based Shotgun Players in 2000, as have other plays by Eichelberger. In addition, Eichelberger's impact has been kept alive by significant contemporary artists, such as 2009 Ethyl Eichelberger award winner and Circus Amok founder Jennifer Miller.

However, the question still remains as to the direct relevance of such works outside of their historical moment and unique artistic community. These works may have belonged to the artist who created them to such an extent that later productions would mean differently than they would have in their original place and time. And yet, they do something provocative and potentially profound: they ask the performer to play a role with which he or she might not feel fully comfortable—be brave enough to accept the performative nature of identity. Eichelberger allowed the vulnerability of the self to come through the character being portrayed, forcing the performer of the role to show themselves to the audience in a provocative and profound way.

Eichelberger did not set out to be a playwright or to leave a canon of play texts for others to perform. Much like the live presentations of Jack Smith, these works might not make complete sense performed out of their historical context by another artist. This extreme ephemerality seems an important thread of the Ridiculous history; beginning with H. M. Koutoukas's camp spectacles at the Caffe Cino, meant to be performed once and then have their texts destroyed,[64] the artists looked at thus far seem primarily preoccupied with creating the act of performance as opposed to the performance text. The former is ephemeral, something that cannot be created exactly the same a second time. The latter, however, can have lasting artistic impact and can help an artist or artistic movement achieve a long-term legacy even after its own historical moment has passed.

This interest in the ephemerality of live performance certainly links the Ridiculous with much of the historical avant-garde. The Dadaists, for example, who were very committed to live performance as a mode of artistic creation, were also entirely disinterested in creating literary dramatic texts. Tristan Tzara's version of Dada was entirely a-literary; Kuenzli notes, "Dada opposed society's sense and logic by creating non-sense in the form of anti-art and a-art. Unlike Cubism, Futurism, or Surrealism, Dada is, as Tzara insisted, 'not a literary school,' denotes not a certain artistic style, but a rebellious, playful 'state-of-mind' that dissolves fixities, truths, and myths."[65] The same could potentially be said of the Ridiculous; it is almost anti–Ridiculous to call something "Ridiculous." The term must be used with irony—even mockery—to be used appropriately. The writers derided their own texts by calling them Ridiculous; by extension, how could the "Ridiculous" be part of a larger literary program for creating works of dramatic literature?

However, without a collection of "Ridiculous plays," the movement has been continuously overlooked in histories of American drama. Eichelberger, for one, may be remembered as a drag performance artist, but his written works are rarely included in collected editions and other artists do not regularly recreate his performance pieces in the contemporary moment. The Ridiculous is almost solely remembered because of the playwright-director-actor-producer Charles Ludlam, Eichelberger's mentor, Vaccaro and Tavel's one-time collaborator, and Jack Smith's unwanted artistic protégé. One reason for Ludlam's canonization is that he, unlike Eichelberger or Smith, wrote plays that were literary in their structure and separated enough from his self as a performer as to invite interpretations by other artists. Ludlam also theorized the term "Ridiculous" in ways Tavel did not, even if Tavel was its initial creator. Therefore, in some sense, all legacy of the Ridiculous, not just Eichelberger's performance career, can be credited back to Charles Ludlam.

But what does this connection with Ludlam do to the progressive quality of the Ridiculous? Ludlam, unlike Smith or even Eichelberger, was certainly concerned with commercial theatrical success, a shift from the Ridiculous's earlier preoccupations. Indeed, Ridiculous Theatre was born as a truly underground movement, one that asked its participants not only to make art in a new way, but to live their lives in a new way as well. Stefan Brecht continues, "The theatre of the ridiculous is produced by a family or families of approximately free persons as part of their family life. Its members adopt and act roles as the f.p. playfully assumes his identity—without identifying and only for the sake of playing them."[66] In fact, Brecht was even a relative of this Ridiculous family; his wife Mary created costumes for Ludlam, making her a part of his clan. All identity in this Ridiculous landscape was meant to be performative; nothing was fixed and all sense of self was always in flux, always to be performed, even in one's personal life. Selling these performed identities to commercial audiences seems disingenuous to this original Ridiculous ideology.

In this way, Eichelberger was the quintessential Ridiculous downtown underground performer; his works altered our understanding of performance through their assertion of the principles of gender theory, even though much of his work predates these theoretical texts. What would happen, then, if this performative approach to character building associated with the Ridiculous began to move uptown? And, when the Ridiculous aesthetic did move to more commercial spaces, as it would with artists like Charles Busch, what became of its more radical flare? Were these works simply the "farces" that Jack Smith bemoaned his style becoming because of Ludlam? Or were they able to maintain their subversive quality despite their more mainstream locales? I tackle these questions in the next chapter, where I look at artists who have clearly credited Ludlam as a source, such as the aforementioned Busch and Pulitzer Prize-winner Tony Kushner. When discussing the importance of the Ridiculous, legacy cannot be ignored: it is the key way in which this theatrical form has survived.

Legacy is hugely important when discussing the Ridiculous—Sean F. Edgecomb's recent book *Ludlam Lives!*, which focuses on artists such as Taylor Mac, proves this. There is a whole new generation of artists working in the Ridiculous style and bringing this queer aesthetic to 21st-century audiences. Therefore, Eichelberger was not the last bit of legacy of the Ridiculous scene; rather, his work was only the beginning of a new generation of artists who were inspired by the works of Ludlam and other Ridiculous creators. In the case of Eichelberger, this connection with the next generation is quite a literal one; both Mac and Peggy Shaw, who I will discuss in the next chapter, have been awarded The Ethyl Eichelberger Award, which "is given to an artist or group that exemplifies Ethyl's larger-than-life style and generosity of spirit; who embodies Ethyl's multi-talented artistic virtuosity, bridging worlds and vitalizing those around them."[67] This shows that the legacy of the Ridiculous, while forever tied to the fame of Charles Ludlam, is actually perhaps best preserved by the impact of Ethyl Eichelberger. Exemplifying Ethyl's spirit and ideals can lead to funding and support which will ultimately lead to theatrical creation and presentation. The ghost of Eichelberger keeps Ridiculous innovation happening and therefore haunts the legacy of this theatrical form.

SIX

The Ridiculous Aesthetic
Across Generations
The Descendants of the Ridiculous

Indeed, the significance of legacy cannot be denied when discussing the Theatre of the Ridiculous. Ethyl Eichelberger, whose impact has already extended far beyond his own moment of artistic productivity through his namesake award, was preoccupied with this concern. "I do want to leave a legacy," Eichelberger contends, "Of whatever, for anyone who'd be interested.... One would hate to think that one has passed through this world and left nothing. It's not even so much leaving something, it's having done something to better the world. I hope I've opened a lot of doors."[1] From this angle, studying the Ridiculous takes on a deeper significance: these artists need to be reinserted into the history of drama in order to show that they achieved these goals of leaving a lasting impression and creating paths for other, similar artists to create innovative work in the future.

Despite being a unique and self-contained artistic movement, it makes sense to discuss the Ridiculous in context; it has antecedents in the historical avant-garde as well as descendants in the contemporary theatre scene. Uzi Parnes suggested, "The Ridiculous is just one form of Pop Performance."[2] For many, Ridiculous Theatre is often discussed as a part of the Pop Art scene, as opposed to as its own form. Aspects of its aesthetic appear in movements that long predate it—such as Dadaism—and continue to exist in contemporary art. In order to understand why the Ridiculous is such a significant artistic movement, it is useful, then, to track its legacy. Many innovative artists credit the Ridiculous as a key influence. Without the impact of Ridiculous theatre—without exposure to the Ridiculous aesthetic—these contemporary visionaries might never have continued to innovate in the ways that they have.

Indeed, at least Ridiculous acting style has found methods of adapting to our contemporary moment. Ridiculous performers like Black-Eyed Susan and Everett Quinton are still performing in New York. Even a play like *Reid Farrington's A Christmas Carol*, which starred Quinton during the 2012 holiday season, showed evidence of his Ridiculous training. He was able to incarnate each of the Scrooges referenced, both the ones of great artistic merit and the ones from children's entertainment, a Ridiculous remix in its own right.

Quinton's acting style also betrayed an over-the-top quality, which worked perfectly for the "trippy performance."[3] Certainly, this sort of acting style has always been associated with Ridiculous Theatre and now, in a seemingly post–Ridiculous world, it has carried over into Ridiculous artists' non–Ridiculous performances. In the contemporary downtown scene, which often honors "weird" aesthetic choices, albeit without an organizing principle provided by a manifesto, this sort of acting absolutely works, no matter the subject matter or intended audience for the show.

In addition, sites associated with Ridiculous theatrical production, such as La MaMa E. T. C., are still very much alive and producing Ridiculous Theatre: Ludlam's *Conquest of the Universe* was produced in the fall of 2017 under Quinton's direction. The LaMaMa archive lists the important queer production *Son of Cockstrong*, written by Tom Murrin and presented by the "Playhouse [*sic*] of the Ridiculous" as opening on February 20, 1970,[4] a fairly early date in the Ridiculous history, reminding us that Ellen Stewart's La MaMa is as Ridiculous a site as any other theatre previously mentioned, both because of the Play-House's residency and because of Stewart's continued encouragement of new and experimental artists. Yet, this site also seems bigger than many other Ridiculous landmarks; it was a producing house, not a company, and therefore was able to adapt as the Downtown Scene changed over time. This quality allows it to remain operational, while other Ridiculous sites have been forced to change entirely. Ridiculous Theatre, then, more evidently lives on in particular theatremakers as opposed to theatre spaces themselves.

Ludlam's Followers: Charles Busch and Tony Kushner

Busch's Ridiculous Theatre:
Vampire Lesbians of Sodom

Indeed, the Ridiculous has direct inheritors, that is, individuals who claim that Charles Ludlam and the Ridiculous directly influenced their work. Charles Busch, for one, noted, "My life changed at that moment," when he saw 1971's *Eunuchs of the Forbidden City*, which he considered a "decadent, filthy play." Busch related, "I had never seen anything like that" which prompted thoughts of "this is what theatre could be." Because of this Busch "started seeing all of the [Ludlam] plays"[5] and Ludlam became a key early influence on him.

Busch, therefore, began his theatrical career with Ludlam as his idol. Busch said, "I kind of wanted to emulate myself after Charles. That was kind of a fantasy of mine."[6] Based on his unsuccessful college acting career, Busch contemplated focusing on playwriting, while learning to embrace his own androgyny for purposes of performing. By seeking a performance path that allowed him to write roles that would work for his own particular skill set, Busch found that "Ludlam was a template, in a way, that I could maybe create my own career." Busch also admits, "I didn't want to be a member of his company. It meant a lot to me for him to think I was talented."[7] Because of this, Busch pursued performing his own solo work at Ludlam's Sheridan Square space, though he did collaborate with Ludlam a few times during his career.

Yet, Busch notes, "it was never my dream to work with him."[8] Rather, Busch was interested in creating a place for himself, like the one Ludlam held, in the downtown theatre community. Although he had these early connections with Ludlam and his company, Busch's real entrée into the Downtown Scene would come later when he both accepted his talent for playing female roles and found the right sort of space for his voice to be heard. After performing solo works that read like "screenplays," in which he wore neutral dress and played both male and female roles, he realized that "the sort of unspoken truth was that the female characters were by far the most successful." Ludlam happened to be the one to articulate this reality to Busch by saying, "'Why don't you just play female characters? Why play men at all?'"[9] After this, in 1984, Busch discovered the sort of space in which he wished to perform: the "after-hours bar/art gallery way down in Alphabet City, in the Lower East Side, the Limbo Lounge." Busch recalled, "I was so entranced with this place, it felt like Berlin in the twenties.... It was sort of gay, but kind of straight, but kind of punk."[10] In addition, Busch recognized that this was the perfect time to get into the Lower East Side scene; "that neighborhood was so funky and mostly abandoned buildings and here and there there would be a kind of a very interesting theatre club or art gallery.... It was a very exciting area that we had discovered.... I was in the right place at the right time because Alphabet City, the East Village was suddenly rediscovered in the six months that I was there."[11] Because of his early encounters with the Ridiculous Theatrical Company, and because of his journeys performing throughout the landscape of the Downtown Scene, Busch would go on to adapt and expand Ridiculous Theatre, as a style and as a movement, with his own dramaturgical contributions.

Indeed, what could be more Ridiculous than a play entitled *Vampire*

Lesbians of Sodom? The title alone suggests that we are still clearly grounded in the age of Theatre of the Ridiculous. In "The Tale of Charles Busch," Don Shewey narrates:

> In the early 1980s, he [Busch] and director Kenneth Elliot assembled a loose company of performers who put on shows at an East Village nightclub called the Limbo Lounge. "I wrote according to what would be acceptable in that space," Mr. Busch recalled. "We performed on an empty stage because we had no place to store furniture. And half the audience was standing up drinking beer, so you couldn't do an elaborate two-act piece."[12]

This sort of "make-do-with-what-you-have" theatre-making is much in line with what his Ridiculous contemporaries were doing (and, indeed, Ludlam was frustrated to see Busch making a play that seemed to plagiarize his own style).[13] From one angle, Busch's early work is a clear continuation of Ridiculous theatre-making.

However, it is the differences between the plays of Ludlam and Busch that are most compelling, not their similarities. In a discussion of Busch's *The Lady in Question*, Frank Rich points out both the connection and distinction between the two Charles' bodies of work:

> While Mr. Busch's plays are often linked with Charles Ludlam's lighter efforts, such generalizing distorts the artistry of both. Mr. Ludlam, a theatrical classicist and a political iconoclast, usually had a second agenda, ideological or esthetic percolating within his gender-flipped sendups. Mr. Busch's attitude is the simpler one of "Hooray for Hollywood!" The man revels in trash. "The Lady in Question" mimics its source material so accurately and affectionately that it is as much homage as parody; the tone is closer to "Dames at Sea" or a Mel Brooks film than it is to the Ridiculous Theatrical Company.[14]

Busch's plays can be said to operate like his Ridiculous contemporaries' efforts; they explore sexual polyvalence, they are episodic in nature, and they make jokes on subjects not usually the source of great comedy. Busch agrees that "all my genre parody plays that I've done over the next 30 years [since *Vampire Lesbians*] do owe a big debt to Charles, doing theatrical parody on the stage involving drag and pop culture references. He was the biggest stylistic influence on me" even though Busch "would like to think" that he has "developed his own voice" in the years since his interactions with the older Charles.[15]

However, just calling Busch's plays "Ridiculous" is probably disingenuous to both his work and the term itself. Busch's work, according to Rich, lacks the edge of mockery present in Ludlam's plays. Without this quality, in Rich's estimation, there is no radical statement being made. Yet, Busch did not see Ludlam's work as political; he "would read these reviews and think, 'What Ludlam are they inventing?' They were saying that I lacked the political edge of Charles Ludlam and I thought, 'political, really? What political edge did he have?' I didn't think he had a political agenda."[16] Busch sees the difference between his plays and those of Ludlam as having its basis in the "physical" differences between himself and Ludlam as performers, especially since Busch has "almost exclusively" performed drag roles whereas Ludlam more often performed male roles. Busch noted, "I always looked really beautiful in drag.... I could look like the ladies that I was emulating."[17] Because of this, he did not need to draw the kind of attention to the gender performance that Ludlam and others had to in their "stylized performances," like "Camille with the hairy chest," in order to make the performance work.[18] Busch could do a realistic impersonation; Ludlam found other modes for using gender performance in his plays.

Vampire Lesbians, the play Busch created to get his foot in the door at the Limbo Lounge, is clearly a Ridiculous play. It was first performed in 1984 and, like its Ridiculous contemporaries, mocks surrounding culture while continuing to refuse to take itself seriously. Madeleine states, "As my dear friend Gertrude Stein says, 'My mystery is a mystery is a mystery,'" a high culture reference. Oatsie's reponse? "Hmmm. I wonder if any man has ever pierced your enigma" (70). Rather than taking this high avant-garde poetry allusion seriously, it is dismissed with a dirty joke, couched in a double entendre, one that also winks at the original poet's presumed sexuality. In Vampire Lesbians of Sodom, nothing is to be taken seriously.

Even when a ritual is performed, to exorcise the vampires, it is not the reverent affair of a Jack Smith production; it is an event as open to mockery as any other. There is nothing here to suggest a sacred staging, as even Smith's penguin funeral demanded.[19] When in danger of being attacked by jungle sorcery, La Condesa accepts her fate, poking fun at the whole procedure. "So what do you expect me to do, scream, run around in circles?" she asks. "Do it, get out your voodoo dolls. This modern world stinks. Broadway's dead. My apartment is going co-op, you can't get a decent bialy. I've had it. Give me the jungle phase out. You'll be doing me a favor."[20] The ritual is not a reverent site; it is merely another ridiculous means to an end. Even the violent undertone, taken so seriously in Kenneth Bernard's Play-House works, is dismissed as an easy out from a city going to pot.

In addition, the performative quality of Vampire Lesbians is not to be ignored, as in all Ridiculous Theatre. For example, along with being an aspect of the production style, cross-dressing emerges as a theme in the play. As we find in Eichelberger's gender mashups, gender construction is a complicated process. In the second scene, there is a male character, who may have been a woman, who is then forbidden from wearing panties (74). Gender is layered here while also being unreliable as a marker of identity. In that same scene, it is revealed that the King (also a term for a woman who dresses up and performs as a man) is not who he says he is; according to Madeleine his "real name is Trixie Monahan and five years ago the coppers tossed you in the sex tank for impersonating a woman" (68). Although the King maintains that "drag is a perfectly legitimate theatrical tradition" (68), it has no place in this early 20th-century Hollywood setting. Drag, as a performance practice, has attention drawn to it in the dialogue so that it can be spurned with the same vigor as anything else, while still being implemented within the play itself: a complex Ridiculous remix construction.

On the one hand, as can be seen, *Vampire Lesbians of Sodom* seems to sum up many of the themes and motifs associated with the Ridiculous Theatre. We find double entendres, references to surrounding culture, non-linear structure, and a preoccupation with forms of popular entertainment, both in the play's structure and content. Yet the play also seems to use those techniques because the Ridiculous style had emerged as a marketable format for producing theatre in the Downtown Scene. As Rich noted of *The Lady in Question*, the development of Busch's plays is less in line with Ludlam's so-called "ridiculosity" (to borrow Rick Roemer's term),[21] and more of a tribute to mainstream entertainment forms, like mad-cap comedies and large-scale musical films. The entry describing Busch's work in *Contemporary Gay American Poets and Playwrights: An A-to-Z Guide* elucidates the distinction between Ludlam and Busch well: "Unlike Charles Ludlam's rather highbrow references, absurdist tone, and politically charged drag, Busch shoots for the true subject matter of camp: B movies. His drag characters bring to life the glorious stars of old."[22] Although this entry highlights the differences as a positive in Busch's favor—he is more of a "true" camp performer—ultimately the difference is in the politically subversive quality. Ludlam created larger commentary about drag through his drag performances, while Busch is performing within the great drag tradition.

Busch's Later Work

Vampire Lesbians of Sodom clearly shows how Busch began his career within the Ridiculous landscape. However, unlike many other Ridiculous playwrights, Busch continues to write plays in the contemporary moment. His 2012 production *Judith of Bethulia* possesses many similarities to the earlier *Vampire Lesbians*: it is epic in scope and episodic in structure, it includes both drag performing and cross-dressing within the drama, and it remixes some cultural references from the popular with its larger biblical framework. The back cover of the Samuel French edition asks the reader to "imagine the outrageous Mae West in a Cecil B. DeMille biblical epic."[23] The entire play takes this as its mindset, it seems. On the one hand, it tells the tale of the heroine Judith in her pursuit to help the Jewish people while on the other it is a Ridiculous homage to Hollywood cinema and the power of the double entendre.

Again, gender mashup exists both within the story itself as well is in the production elements. Busch played the title role in drag when it was performed at Theater for the New City. In his cast list, he also notes, "This play can be double cast, as well as cross-gender cast."[24] Yet Busch takes the play with gender a step further, allowing characters within the drama to knowingly don the garb of the opposite sex. Urdamani, a eunuch, decides to enter the city in a female disguise. When his master Holofernes questions this choice and its minimally successful execution, Urdamani admits, "Your Highness, there is much I can learn from you of being a man and a woman" (9). On paper, it is often difficult to ascertain characters' genders simply by reading what is happening in the play. This is a production meant to draw attention to the performative nature of gender identity, especially in its inclusion of a eunuch character: a clear example of what might be considered a "third sex," neither completely male nor female.

This concept, one that is more deeply explored in John Cameron Mitchell's *Hedwig and the Angry Inch*, comes into play later in the drama. As is the case in *Vampire Lesbians*, much of the action of the play indulges in bawdy humor, as many Ridiculous comedies do. Urdamani bemoans having lost his genitalia, "My sacrifice has left me with a mound as bare as the vast desert, with no oasis to provide pleasure. I've an uncomfortable itch to scratch. I, who possess neither penis nor snatch" (42). Like Mitchell's earlier musical, this discussion suggests that a gender binary is insufficient for categorizing all of humankind, but couches that discussion in a dirty poem, making for a fun blend of a serious issue and an immature joke. This recent play shows a real Ridiculous commitment to sexual humor and the off-color as not only a key source of humor but also as an important element of the plot structure.

This play is not, however, as clear an example of Ridiculous remix as some of Busch's other works are, yet its title is borrowed from a 1914 D. W. Griffith film. There are references to popular culture—the Hollywood motif and the invocation of actress West being the clearest—but this is not a collage-style play, meant to invoke the ghosts of the cultural past. Despite being more of an original scripted comedy, one of the most obvious acts of quotation occurs between the two young lovers, the former prostitute Naomi and the virginal Nathan. To his beloved, Nathan says, "Softer than starlight are you. Warmer than winds of June are the gentle lips you gave me" (33), clearly lyrics from the Rodgers and Hammerstein's musical *South Pacific*. This seems a particularly postmodern gesture of Ridiculous remix; it suggests that love is so humorous that it must always be discussed via quotation. This interest in phrases meant to be said with quotation marks around them extends beyond merely quoting from outside material. Naomi and Nathan share double entendres with one another to avoid actually having to say words like "sex" (36). Even in this more recent play, Busch is still working within a Ridiculous aesthetic.

Before he began writing plays like *Judith of Bethulia* for the new Downtown Scene, Busch had made a mainstream impact in the theatre. From his perhaps inauspicious beginnings in the downtown club scene, Busch would emerge as one of the brightest and best-known theatre writers of the late 20th and early 21st century. This was due in large part to his *Tale of the Allergist's Wife* (2000), which was nominated for a 2001 Tony Award for Best Play. In his *New York Times* review, cultural arbiter Ben Brantley declares, "Mr. Busch, it would seem, has swum straight into the mainstream." For Brantley, one of the most notable aspects of this production is the choice for Busch not to portray Marjorie himself; i.e., for this *not* to be a drag performance. Brantley suggests, "Real women, after all, can be just as self-dramatizing as drag queens; they just tend (for the most part) to look less like cartoons."[25] Yet without the presence of cross-dressing, this production loses a key link to its Ridiculous ancestry.

For John Simon, writing in *New York*, this break with its Downtown Scene past is exactly what makes *The Tale of the Allergist's Wife* worth seeing. Simon writes in his introduction to his review, "Who would have expected from a campy downtown playwright a nicely structured, intelligently funny, satirically relevant uptown comedy?"[26] Clearly, Simon is forgetting Ludlam's late plays, such as *Le Bourgeois Avant-Garde*, which are also tightly-plotted, with more highbrow references than lowbrow ones. Still, Busch's 21st-century play is remarkable in that it moved an almost entirely Downtown Scene playwright and performer into the limelight of Broadway. Busch made the transition that Ludlam did not live long enough to do on his own; he took the Ridiculous aesthetic and adapted it tremendously so that it might sell to mainstream and commercial audiences.

The Allergist's Wife, more tightly structured and seemingly realistic than Busch's earlier works, centers on a loose domestic drama about a married couple and the wife's long-lost friend Lillian, now called Lee. Lee brings out secret desires among the family, both for illicit sexual affairs and also for high culture. This blending of high culture references into a comedic play might suggest something Ridiculous. Certainly, this play is episodic and disavows traditional plot progression. Despite this seemingly Ridiculous construction, the play is more heavily marked with highbrow references than with popular or low cultural ones and ultimately is less a Ridiculous remix than a boilerplate drawing room comedy in a mildly absurdist vein.

This absurdist quality is critical to making sense of this play's construction. Dialogue often seems to be organized around non-sequiturs. Because of this structural conceit, one of the most telling literary references in the play is to *Waiting for Godot*. Marjorie fears because "we're Russian peasants from the shtetl"[27] that she and her husband have no right to take in so much high culture. Ira dismisses this complaint, claiming, "You know, that last production of

'Waiting for Godot' affected me deeply. I had a sense that I finally understood what that play was about" (276). But Marjorie cannot accept Ira's statement; she mocks him, saying: "You understood the story. You think it's about two guys who get stranded by the Tappan Zee Bridge. They're not waiting for Triple A. It's about—I can't even explain what it's about. That is my conundrum. I don't understand the play any better than you. I'm a fraud. A cultural poseur. To quote Kafka, 'I am a cage in search of a bird'" (276). This allusion to a classic work of the Theatre of the Absurd does not seem out of place in this drama, one whose dialogue comes across in much the same manner as spoken text in a Eugene Ionesco play might: random topics followed to an illogical conclusion and then traded for the next viable topic of discussion. For example, this discussion of the meaning of esoteric works of art is immediately followed by an exclamation of hunger and a reference to Entenmann's, a commercial consumer product.

This seeming Ridiculous remix behavior does not have the same quality as similar references made in a Tavel or Ludlam play, however. Rather, Ira and Marjorie's argument throws into relief the importance here of making meaning out of a work of art and how, when one fails to do so, one can also fail to be an actual intellectual. Understanding high art matters here, probably more than understanding popular iconography. No longer could a Ban deodorant slogan outrank Shakespeare; one must be an insider to the top echelon of culture to matter in the world of *The Allergist's Wife*.

Indeed, such literary references as this Beckett discussion are rampant in this drama. When describing her own failed attempt at literary greatness, for instance, Marjorie refers to her work as "phantasmagoria," "heavily influenced by Thomas Pynchon," "composed as verse drama," containing "chapters in various historical periods," including characters such as "Plato and Helen Keller" as well as "allusions to 'Anna Karenina'" (286). Of course, on one level this laundry listing of high concept literary references is used as a Ridiculous sort of mockery of the literary process, high literary genres, and intellectualism as a hobby. Yet, Marjorie ends this ranting description with "I was attempting to break away from conventional narrative structure" (286). This idea seems in line with both an Absurdist construction as well as a Ridiculous one. In both cases, we have dramatic literature forms that reimagine what narrative can be. In the Absurd, it is a lack of narrative development that marks the genre; in the Ridiculous, it is an almost overabundance of narrative elements that are at work to create the overall production. The inclusion of the concept of a form of structure here suggests that this idea—reimagining how to organize a play— is as ridiculous a concept as any other. The merit of this practice, one not fully implemented here, is undercut by these characters' dismissal of it. Marjorie sees her Ridiculous remix work as "tangible proof of my own mediocrity" (286), allowing commercial failure to distinguish it as unworthy of being read.

In this slew of referencing, even the Pop Art scene, in which the original Theatre of the Ridiculous was so clearly grounded, makes an appearance. Lee, a true cultured woman of the world, claims to have known Andy Warhol in her more bohemian days. She relates, "He [Warhol] used to come over and we'd share a can of soup. He got such a kick out of the way I used to pile the empty Campbell soup cans on top of each other. I guess you could say, I planted a little seed" (290–91). Lee is implying here that she actually served as the impetus for Warhol's groundbreaking work of Pop Art expression. In addition, though, the fact that Marjorie seems impressed that Lee knew Warhol suggests that he, too, now belongs in the category of high art references. Here, Busch is drawing direct attention to the Ridiculous lineage, showing how it might now be considered high art form.

The Tale of the Allergist's Wife seems to be precisely the sort of play that Lee would have abhorred; one highbrow enough, because of its "downtown"-leaning playwright and its references to Warhol and literature, to appeal to a cultural elite, while not being challenging enough, in either content or structure, to alienate a wider Broadway clientele. Indeed, the most scandalous topic, besides the sexual relations between Marjorie, Lee, and Ira, is Marjorie's mother, Frieda's, suppositories. These are neither relevant to the overarching linear plot nor bizarre enough to be truly Ridiculous. They are like a remnant of a Ridiculous aesthetic in a play that is not, overall, a work of Ridiculous Theatre.

The Tale of the Allergist's Wife may be Busch's most successful and well-known work, despite being a clear departure from his Ridiculous roots. Yet Busch's recent play, 2014's *The Tribute Artist*, pays homage to his Ridiculous ancestry both in its construction and content; it and *Judith of Bethulia* seem more deeply committed to Busch's Ridiculous heritage than his Broadway play. *The Tribute Artist* uses cross-dressing as the main dramatic throughline; a man, Jimmy, who plays female roles is forced to don female garb long-term in order to fulfill a convoluted real estate scheme. Despite only being a cross-dressed performer, because of the nature of the events that this play presents, the audience never sees him in anything but female attire. The play opens with him trying on clothes that belong to Adriana, his elderly landlady, for fun and then turns to more serious cross-dressing: becoming a woman full-time in order to become rich.

Jimmy is the titular "tribute artist"; he has made his career impersonating the same catalog of great film actresses as the Ridiculous performers of the previous generations had. His adamant dismissal of the term "drag queen"—he tells his friends, "I don't wear women's wigs in real life" and "I recreate legendary female performers. I'm an illusionist. I don't do this for fun. I'm a professional entertainer"[28]—suggests that he is aware of the performative nature of gender but also of the connotations that come along with accepting that fact. To this point, he has only *performed* female roles; he has never before *become* an actual woman.

The interest here is less in the crossing of gender and more in the particular types of women that Jimmy portrays. He does impersonations of a particular generation of female stars, one that has less and less relevance to the Las Vegas audiences to which Jimmy still plays. All of Jimmy's references are dated; his cultural allusions seem more in line with the Ridiculous crowd of Ludlam's time than with contemporary audiences. He bemoans, "There is no longer any place for Jimmy Nichols in the Flamingo Hotel's Boys Will Be Girls Revue. I should have seen the writing on the wall. Last year, both my Julie Andrews and Charo were cut. Finally, I was just left with Marilyn. She is my masterpiece but most of that Vegas crowd just thinks I'm doing Christina Aguilera. Everything's fallen apart since this new producer took over. He's a kid. He's forty years old" (6). Although it is quite funny think of a 40-year-old as "a kid," certainly someone of that age would not be nostalgic for the 1950s; his set of references would be from a later decade. Like Eichelberger's *Dasvedanya Mama*, Busch's play is aware that this mode of performing may be a dying form.

However, what *The Tribute Artist* does show is that gender performance is a more relevant aspect of human existence than perhaps any earlier Ridiculous play does. We do not see Jimmy play any role other than Adriana, his recently deceased landlady and friend. And he does not play her merely as tribute; he fully becomes Adriana, assuming her vocal patterns, wigs, and wardrobes, as well as all of her personal history. This sort of gender performance suggests something much deeper about the performative nature of identity than simply playing at being famous starlets. Yet, Jimmy's interpretation of women cannot help but be shaded by his knowledge of famous female stars. His recreation of Adriana is both an honest rendering and proof that the surrounding culture and its archetypes always influence assuming a gender.

The interest in pursuing a deeper contemplation of the performance of self and its relation to gender is further emphasized through the inclusion of the deceased homeowner's grandnephew, an individual who is in the process of transitioning from female to male. Oliver, born Rachel, suggests gender performance is something of much more significance than merely drag performance. Oliver clearly identifies with his in-process state, telling his mother, "I'm not a tomboy. I'm a transman" (21). Yet, Oliver is also comfortable with the ambiguities of gender, declaring, "And I'm gonna continue to do that as I become more comfortable with myself. I'm not ruling out a touch of androgyny. I just might surprise you one day by wearing a skirt" and then clarifies by saying, "More like a kilt" (21). Oliver understands that one's gender identity is a complicated notion and his representation, more so than Jimmy's impersonation of Adriana, displays the progression of our understanding of a gender spectrum, not a dichotomy.

The inclusion of these extended universe characters, such as Adriana's grandnephew and his mother as well as the deceased's former lover Rodney, in addition to the central figures of Jimmy and his best friend, Rita, hearkens back to the kind of parade of crazy characters that Ludlam constructed in *How to Write a Play*. The plot—a seemingly straightforward bait and switch in which Jimmy pretends to be the deceased Adriana until Rita can sell the apartment and they can abscond with the profits—is continually complicated by the web of interactions among this cast of characters. Yet, this play is also a conventional kind of farce; cross-dress is used to achieve a goal and is often the source of humor. It is perhaps more similar to *Love, Sex and the I.R.S.*, a 1979 play by Billy Van Zandt and Jane Milmore, in which a young man must pretend to be his male roommate's wife to further his tax evasion scheme, than like Eichelberger's *Minnie the Maid* or Jack Smith's loft performances. Cross-dressing is used to achieve a particular goal, not because of a commitment to exposing issues related to gender performance. In an interview with Michael Riedel and Susan Haskins for CUNY TV's program "Theater Talk," Busch admits that this was entirely the point:

> I've done so many plays where I just played the female character, the leading lady role and I've always thought it would be kind of fun to do a *Some Like It Hot / Tootsie* kind of story where a fellow actually is impersonating a woman. I thought it would be kind of interesting to see well, what could I bring to that very old convention … through my experiences, first of all being a gay man and being a professional female impersonator.[29]

Because of Busch's unique perspective on this part, this is a much more thoughtful rendering of the cross-dressing plot than other similar dramas. The dramatic irony of the play—that the audience knows the woman is actually a man—serves as the source of most of the humor in both plays.

Still, overall, the play relies on its Ridiculous roots for both its most humorous lines and its most emotional moments. In terms of the humor, double entendres abound. For example, when Adriana asks Jimmy, "Do you receive a form of sexual gratification from dressing in women's clothes? The soft fabrics? The close fitting garments?" Jimmy cries, "No! This is just what I do best. Like juggling. You don't ask a juggler if he finds his balls sexually stimulating. Bad example" (8). The dirty bit of humor undercuts the serious discussion of the justification for drag. Similarly, when the plot goes awry and Jimmy's secret is revealed, rather than relying on the emotional connections that he has built with Adriana's relatives to save him, he falls back on his tribute artist routines. Rita must make him promise, "Are you really crying? You're not doing Meryl Streep or Margaret O'Brien, are you?" (96), and even after doing so, he cannot keep to his word. Even though Jimmy begs, "please don't call me a drag queen" (5), he cannot help but fall into these Ridiculous routines. Writing for the *New York Post*, Frank Scheck finds "Jimmy delivering a series of comic references to old movies that Rita's forced to explain to those too young to have seen them" to be the play's "funniest" moment.[30] The Ridiculous elements are still what shines in a Busch production.

Indeed, like so many of his Ridiculous predecessors, Busch is accused by *Variety* reviewer Marilyn Stasio of creating a play "strictly for the in crowd."[31] The Ridiculous may be alive and well in the theatre, but it may remain for a particular audience only, no matter its prevalence. Yet, this play still seems much more accessible than earlier Ridiculous plays, even Busch's own *Vampire Lesbians of Sodom*. Busch refers to this play as a kind of "middleground between my camp movie genre spoofs and then my sentimental Jewish comedies, like *The Allergist's Wife* because it's kind of a naturalistic play."[32] This play suggests a Ridiculous remixing of Busch's own style, bringing in his interest in the mainstream theatre with his Ridiculous ancestry. Scheck refers to *The Tribute Artist* as "a minor effort to be sure. But even a lesser Busch is more."[33]

Kushner's Theatre of the Fabulous: *Angels in America*

More complicated still in terms of the connection of his plays with the Ridiculous scene that he claims inspired them is Tony Kushner who, in his introduction to *The Mystery of Irma Vep and Other Plays*, pays tribute to his theatrical hero. Kushner reminisces, "I had a mad crush on Charles Ludlam."[34] Kushner then walks the reader through his numerous encounters with the Ridiculous Theatrical Company, never losing his wistful, nostalgic tone. This is clearly work for which he cared deeply and an artistic influence that he tries to incorporate within his own dramatic creations.

Kushner draws a direct link between the work he saw at sites like One Sheridan Square and his own dramatic practice. He suggests that from this admiration for Ludlam and the Ridiculous came the next tradition in gay theatre, which he calls "Theatre of the Fabulous." Kushner sees "fabulousness" as the style toward which gay and lesbian drama is moving in a post–Ridiculous world. He writes, "If the great antecedent form of gay theater was theater of the ridiculous, then the new theater that … all of us who are lesbian and gay and working in theater now are creating is something that I'm calling 'theater of the fabulous.'"[35] In "Thinking about Fabulousness," a conversation with novelist Michael Cunningham, Kushner notes a concept that is very close to Ridiculous ideology. He states, "Theater is as much a part of trash culture as it is high art…. And it's incredibly important for people who are working in theater to always remember that it's show biz and it's sort of sleazy, and ... a lot of the ways that you have at your disposal for telling a story are ways that were developed by, incredibly, sort of lowbrow, popular entertainment."[36] This clearly explicates how the Fabulous builds on the Ridiculous; it also recognizes the value of using the lowbrow elements in the production of theatre.

Kushner draws a line from Ludlam's work to his own contemporary dramas, stating, "Our great antecedent is Charles Ludlam ... who was, in addition to being the funniest man who ever lived and a brilliant consumer and regurgitator of theatrical style and legend, the founder and chief arbitrator of the Theater of the Ridiculous."[37] For Kushner, with the Ridiculous as a "great antecedent," "'theater of the fabulous'... [includes] an issue of investiture, that you become powerful because you believe yourself to be. In a certain sense, the people in the theater are all fabulous at the moment that Prior [the protagonist of *Angels in America*], who has become invested by the audience with a moral authority and a kind of prophetic voice, blesses everybody—they're fabulous, whether they want to be or not."[38] Kushner is saying that in the Theatre of the Fabulous, there is meant to be a real connection between what happens on stage and what the audience is meant to do in the actual world. In the Ridiculous, a spectator might only be confronted with the silliness and failure of the surrounding culture to best express their community's view of issues and circumstances. But Kushner asks his audiences to take something away from the theatrical experience and, as they might after attending an Epic Theatre production by Bertolt Brecht or Erwin Piscator, use that information to interpret and affect the world around them. To be Fabulous, then, is not just to laugh *at* the world, but to engage in the "Great Work," to riff on Prior's blessing, that must occur *in* the world. Because of this, as in Prior's final blessing, there is an active and activist quality to Kushner's plays.

Kushner has been creating work in a very different climate than the one in which Ludlam worked, yet he sees the trajectory from the raucous and irreverent, politically charged 1960s to the world of AIDS crisis America in the 1980s and its aftermath in the 1990s. In a way, it is impossible to discuss the Ridiculous without reflecting on the toll the AIDS epidemic took on the movement. Indeed, it is likely that one reason Ridiculous Theatre is often overlooked in American Theatre Studies is the fact that, at the height of their productivity, many of the greatest artists associated with the Ridiculous were victims of AIDS. Of course, nowhere is this effect clearer than in the case of Charles Ludlam, but Jack Smith died from complications from AIDS and Ethyl Eichelberger committed suicide before the virus could take his life from him. In a sense, discussing the legacy of the Ridiculous is *only* essential because of the toll that AIDS wrought; if Ludlam, for one, had lived, it is certainly possible that the movement as he participated in it would have moved uptown itself, rather than leaving that journey for theatre work created by those who were inspired by him.

AIDS became a great source for dramatic production in its own right. Plays from Larry Kramer's emotionally melodramatic *The Normal Heart* to Jonathan Larson's commercialized Broadway musical *Rent* took up the crisis as subject matter. Perhaps no AIDS play became more famous or influential than Kushner's "Gay Fantasia on National Themes," *Angels in America* (1993). The play won consecutive Tony Awards for Best Play (each part being awarded in its year of premiere) and a Pulitzer Prize, and continues to be one of the most celebrated recent American plays, with a 2010 production at the Signature Theatre playing to sold-out crowds for months and a National Theatre production transferring from London in 2017 to the Great White Way in 2018. Clearly, Kushner's play has now been accepted into the American theatrical canon. In his positive, if slightly underwhelmed, *New York Times* review of the 2010 production, Ben Brantley notes:

> We've grown accustomed to the theatrical audacity and intellectual reach of this study of the intersection of personal, political and cosmic crises in the early days of the AIDS epidemic. The play has never left our cultural consciousness. It is performed regularly in schools and local theaters; it is on the syllabuses of university English and drama classes, and the star-filled 2003 HBO adaptation, directed by Mike Nichols, is in many a home-video library.[39]

Angels in Amercia is now a familiar work, one that reflects on the past as opposed to confronting its audiences with the realities of the present.

When the show first opened it was something of a theatrical revelation. In his review, longer than the average reflection on a theatre piece, Frank Rich attempts to give a reader a sense of what it will be like to see Part One of Kushner's epic, entitled *Millennium Approaches*, while admitting that such a feat may be impossible unless one has seen the show. I quote Rich at length, as his praise helped to create the undeniable significance of the play. Rich lauds:

> "Angels in America" is a work that never loses its wicked sense of humor or its wrenching grasp on such timeless dramatic matters as life, death and faith even as it ranges through territory as far-flung as the complex, plague-ridden nation Mr. Kushner wishes both to survey and to address. Subtitled "A Gay Fantasia on National Themes," the play is a political call to arms for the age of AIDS, but it is no polemic. Mr. Kushner's convictions about power and justice are matched by his conviction that the stage, and perhaps the stage alone, is a space large enough to accommodate everything from precise realism to surrealistic hallucination, from black comedy to religious revelation. In "Angels in America," a true American work in its insistence on embracing all possibilities in art and life, he makes the spectacular case that they can all be brought into fusion in one play.[40]

In what Rich earlier refers to as "the most thrilling American play in years," there are all of the qualities I have associated with the Ridiculous: a polyvalent approach to gender identity and sexuality; the raising of spirits and ghosts for worship and interaction; and a blending of both the political and the popular, high culture and low. In including many of the key aesthetic elements that I associate with the Ridiculous, one could call *Angels in America*, if not a Ridiculous play, then certainly a play created with a reverence for the Ridiculous dramaturgy.

Without belaboring either the plot or the extensive production history of this important play, it is worth noting some ways in which it overlaps with the larger Ridiculous aesthetic. It involves the evoking of spirits and angels— quite literally—as well as Ridiculous remix, constructed of a slew of popular culture and high culture references, ranging in subject matter from *Come Back, Little Sheba* to *The Wizard of Oz* to the House Un-American Activities Committee. Cross-dressing is also present; the same woman who plays a mother and Ethel Rosenberg also dons the garb of a male rabbi. Yet, this is not quite gender mashup; the journeys across the gender divide are meant to be believable and complete. In all of this, we find the evocation of the ghosts of a haunted stage, a remixing and blending of highbrow and popular culture alike, and a configuration of gender that is, if not mashed up, then certainly on some level performative: all aspects that can be associated with the Ridiculous. Despite these loose connections, it would be a stretch to ground this play in the Ridiculous landscape. *Angels in America* more clearly evokes the effect of the Ridiculous on Kushner's playwriting than stands as an example of Ridiculous Theatre itself.

Kushner's plays seem preoccupied with something larger than just aesthetic concerns. Although *Angels in America*, constructed of two multi-act plays that take over seven hours to perform in their entirety, has a grand epic structure, the larger themes of the play, such as religion and faith, personal journeys, disease and suffering, seem much more in tune with political drama than farce. Even though humor is a present force throughout the drama, the overall production does not come across as ridicule in the same way that a Ridiculous play on dark subject matter, such as *The Magic Show of Dr. Magico*, might. Thus, despite many light moments in the two-part work, the overall piece is still a serious play, not a mockery of the surrounding culture on which it comments. *Angels in America* does not possess the mocking humor of Ludlam's and other Ridiculous playwrights' works.

Although magical and imaginative and calling for some level of cross-dress, *Angels in America* is too realistic of a play and too tightly scripted of a drama to be "Ridiculous" in the way the works of Tavel and Smith are. Many of the characters are meant to be real people engaging in real world challenges and meeting or failing to meet those callings, facing whatever consequences come their way. And despite its dream-like quality, and its acceptance of the presence of angels and an afterlife, it is neither a Smith-ian ritual, with its demand for audience participation, nor a nightmarish carnival through the darker aspects of the human psyche, as a Kenneth Bernard play might be.

Using Kushner's term "Fabulous" to describe *Angels* reminds us that this play is a development beyond the Ridiculous, not an example of it. According to Ken Neilsen, "Fabulous in one sense evolves beyond ridiculous in the way that fabulous becomes a rejection of the weakness inherent in being stigmatized as ridiculous. Fabulous rejects being perceived as weak or suffering in relation to oppression."[41] In a sense, Fabulous adds a politically active quality to the Ridiculous; there is no longer acceptance of being the butt of a joke. Rather, there is delight and celebration in spite of it. Indeed, *Angels in America* is a Fabulous construction by all possible interpretations of the term. This play includes such a spectacular *coup-de-theatre* as an angel crashing through the ceiling at the end of its first part while also allowing its protagonist to journey to and through heaven, which is both a paradise and warzone.

The "Fabulous" quality of *Angels in America*, ultimately, serves a real-world function, to show (as Prior contends at the play's conclusion) that life still has value and that there is something more to existence than suffering. Prior states, "This disease will be the end of many of us, but not nearly all, and the dead will be commemorated and will struggle on with the living, and we are not going away. We won't die secret deaths anymore."[42] Theatre of the Fabulous goes beyond Theatre of the Ridiculous because it already accepts that although life might be worthy of being mocked there is still something much more magical about it than that. Life is something worth fighting for and fighting is a key aspect of what it means to be alive.

Kushner's plays should be seen as building on the work of Ludlam, acknowledging his influence but moving in a new direction. Ludlam saw his work as moving beyond the minimalism of Beckett[43] and Kushner seems to move beyond the mockery of the Ridiculous. Kushner is always making a larger, if not political then certainly social, comment in his plays. He wants to show his audiences not only that they can laugh at the world, as they might learn from watching a Ludlam farce, but also that they can embrace it and, ultimately, change it. This celebratory perspective elucidates what is meant by Theatre of the Fabulous, clearly linking it to its comic antecedent, Theatre of the Ridiculous.

In the case of both Charles Busch and Tony Kushner, we see theatrical creators who are deeply indebted to Ludlam's theatrical tradition. Yet, they each clearly have adapted that form to their own ends: Busch seems more in line with Ludlam's emphasis on entertainment and popular culture while Kushner elucidates the possible progressive thread that was always thinly veiled in the queerness of Ridiculous productions. While these two playwrights acknowledge their debt to Ludlam, his influence seems even wider spread in a contemporary theatrical scene in which *Hedwig and the Angry Inch* and the performing duo Kiki and Herb found homes on Broadway. When considering the impact of Ridiculous Theatre, it is important to extend that discussion to works that are aesthetically indebted to the work of Ludlam and his contemporaries, even if they do not address that connection directly.

SEVEN

The Ridiculous Aesthetic Across Generations
The Inheritors of the Ridiculous

The legacy of the Ridiculous is rich and varied, including both practitioners who deliberately worked with or against the form as well as creators whose work feels indebted to the contributions of the Ridiculous, even if their work itself is not called Ridiculous. Certainly, the Ridiculous aesthetic has carried through into contemporary downtown performance, as Sean F. Edgecomb discusses in *Charles Ludlam Lives!*; performers like Taylor Mac, who is one of the artists on whom Edgecomb focuses, creates performance work that clearly possesses a Ridiculous quality. Mac's recent portrayal of Shen Te/Shui Ta in the Public Theatre's *Good Person of Szechwan* "suggest[ed] mischief in the making."[1] Mac ultimately used drag to similarly complex and meaningful ends regarding the stakes of the performance of gender as Ludlam and Ethyl Eichelberger had before him. In addition, the Ridiculous can be seen to have brought its use of gender bending and cultural remixing as far uptown as Broadway stages. Productions such as *Kinky Boots* (Broadway opening 2013) and *Hedwig and the Angry Inch* (Broadway production 2014) seem to owe a great deal to their Ridiculous forebears.

On one hand, this movement away from their original place and time of production may diminish the progressive power of these aesthetic techniques. On the other, the use of these techniques by commercial stages shows how queer performance has entered into discussions of even the most mainstream of theatrical forms. How we understand American theatre is shaded by Theatre of the Ridiculous. Knowing its key elements helps the contemporary theatre fan interpret the works being produced at the current moment. Productions such as Charles Busch's *The Tribute Artist* at 59E59 in the winter of 2014, as well as the Broadway production of *Hedwig and the Angry Inch*, which opened in 2014 as well, all display the pervasiveness of Ridiculous theatrics in contemporary performance.

As a document of what the Ridiculous brought to the history of performance, these works influenced by Theatre of the Ridiculous serve as a wealth of knowledge on the subject. They provide contemporary audiences with as close an experience to seeing the Ridiculous live as they might be able to get while highlighting the innovations that these practitioners brought to American stages. As a commercial entity, however, the Ridiculous changes; it is no longer a subversive form scrutinizing both gender construction and cultural hierarchy, but instead a postmodern form that embraces the performativity of all things insofar as this aesthetic can be used to appeal commercially to a contemporary moment and culture. Legacy is a double-edged sword for the Ridiculous; it serves to remind us of the important contributions of these artists/companies while at the same time overshadowing them. It often contains our only live and active traces of this aesthetic while continually obscuring them.

What legacy does prove is that the ghost of Theatre of the Ridiculous is still quite present in the contemporary theatrical scene. *Ruff*, conceived by Peggy Shaw and Lois Weaver, of Split Britches fame, and performed by Shaw, makes this quite obvious. LaMaMa ETC, as a performance site, is also a logical space for this sort of raising the dead to occur; many of the most famous Ridiculous productions were presented there during the heyday of Ridiculous Theatre. It also follows that it should be individuals like Shaw who are evoking these ghosts, as Split Britches is one company that could belong in a discussion of the Ridiculous, though their work has been discussed in many other aesthetic and cultural contexts. Although not Ridiculous practitioners per se, there are certainly key aesthetic overlaps between the works of Split Britches and Ridiculous Theatre.

In response to whether she considered her work Ridiculous, Peggy Shaw stated, "No, I see my work as a combination of Hot Peaches and Spiderwoman theater, I did not think of my work as ridiculous. I thought of it as garbage aesthetic, and exploring gender and queerness by being myself, and celebrating my otherness and my lesbianness, which was highly unexplored. Everything was up for grabs, and I wanted to make lesbians funny, and a 'given' onstage."[2] I do not wish to contend that Split Britches was something it was not—Shaw was clear that her work was not Ridiculous. In fact, Shaw contends that she "didn't consider [the works of Ludlam and those around him] as a movement." Rather, she states, "there was a type of convergence of talent in the GAY scene, and it was all soooo new, and sooo exciting, and reacting to years of feeling oppressed by straight theater content as well as format and hierarchy."[3] Perhaps it was because of this that, although not specifically operating as a cohesive theatrical movement might, both the plays of Split Britches and Ridiculous Theatre productions often include cultural references from both highbrow and lowbrow culture—a definite Ridiculous remix—while always including some form of gender mashup performance.

Shaw invokes the Ridiculous in *Ruff*, blending references from all over culture, including her own history, in order to talk about experiences related to her stroke. In this production, Shaw and Weaver emphasize the need to laugh in the face of the terror of human mortality. The play suggests a post-absurdist perspective; if the absurdist playwrights had exposed our human condition, then it seems up to the Ridiculous performers to embrace the fact that there is nothing we can do in light of it but laugh. This one-person show is incredibly funny, yet it is punctuated with some serious moments, moments that remind one of the ritualistic quality of early Ridiculous theatre as it was performed in Jack Smith's apartment.

Shaw does not shy away from the ghosts of her past; rather, she invites them on stage with her. In discussing facing her own mortality, she also engages the mortality that took so many of her friends and collaborators in preceding years. She links her own stroke to the death of Ellen Stewart, saying, "The day Ellen Stewart died/I dreamt she was pulling me with her,/her silver fingernails digging into my shoulders and arms, dragging me down with her cause she was lonely."[4] As the piece was performed in Stewart's La MaMa, it is hard not to feel her presence in the space with Shaw and her audiences. Yet Shaw allows this ghosting to go further, dedicating the piece to Ethyl Eichelberger and using a video of his performances as a backdrop, even as a co-performer, at one point in the night's proceedings. Like Smith's "expanded cinema," the use of this video backdrop allows a ghost literal access to the stage space. The presence of Eichelberger seems to be everywhere in this play, not only in that video recording: he is present in the use of accordion music, in the interest in drag as a performative practice, in the overall theme of how one lives in the face of medical tragedy. Shaw may ostensibly be performing on her own, but she opens her stage to the spirits of all those who had performed with her and gone before her.

Like in an Absurd drama, there seems to be a maddening quality to objects and their proliferation. At one point, Shaw stuffs her face with pieces of bubble gum. Yet, Shaw allows her performance to go beyond absurdity to become something more complex, as much Ridiculous Theatre had. While narrating a dream about jumping off the George Washington Bridge, inflatable fish join Shaw on stage. Rather than being simply a silly moment, Shaw takes this opportunity to invoke the names of some of those she might see if she actually did journey to the other side.[5] During the performance I saw, on January 9, 2014, one of those names was that of Charles Ludlam. Somewhere, it seems, the Ridiculous landscape might continue into the great beyond.

In true Ridiculous fashion, this moment is not left on a sentimental note. Rather, popular culture returns to have the last word on Shaw's predica-ment. This use of a pop culture joke somehow plays with great profundity. Shaw describes a character from *South Park* named Mr. Hindsight who "lists all the things that could have been done to avert the tragedy in the first place."[6] Mr. Hindsight is no Superman; he does not come in at the last minute and save everyone. Instead, he explains how those about to die in a fire could have avoided that fate, if only there had been a fire escape or a larger alleyway between buildings. The anecdote has a very humorous quality—indeed, on the original animated television program on which it aired, it was likely a solid punchline. In this play, however, it also manifests emotions about not only the situation from the cartoon, but the larger issues surrounding crisis and mortality with which Shaw has dealt throughout the performance. We never know what will happen and only seem to have all the answers once tragedy has occurred.

There is a powerful Ridiculous quality to what Shaw has created here, but in its themes and meanings, this show suggests how elements derived from the Ridiculous aesthetic can be used to get beyond mere Ridiculous mockery. Unlike many Ridiculous companies and artists, the life and work of Split Britches has been covered in great detail elsewhere[7] but their link with Ridiculous Theatre is worth reiterating. Shaw, Weaver, and earlier con-tributor Deb Margolin had a direct connection with the Ridiculous scene. They worked in the Downtown Scene, like their Ridiculous contemporaries, at sites such as the WOW Café Theatre, a theatre for women that was run as a collective. Although Hot Peaches is cited by Alexis Clements in *American Theatre* magazine as Shaw's practical start in queer theatre, Clements acknowledges that it was the theatre of Charles Ludlam that first turned Shaw on to the downtown New York artistic scene. Clements writes, "After finishing a fine arts degree in Boston in 1967, she [Shaw] moved to New York City, where early on she was impressed by downtown impresario Charles Ludlam's *Bluebeard*, mounted by his Ridiculous Theatrical Company."[8] Shaw elucidated this history further, admitting, "I stumbled upon Ludlums [*sic*] work by mis-take, and right after, Hot Peaches, a group I was a part of for many years. Ludlum [*sic*] was actually rather conventional theater in a way, not necessarily creating a questioning of gay as much as a venue for mostly gay men to the-atricalise themselves without actually having a known gay consciousness."[9] Although Shaw may have gotten her jumpstart from seeing Ludlam's work, she was also able to recognize the limitations of those plays for her objectives and used her own work to expand the possibilities of this sort of perform-ance.

The plays of Split Britches, then, show a Ridiculous aesthetic in their con-struction and presentation style, used in order to problematize issues of per-formativity, especially as they relate to gender. These plays emphasize performance over all—"Shaw and Weaver assert that theatrical rather than political concerns have always been foremost in their creative work"[10]—while many scholars still highlight their dismissal of gender norms and traditional narrative structures as "a radical act."[11] Their 1991 play, *Belle Reprieve*, can be seen as a variety of Ridiculous remix, filled with a blending of a canonical theatre text with many low culture references. The play also shows elements of gender mashup, including the practice of cross-dressing as an aesthetic and performative choice. As Mary F. Brewer puts it, "The work of Split Britches problematizes the concept of a single feminine or masculine gender."[12] In *Belle Reprieve*, Shaw played the role of Stanley, for example, while the role of Blanche was played in drag as well. Of course, the title is a play on "Belle Reve," the ancestral home of the DuBois women in Tennessee Williams's classic, *A Streetcar Named Desire*. The play is preoccupied with the film; Sue-Ellen Case argues, "*Belle Reprieve* is based on the film iconography of *Streetcar*, more than the script."[13] This interest in Hollywood over theatre suggests a Ridiculous preference for the popular over the canonical, a nod to the reverence Jack Smith held for Maria Montez.

There is a violent undertone even in Williams's original play—Blanche is raped, after all—that Split Britches had to contend with in their more humorous interpretation. Case describes, "The cast stressed this attribute as specifically macho het-male, in its stereotypical representation."[14] Here, we find the interest in exposing performative gender stereotypes being linked with some of the darker elements present in other Ridiculous plays, such as those of Ronald Tavel and Kenneth Bernard. In the work of Split Britches, we often see the post–Absurdist quality, which Tavel had previously argued for, reaching its apotheosis. These plays present the violent and cruel world in which human beings find themselves, only to approach that human condition with humor.

Indeed, it would seem that in many ways the Ridiculous is alive and well in the New York theatre. Besides Split Britches, who are more coincidentally similar to the Ridiculous than inheritors of the form, we can view many artists' work through a Ridiculous lens; Sean Edgecomb, for one, argues that we may be able to find the Ridiculous in more places than we initially realize.[15] The Ridiculous has a rich legacy, made of those who it touched directly with its flamboyant aesthetic and those who seem to have discovered the work through their own experimental processes. In either case, the Ridiculous has many inheritors, both direct from the period and beyond.

Yet, just because it seems to have an influence throughout the Downtown Scene, the Ridiculous has its critics, even from that territory. Certain contemporaries of the Ridiculous, even, find the work lacking in terms of a progressive "gay" or "queer" agenda. Medusa's Revenge performer Ana Maria Simo, in the same discussion as the one in which RTC contributor Lola

Pashalinski claimed political potential in aesthetic choices, states, "Where I was in 1981 had absolutely nothing to do with the Ridiculous Theatre in that I was never aware that the Ridiculous Theater was gay. To me, the Ridiculous Theater was a theater that was using a theatrical form that had always been used, which is, men in drag."[16] To some viewers, the Ridiculous is not all that radical, as it uses certain tropes that have existed in drama for centuries, as opposed to innovating new styles.

For artists of the same period and from the same so-called downtown "community," the work of the Ridiculous can seem as mainstream as any other theatre work—not just those happening at the time, but throughout history. What then is the valence of a Ridiculous legacy? How is the potential radical quality of this work undercut by tracing its ubiquitousness? Does legacy improve the Ridiculous geography? Or does it somehow diminish it?

Contemporary Cross-Gendered Performance and the Ridiculous

Even in the case of artists like Charles Busch and Tony Kushner, whose work arguably resembles Ridiculous Theatre but who also credit Ridiculous Theatre's creators as important influences, there seems to be a disconnect in the development of the style. The work of these artists is, whether for better or for worse, a departure from the Ridiculous aesthetic. This difference is only further accentuated when one considers companies or artists whose work seems to be in the Ridiculous style, even if the associated theatre makers do not directly espouse Ridiculous Theatre as an influence. Both the performance pieces of Kiki and Herb and the off-Broadway musical (and later independent film and then Broadway production) *Hedwig and the Angry Inch* appear to have elements of the Ridiculous in their aesthetic. And yet, in both cases, the final product is something that is also much removed from true Ridiculous Theatre.

Possible Ridiculous Inheritors: Kiki and Herb

Kiki and Herb began in the same "post–Ridiculous" landscape of other artists mentioned in this chapter. Justin Vivian Bond and Kenny Mellman, respectively, joined forces in 1992 and began their avant-garde drag cabaret act soon after. According to James Wilson, Kiki and Herb were more distinctly political in their performances than most of the Ridiculous and Ridiculous-esque artists heretofore mentioned. Wilson suggests, "This political aspect is a primary characteristic of Kiki and Herb and derives from Bond and

Mellman's background in AIDS activism and political street theatre. Kiki and Herb are washed-up, ridiculously irrelevant lounge singers and perpetually on the comeback trail, but they were created within the turmoil caused by AIDS and the in-your-face theatrics of Queer Nation and ACT-UP.[17] Indeed, they are certainly ridiculous, but they also have specific political opinions and ideas they wish to convey.

Once again, we find AIDS playing an active role in the development of this aesthetic. In this case, as with Kushner, it pushes these Ridiculous behaviors from being radical only in their aesthetic choices to being radical in their actual statements as well. Ridiculous remix is used as a means to very specific and direct political ends. One track from "Kiki and Herb Will Die for You," their live Carnegie Hall show, mashes up everything from Wu-Tang Clan to Eminem with their usual cabaret look and aesthetic. "The Revolution Medley" has strong political overtones, ending on the suggestion that "the revolution will be live."[18]

Despite the political nature of some of their antics, Kiki and Herb were able to translate their shtick to larger audiences than the limited Downtown club scene would allow, performing a concert at Carnegie Hall, recorded for album release; appearing in a film featuring such stars as Sigourney Weaver[19]; and even creating a full-scale two-act Broadway production. This work, titled *Kiki and Herb Alive on Broadway* (2006), featured Bond's gender mashup construction of the character of Kiki who occupied audiences with her usual rants about love and motherhood, her incessant drinking, the history of Herb as a "gay-Jew-'tard," as well as more biting political commentary—about then president George W. Bush—and references to her own presence at the birth of Christ. This remix of elements was all punctuated with the duo's song stylings, covering great hits in their unique style, as they had done at Carnegie Hall.

For critics, this production transcended its downtown roots. In Ben Brantley's extremely positive *New York Times* review of the 2006 production, he both singles out Kiki and Herb's downtown past while celebrating their transcendence of it: "And a performance that should, by rights, be just a night of imitative song and shtick from another pair of happy high-campers from the alternative club scene becomes irresistibly full-bodied art."[20] Apparently, just role-playing in drag on stage would not have had the same impact of this piece, in Brantley's estimation. Kiki and Herb are worthy of his praise because they created something that went beyond their "club scene" roots. Ultimately, they were able to use the scene that they came from to create a piece that would be appealing to broader audiences than just those that partake of "Downtown" theatre.

For Brantley, what is best about this production is not what it shares with the Ridiculous, but the degree to which it moves beyond the boundaries of the tradition that it inherits. The potentially radical constructions of

Ridiculous remix and gender mashup are here seen as something that has already been done. That style—over-the-top drag performances marked with pop culture references—has lost its edge in Brantley's estimation:

> Fakery is often more real than reality in the glamorous and tawdry world of theater. I should probably state, for the uninitiated, that the ultrawomanly Kiki is channeled by a man named Justin Bond. Herb is the alter ego of a truly inspired pop musicologist named Kenny Mellman. This sounds like regulation tacky countercultural standup, laced with the overemotional kitsch that drag queens borrow from old movies, right?[21]

Here, Brantley does not take into consideration that Bond does not identify as a man; Brantley may be misreading the production on which he is commenting. The drag tradition which Brantley references is the same one that Eichelberger mocked in his productions, but it also includes the practices with which he and other Ridiculous artists were associated. As I have mentioned, both cross-dressing and a preoccupation with performance as a career are essential elements in Ridiculous Theatre. Yet, Kiki and Herb's act does seem to be something more than just a Ridiculous mockery of surrounding popular culture. Their *Alive on Broadway* show confronted real hard-hitting topics, like religion and politics, not just for humor, but also in order to use humor to expose larger, very unfunny, realities. Indeed, as Brantley notes, "they use the surface of camp as a tool for detonating surfaces."[22] Like Kushner, Kiki and Herb built on their Ridiculous predecessors for very political ends. In this way, although they share many aesthetic elements with Theatre of the Ridiculous, they are some new version of the form, one more applicable to the 21st century and mainstream audiences, while being more politically abrasive.

Possible Ridiculous Inheritors: *Hedwig and the Angry Inch*

Hedwig and the Angry Inch is another show that developed out of a similar drag and club aesthetic as the one that gave life to Kiki and Herb. "Don't you know me? I'm the new Berlin Wall!"[23] exclaims Hedwig, the protagonist of John Cameron Mitchell's musical. (S)he is iconic of the divide between genders, the political divides between people, and the strange line between high and low culture, while being, once again, a politically charged Ridiculous descendent. In his "Author's Note" to the published edition, Mitchell notes the importance of site to his work. He writes, "We deliberately developed it [*Hedwig*] over a number of years in non-theatrical venues—rock clubs, drag bars, birthday parties, friends' patios—in order to keep it free-flowing, improvisational, alive."[24] This show, like the works of Eichelberger, is a work that is deeply indebted to the downtown club scene and the kind of free-form culture-blending theatre associated with it.

The show, about Hedwig, a victim of a botched male-to-female sex change operation, and her failed love affair with now mega-star of the music world Tommy Gnosis, includes much of what I have already demonstrated to be key elements of the Ridiculous stage. A performer of either gender can play the lead role because, no matter who dons Hedwig's wigs, he or she will be forced to cross genders. Hedwig is both male and female, while being neither sex biologically: inherently a gender mashup. In its earliest versions as well as briefly on Broadway in 2015, Mitchell played the lead role, in a similarly flamboyant mode of dress as that once worn by Smith or Eichelberger. The songs are pure Ridiculous remix, born of a love affair with both the most pop culture of references—such as Farrah Fawcett—and a high cultural knowledge—like "The Origin of Love," a song about Aristophanes's contribution to Plato's *Symposium*.

This show, like the performances of Kiki and Herb, is built upon a Ridiculous foundation. Yet, like the performances created by Bond and Mellman, for better or for worse, *Hedwig* goes beyond its Ridiculous inheritance. In his *New York Times* review of the original Off-Broadway production, what Peter Marks celebrates is the way in which Mitchell's show transcends its drag show roots, as had been lauded in Kiki and Herb's performance as well:

> The most impressive achievement, however, is by Mr. Mitchell, who transforms what might have been just another campy drag act into something deeper and more adventurous. His Hedwig, all glittered up in her denim outfit with the pink leather fringe, is in hiding up there in front of us. Embittered by a sexually confusing German childhood and a lifelong series of disappointments, especially the mutilating surgery that leaves him/her with an "angry inch," Hedwig spends her time onstage coming to terms with the implications of mistakes she made, of her self-denying masquerade.[25]

This show allows its character to explore the complications inherent in crossing the gender divide and what it means to do so incompletely. In so doing, it hearkens back to the real theoretical concerns to which drag draws attention: what aspects of the self could really be seen as being essential or innate and to what degree are all elements of selfhood performed or performative. The larger concerns seem to be what is of value in experiencing such a performance on stage. Yet, Marks ends his review by suggesting that "to solve a problem like Hedwig? You sit back and enjoy her show. In the end, that's really all she asks."[26] Like its Ridiculous ancestors, then, one element of this show that really matters is the extent to which it is able to entertain.

Because of its appeal to both countercultural and mainstream audiences, the musical was quite marketable, both with other performers, such as Ally Sheedy, in the lead role, as well as in the form of a full-length feature film. In his *New York Times* review of the cinematic version, Stephen Holden questions whether "the world [is] ready for Hedwig ... [an] allegorical semi-drag show that calls itself a 'post-punk-neo-glam rock musical' [that] bears an uncomfortably subversive message about the fluidity of sexual roles, disguise and self-invention in rock music."[27] Holden is able to celebrate the entertaining performances, costumes, and songs in the film, while staying somewhat elusive about the overall production's meaning or importance.

Holden seems uncertain about a story with these themes, presented with this aesthetic style, being marketed for a conventional audience. For Holden, what this film suggests is that this sort of self-performance has now arrived in a mainstream way, whether he likes or not. Holden contends:

> In such a climate the Hedwigs of this world are beginning to seem less like freaks and more like brave individualists mapping out an emerging frontier where boys can be girls and girls can be boys, and everyone has the freedom to couple however he or she chooses. If the glam-rock era is long gone, "Hedwig" reminds us, its subversive spirit, which has percolated under the surface of rock culture for more than two decades, lives on.[28]

According to Holden, what was once most subversive about this sort of performative gender play on stage is now a normal form, one that includes all of us, insofar as we accept that we are always performing ourselves. If this type of drag performance is no longer something unique to a particular setting and aesthetic, what then does that mean for Ridiculous Theatre? Is there a place for it in the contemporary mainstream, commercial theatre? Like Kiki and Herb before, *Hedwig and the Angry Inch*, originally a downtown club act, found a way to be adapted to Broadway.

The spring 2014 Broadway production, which opened with television superstar Neil Patrick Harris in the titular role, proved that the Ridiculous aesthetic is not only still applicable, but also still quite meaningful for contemporary audiences. In anticipation of playing the role, Harris, according to a *New York Times* feature, "[feels] anxious, but [his] fearless quotient is higher than it's ever been" to perform the demanding musical score.[29] This *Hedwig* exemplifies what a 21st-century incarnation of the Ridiculous might look like. From the moment one enters the Belasco Theatre, it is clear that we have entered an at least semi-Ridiculous space. The stage setting, supposedly constructed of abandoned set pieces from the previous night's opening of the theatrical flop *The Hurt Locker—The Musical*, hearkens back to Jack Smith's junk-filled loft, while still being constructed of a joke about a work of contemporary pop culture. Center stage is marked with a "junker" sort of car, which seems to have reversed into the backdrop, as its back half is scattered in the air behind. This deconstructed piece of junk, which causes the stage to be filled with even more clutter, suggests a potential similar reverence for the valueless that Smith once possessed. This show, like Smith's late-night loft performances, attempts to turn trash into treasure through the ritualistic alchemy of theatre.

In addition, this production does not allow for a distinct separation between actors and audience. Hedwig knows we are present and enters the audience space, even to the point of discomfort, gyrating over and spitting on members of the first row. To make the play relevant to a contemporary audience, and to maintain Mitchell's idea of the piece as a living breathing adapting thing, the popular culture references have been updated, both to take in the play's current setting (referring to the history of and myths about ghosts of the Belasco) and the current cultural scene (with jokes about current celebrities and events). Gender is layered not only in the figure of Hedwig but also in his husband, Yitzhak, a woman playing a man who wishes to wear wigs and perform in drag. The two main characters are figures who defy gender, with Hedwig's over-the-top makeup and costume elements, and her botched biology, and Yitzhak's beautiful feminine voice shining through the male attire.

What could have been a silly drag stand-up act or an entertaining but pointless star vehicle maintains its status as a relevant commentary on the struggles of finding oneself in the contemporary world. Neither the aesthetic elements nor the discussion of the Berlin Wall seem out of place here. Rather, *Hedwig* on Broadway is a powerful production about identity and love. It is marked by many of the elements that could be considered Ridiculous, proving that the Ridiculous has a place on Broadway and that it can use that important cultural location to make meaningful statements about serious topics.

When Cross-Dressing Becomes Commercial

Certainly, much of contemporary Broadway and off-Broadway theatre would suggest that there is now room in commercial theatre for the aesthetic elements that were honed in the Ridiculous Theatre. For example, the quotation, "Ladies, gentlemen, and all those who have yet to decide"[30] comes directly out of the Broadway musical *Kinky Boots*, a show that suggests exactly how far this sort of "Ridiculous" performance has come in the past few decades. This show has been considered so conventional that it not only won the Tony Award, but was also a marquee performance at the "family-friendly" Macy's Thanksgiving Day Parade in 2013. Ben Brantley feels like the motif— of having a big brassy drag queen make the protagonist and the audience fall in love with "her" via performance and charm—is already a bit played out. Of *Kinky Boots*, Brantley writes, "It's a shameless emotional button pusher, presided over—be warned—by that most weary of latter-day Broadway archetypes, a strong and sassy drag queen who dispenses life lessons like an automated fortune cookie."[31] On the one hand, *Kinky Boots* inclusion in the Thanksgiving festivities suggests that as a culture, Americans are at a point where a play about drag queens is considered general entertainment, where a Ridiculous sort of gender mashup blended with a Ridiculous remix kind of adaptation musical is no longer something radical.

And yet, this presentation created a minor uproar among social media-using conservative Americans. *The Huffington Post* reports that "although the show's message is of acceptance and tolerance and the performance was relatively tame … right wingers across America took to social networks to voice their outrage at NBC for broadcasting it," citing tweets that remark on how "disgusting" or inappropriate inclusion of the sequence was.[32] There may be a place for such gender-bending performance in mainstream New York culture, but American culture at large still seems somewhat resistant to such presentations.

The potential radical quality of *Kinky Boots* was perhaps best evident during Todrick Hall's run as Lola in the winter of 2017. Hall experienced first-hand the political potential of this work. In numerous interviews about playing the part, he addressed audience response to the show and its relevance to the historical moment. Of more recent reactions to the show, he related:

> But I think the coolest thing was the day after they announced who was going to be our next President. The energy in Times Square was just insane. I've never seen it so full of people, yet so lifeless. It was crazy. It felt like a bunch of zombies walking around. We had two shows that day, and it was really hard. I'd never experienced anything like that before. The audience got up and they were crying, like women from middle America, and families who were crying because they thought the show was so beautiful. That was really awesome.
>
> A couple weeks after my opening, I met a lady from Utah who said that her and her husband were there on my opening night, and didn't know who I was but had just bought tickets, and had never experienced an energy like they had the night in the theatre. So, they ended up flying back the following weekend with all of their kids. They had four kids, and all of them came back and saw the show![33]

Clearly, *Kinky Boots* was providing something that audiences found meaningful, even essential, during this tumultuous historical and political moment. Even in its commercial entertainment format, this sort of cross-gendered celebratory performance has something poignant to say to its audiences.

Of course, cross-dressing has been a part of the Broadway stage practically since its inception. Yet the drag performing in a musical such as *Kinky Boots* is not the sort of cross-dressing that we would associate with Broadway in its golden age. It is not being done simply as a joke, as in, say the film *Some Like It Hot*; rather, these "crossed" identities are meant to be the individual's actual self. He/she lives as the opposite gender, as opposed to merely dressing up this way to achieve a particular goal, as in a show such as *Victor/Victoria*. The cross-dressed individual in these more contemporary Broadway musicals creates an identity that defies a binary gender system. In the case of a show like *Rent*, for example, the character Angel identifies more as a female than as a male. In his tribute to Angel upon the occasion of his death from AIDS, Mark must correct himself in his usage of the gendered pronoun "his" for its feminine counterpart.[34] In shows like the aforementioned *Kinky Boots*, the gender performance is not about simply becoming the opposite gender identity, but about revealing the performance of self, drawing attention to how the putting on of sexy sequined boots can give one the chance to redefine one's identity outside of a male-female dichotomous system.

Cross-dressing on its own, then, does not Ridiculous Theatre make. On the contemporary Broadway stage, cross-dressing, when associated with sexual orientation, is less controversial or outlandish than it perhaps has ever been.[35] *La Cage Aux Folles* reminds its viewers that "life ain't worth a damn 'til you can say 'I am what I am,'"[36] a proclamation provided in a show which features an ensemble of cross-dressed chorus girls, while *Hairspray* allows a man-impersonating-a-woman to stand in for the lead character's mother without much questioning of the situation. Brantley writes of Harvey Fierstein in the cross-dressed role, "Big (Mr. Fierstein wears a fat suit), burly and tart-tongued as she sweats over the laundry she takes in, Edna is not just a cross-dressing sight gag. She's every forgotten housewife, recreated in monumental proportions and waiting for something to tap her hidden magnificence."[37] The cross-dressing is at the heart of the artistry, an element of character that is not questioned or explained by the narrative.

Some of the Broadway works that unknowingly seem to borrow from the Ridiculous are not quite this provocative or profound. Rather, they display a commercialization of the drag queen heroine, and the sort of cultural mixing that we find in the Ridiculous is now a staple of jukebox musical construction. Of 2011's Broadway production of *Priscilla, Queen of the Desert*, Charles Isherwood writes for the *New York Times*: "It's the kind of mix you might find blaring from the jukebox in a Florida gay bar if patrons of varying ages and argumentative tastes were on hand: everything from Dionne Warwick to Donna Summer and the Village People, Madonna, Cyndi Lauper and Pat Benatar. Let's not forget the contribution from that immortal dance-floor diva John Denver."[38] Here, again, we have what seems to be the semblance of a Ridiculous motif: cross-dressing characters who love to cite from their surrounding culture, though the sum total does not seem quite to add up to the cutting commentary on its time that a Vaccaro production might.

By moving to Broadway, it would seem, these Ridiculous aesthetic elements toe a thin line between being radical and being a gimmick. As Hall's run in *Kinky Boots* proved, the traces of Theatre of the Ridiculous that can be found uptown allow the radical messages to reach a much wider and more diverse audience than ever before. How, then, is legacy useful in discussing the significance of the Ridiculous? If we can claim to find its traces everywhere, does this then dissipate its importance as a moment in theatrical history? Or, does it offer us a useful thread for locating the Ridiculous—and, by extension, its radical valence—in our contemporary moment?

Conclusion
Radical Ridiculous Theatre?

"No Charles Ludlam," according to Everett Quinton, "no RuPaul being taken seriously."[1] Ludlam's influence, even if not obvious to everyone, can be felt in a wide range of places in 21st-century culture. Although not every theatre expert might know the names of all its key practitioners, even the most uninformed theatregoer could recognize many of its tropes, as the popularity of Broadway shows such as *Kinky Boots* has proven. As Gregory J. Seigworth and Melissa Gregg explicate of Spinoza's theory of affect, "the capacity of a body is never defined by a body alone but is always aided and abetted by, and dovetails with, the field or context of its force-relations."[2] A thing is not only known by what it is, but is also understood by the interactions it has with the world around it. Indeed, the Ridiculous is a clear example of this phenomenon; its growth as a concept was always negotiated via "its force-relations" between and betwixt the varied artists who shaped its theoretical boundaries in their various places of performance.

Yet, the power of affect in the Ridiculous does not necessarily contribute to its progressive quality in the way one might think it would. It does not declare the Ridiculous's radical quality; it instead exemplifies it in its theoretical construct. As Seigworth and Gregg argue, "affect instead bears an intense and thoroughly immanent neutrality."[3] For Seigworth and Gregg, who read neutrality via Roland Barthes, this allows affect to be separated from binaries as "the neutral is not bound to the formed/formal matters of space or time nor has it anything to do with linearizing axes and abrupt angles of structuralism."[4] Like the Ridiculous Theatre itself, the presence of its affect is not clearly one thing or another; what its presence does is force its audiences to reconsider their own structuralist interpretation of the world. Charles Ludlam's Camille is neither specifically male nor female; she is something else entirely. Similarly, the effect of the Theatre of the Ridiculous is neither the

Ridiculous itself nor is it its legacy; it suggests an in-between space, what is left when an inherently ephemeral act of performance ends before its next incarnation begins. The Ridiculous was a theatre movement because we can find evidence of it everywhere; Sean F. Edgecomb's book *Ludlam Lives!* proves that many significant contemporary performers are keeping the Ridiculous flame alive in their artistic practice. However, as powerful as the impact of this legacy might be, these traces are not Ridiculous Theatre in and of themselves. Rather, the purpose that they serve is to remind us to look back for their source, serving as important echoes that must be heard in order to bring the Ridiculous, as it was practiced in the mid to late 20th century, back into theatre studies.

Indeed, discussions of affect are a critical tool in ascertaining the significance of the Ridiculous, as the form itself has not been nearly as well recognized as its effect on subsequent theatremakers has. To build the context of this affect, it is useful to return to the seemingly amateurish quality of many Ridiculous performances. These performances were in fact anything but amateur; they were instead sophisticated reinterpretations of how character can be created on stage. These performers also provided a critical lens on the act of performing itself, showing how crossing all lines of identification in performance exposes the reality of the performance of our everyday lives. In distinguishing "shame" from "guilt," Eve Kosofsky Sedgwick establishes, "Transformational shame, *is performance*. I mean theatrical performance. Performance interlines shame as more than just its result or a way of warding it off, though importantly it is those things. Shame is the affect that mantles the threshold between introversion and extroversion, between absorption and theatricality, between performativity and—performativity."[5]

If "shame and exhibitionism are different interlinings of the same glove,"[6] then the queer construction of "failure" once again seems applicable. On the one hand, a traditional performer might have been embarrassed by the kind of the play-acting that marks Theatre of the Ridiculous theatrical production. But the Ridiculous practitioners found a way to play *within* this affectual space, exploring the pleasures of displaying the shameful side of character portrayal, the inabilities to fully become another human being. This quality, perhaps beyond any other in the Theatre of the Ridiculous, exposes its radical potential. Ridiculous Theatre may not have changed the political landscape or the way in which we live in the world directly, but it certainly altered how we understand the performance of identity on stage. It is no longer necessary to effectively become someone else on stage; rather it is equally and perhaps even more valuable to explore the experience of *becoming* on stage. It is important to explore the interface between all levels of cultural production.

The Fall of the Theatre of the Ridiculous?

In embracing new performance techniques, the Theatre of the Ridiculous created a remarkable mode for theatrical production, one whose traces still affect modern theatre, at all levels of experimental and commercial production alike. The Ridiculous cannot be said to be only present in its legacy, but certainly understanding its inheritors can help us find our way back to the Theatre of the Ridiculous. While the contemporary moment feels rife with a Ridiculous Renaissance, there was certainly a period in the 1990s in which it felt as though Ridiculous Theatre were coming to an end.

Eichelberger's 1990 *Dasvedanya Mama* is key evidence of this—and perhaps the clearest reflection of the effect of the AIDS epidemic in the form. *Dasvedanya Mama* operates on one level as an homage to the lost glory days of Ridiculous Theatre. The final song, ostensibly from Vaslav to his recently deceased mother Olga, played by Eichelberger, has particular resonance in this context. Vaslav intones, "Dasvedanya, Mama/My lover and my friend/I'll cherish your sweet memory/Until I reach the end/Of this strange life I'm leading/I know I've been a beast/But when I'm gone it's famine/And when I'm here it's feast."[7] If we remember that Eichelberger saw Ludlam as not only an influence but also as a mentor for his work and know that Ludlam had died only about three years before this show premiered, it becomes clear that this lament could be meant for him and the artists like him. These artistic greats were lost before their time, leaving their Ridiculous fellow travelers behind to be artists out of time, working in an aesthetic that had appealed to a community of individuals who were aging, dying, or simply moving on.

This seeming death of the Ridiculous is very much intertwined with the deaths of its great artistic minds. Ludlam, for one, begged his partner—both theatrical and romantic—Everett Quinton to continue his theatre, the RTC. Ludlam recorded a version of their negotiations, in which Everett fears, "But they won't do what I tell them." "They will if you pay them," Charles responds. Although this was true for a time, and audiences did accept Quinton's brand of Ridiculous Theatre, despite his fear that "the audiences want *you*,"[8] meaning Ludlam, he could not sustain the company for as long as Ludlam had. James Fisher credits Quinton with keeping the company running at One Sheridan Square until 1997,[9] with the Axis Theatre taking over the space in 1998.[10] Obviously, the loss of key artists, like Ludlam, did not help the situation; how could a form exist without its preeminent practitioners?

Additionally, however, the mid-1990s were a very different time from the mid-1960s, the era in which the Ridiculous was born. By 1997, New York rents were higher and theatre was more of a commercial commodity, even in its off-Broadway incarnations. In *Selling the Lower East Side*, Christopher

Mele discusses this "renaissance" or "death" of the Lower East Side—depending on one's perspective on the matter—in terms of an undoing of earlier stereotypes associated with the locale. Instead of being a site for the lower classes or a minority ghetto, by the 1990s, "the real estate sector and state actors consistently put forth notions of a desired, revitalized East Village or Lower East Side that contradicted existing sociocultural conditions."[11] This new vision of lower Manhattan encouraged a more bourgeois clientele to snatch up property in the area. The changing face of the Village led to changes in the artistic scene, creating a landscape less conducive to a Ridiculous Theatre, both socially and economically.

Ridiculous Theatre, in its original form, can be seen as a product of its own historical moment. It was born of a time when gay rights were coming to the forefront and when downtown New York was a renowned site for experimental art-making. If Wendell Stone is correct, and the Caffe Cino was the "birthplace of off-off-Broadway," it is likely because Greenwich Village was, throughout the 20th century, "a hub of nontraditional politics, art, and thought in the United States.... In the 1960s it would be rivaled only by San Francisco's Haight-Ashbury as the center of the counterculture movement."[12] This particular locale lent itself perfectly to work, both artistic and political, that questioned the status quo. If its legacy is to live on in the 21st century, its practitioners will need to continue to innovate in ways that will speak to and of the contemporary moment.

Even if Ridiculous plays were not political in a didactic way, they were certainly subversive, through their aesthetic choices if nothing else. When asked whether he thought of the work of Jack Smith and Ethyl Eichelberger as "political," Parnes claimed that they were "not in the ... hit you over the head with a brick kind of political, but in the Brechtian concept of ... as a subterfuge in the plot and somehow that coming through as the message.... It could be hysterical but it was still inherently political."[13] These works do, in fact, share in an inheritance from Brecht; they find a way through their artistic construction to present the audience with issues worth considering. As Ludlam claimed, you might laugh or cry at his *Camille*, but in either case, (s)he affected you.

In addition, as Edgecomb eloquently argues in *Ludlam Lives!*, the Ridiculous created a kind of "queer legacy," which is "self-selected, extended, and expanded, but," like all queer legacies, "also often forgotten, hidden, or lost."[14] The Ridiculous inheritors, according to Edgecomb, each took their own unique path to becoming "neo–Ridiculous." Yet, for Edgecomb, the paths of Charles Busch, Bradford Louryk, and Taylor Mac are uniquely indebted to and consciously recognizing the Ridiculous, and therefore can be classified as such; he contends, "The Ludlamesque Ridiculous sensibility has influenced many performers, but just because a performer is influenced consciously, subconsciously, or inadvertently by one or many Ridiculous tenets or characteristics does not necessarily make him part of a Ridiculous legacy."[15] While I agree that not every artist inspired by the Ridiculous is necessarily Ridiculous themselves, I do think that the presence of the Ridiculous aesthetic in varied and often commercial forms of performance is worth acknowledging as a strange off-shoot of the Ridiculous lineage. Edgecomb acknowledges the presence of what he calls "'Ridiculous-like' works ... [that] float around but not are not connected to the web of gay sensibility," admitting that there is "a recessive gene ... in the Ridiculous legacy that allows for such inspired works to exist beyond Ludlam's direct lineage."[16] In my opinion, it is worth studying those impacts, as I have done in the preceding two chapters, as they show the degree to which the Ridiculous has shifted over time; its ability, if you will, to, as Ludlam once quipped, "expand the definition of the Ridiculous" with new visions and contributions by a later generation of artists working within the lexicon of their own time and place. The Ridiculous is, in my estimation, a product of its unique historical moment and location; why would it not be able to adapt to later eras, locales, or individual sensibilities, so long as these remain within a queer framework?

The Ridiculous Has Moved Uptown: So What?

Indeed, many, varied, contemporary artists credit the "effect" of the Ridiculous for the experimental artistic work that they would go on to create. Robert Wilson and Richard Foreman, for example, both single out Jack Smith as an important precursor to their own esoteric work,[17] while both Charles Busch and Tony Kushner cite Ludlam as a key influence on the plays they have created. Yet plays by Wilson, Foreman, Busch and Kushner have all garnered far more substantial critical and commercial success than either those of Smith or Ludlam ever did. What does this increased cultural impact do to the claims that this work was subtly political in its aesthetic construction? In other words, what happens to this aesthetic when it is moved uptown?

The answer is not a simple one. Someone like Ludlam would have been thrilled to see his theatre move uptown and become profitable; Ludlam sought commercial success and recognition, even if he was suspicious of the Broadway model of theatre-making: "I want a big commercial success, I do. It's very hard for an artist to make a living. I wonder if at a certain point we'll have to charge a hundred dollars per ticket."[18] On the other hand, however, Jack Smith eschewed this sort of limelight. In Smith's case, his main fame is in influence, not actual practice. Yet, as Sally Banes notes Smith may have inspired contemporary performance art, but he was able to do something with his aesthetic choices that the artists around him could not master:

Smith's performance used the iconography of Disney cartoons, movie stars, exotic dancers, of musty junkpiles whose particulars were hard to discern in the gloomy auditorium. But, unlike his contemporaries, the Pop artists, who took a cool, ironic stance in relation to this kind of imagery, unlike the Lower East Side cabaret acts of the 1980s, whose imitations of popular entertainers use distancing to either comment on or simply assimilate mainstream commercial art, Smith is a kind of alchemist.[19]

Smith accomplished something in his live performances that has proven difficult for others to recreate. Rather than being remembered as inspiration to others, a commercial success may have allowed these artists' plays to be remembered in their own rights, not just for what and whom they inspired. Despite this, however, avoiding commercialization preserved what was most radical about these Ridiculous artists.

It is uncertain what the Ridiculous artists would have made of finding elements of their downtown aesthetic on MTV, social media, and on Broadway. Ludlam would likely not have been *that* upset about this, so long as he was profiting from it himself; he pursued a commercial career. At the time of his death, he was actively trying to break in to mainstream cinema, television, and theatre. Ronald Tavel was a bit more academic in his imaginings of the Ridiculous, but what would this extreme commercialization and commodification have meant for the development of that style? If Tavel did indeed design Ridiculous Theatre as a reaction to Theatre of the Absurd, then Ridiculous-ism would be rendered irrelevant anyhow, as the Absurd, too, is largely a dated movement, a product of a post-war World War II world that has been reshaped time and again since.

Where, then, does that leave the Ridiculous? Is it applicable to the NEW New York of the 21st century, with its high rents, especially below Fourteenth Street, as well as its abundance of theatrical performances of all sorts? Or is the Ridiculous more important as a product of its time? On the one hand, what the examples presented in the two preceding chapters suggest is that the moment for the Ridiculous has arrived; it has the possibility to be more popular and to reach more audiences than it ever did before. On the other hand, however, its most essential quality—its radical questioning of the status quo through its preoccupation with popular culture and the representation of unstable gendered identities—may have been lost in its commercialization. In many cases, it has become nothing more than another humorous cliché, used not to alter perceptions but to sell tickets and fill seats. In either case, through the presence of a rich and varied legacy, we can say that the Ridiculous may have ended, but its legacy lives on.

How we can interpret performance has forever been changed by the Ridiculous landscape; this movement showed the value of blending cultural references and gender iconography, which is very common in both contemporary performance and multimedia practices, in order to create something not only innovative but also potentially radical. It means that we can still make theatre in the Ridiculous aesthetic—as Taylor Mac and others are continuing to do, quite successfully—and still find that it has something meaningful to say, even if that meaningful quality is born of nothing more than a silly joke based on a reference to a ghost (even of a B-movie star) of a long-forgotten cultural past.

Chapter Notes

Preface

1. Aristotle, *Poetics*, in *Theatre, Theory, Theatre*, edited by Daniel Gerould (New York: Applause Books, 2003), 49.

2. Sean F. Edgecomb, *Charles Ludlam Lives! Charles Busch, Bradford Louryk, Taylor Mac and the Queer Legacy of the Ridiculous Theatrical Company* (Ann Arbor: University of Michigan Press, 2017). For more on Taylor Mac's "Genius Grant," see http://variety.com/2017/legit/news/2017-macarthur-genius-grant-winners-1202586951/.

3. Oscar G. Brockett and Franklin J. Hildy, *History of the Theatre, Tenth Edition* (New York: Pearson, 2008), 544.

4. Edgecomb, *Ludlam Lives!*, 37.

5. *Ibid.*

6. Jack Halberstam, *In a Queer Time and Place* (New York: New York University Press, 2005), 2.

7. Charles Ludlam, *Scourge of Human Folly* (New York: Theatre Communcations Group, 1992), 131.

8. Jack Halberstam, *The Queer Art of Failure* (Durham: Duke University Press, 2011), 89.

9. http://www.warholstars.org/ridiculous.html.

10. Charles Ludlam, "Manifesto: Ridiculous Theatre, Scourge of Human Folly," in *Ridiculous Theatre: Scourge of Human Folly* (New York: Theatre Communications Group, 1992), 157.

11. *Ibid.*, 158.

12. Halberstam, *In a Queer Time and Place*, 78.

13. Stephen J. Bottoms, *Playing Underground: A Critical History of the 1960s Off-Off-Broadway Movement* (Ann Arbor: University of Michigan Press, 2004), 11.

14. *Ibid.*, 14.

15. Moe Angelos, et al., "From the Invisible to the Ridiculous: The Emergence of an Out Theatre Aesthetic," *The Queerest Art: Essays on Lesbian and Gay Theatre*, edited by Alisa Solomon and Framji Minwalla, 135–51 (New York: New York University Press, 2002), 150.

16. Benjamin Shepard, *Queer Political Performance and Protest* (New York: Routledge, 2009), 7.

17. Jill Dolan, "Building a Theatrical Vernacular: Responsibility, Community, Ambivalence, and Queer Theatre," in *The Queerest Art: Essays on Lesbian and Gay Theatre*, edited by Alisa Solomon and Framji Minwalla, 1–8 (New York: New York University Press, 2002), 5.

18. Stefan Brecht, *Queer Theatre* (Berlin: Suhrkampf, 1978), 42.

19. Halberstam, *Queer Art of Failure*, 96.

20. Bottoms, *Playing Underground*, 215.

21. Halberstam, *Queer Art of Failure*, 2.

22. Tavel, qtd. in Bottoms, 220.

23. Halberstam, *Queer Art of Failure*, 3.

24. Bottoms, *Playing Underground*, 215.

25. Fabio Cleto, "Introduction: Queering the Camp," in *Camp: Queer Aesthetics and the Performing Subject—A Reader* (Edinburgh: Edinburgh University Press, 1999), 26.

26. Halberstam, *Queer Art of Failure*, 19.

27. Adam Salandra, "'Queer Ghost Hunters' Is Back to Wake the LGBT Dead for Second Season," *Logo*, June 27, 2017, http://www.newnownext.com/queer-ghost-hunters-season-two/06/2017/.

28. Moe Meyer, *The Politics and Poetics of Camp* (New York: Routledge, 1993), 3.

Chapter One

1. Robert Chesley, "Dialogue with the Ridiculous," *Omega One*, January 19, 1979, 23. Found in the Charles Ludlam Papers in the Billy Rose Theatre Collection at the New York Public Library for the Performing Arts, call number 8-MWEZ+n.c. 29.277, folder #2.

2. Everett Quinton, interview with the author, February 27, 2014, via telephone 2–3 p.m.

3. Charles Ludlam, *Ridiculous Theatre: Scourge of Human Folly*, edited by Steven Samuels (New York: Theatre Communications Group, 1992), 131.

4. David Savran, *A Queer Sort of Materialism: Recontextualizing American Theatre* (Ann Arbor: University of Michigan Press, 2003), 58.

5. Charles Ludlam, "Camp," in *Scourge of Human Folly* (New York: Theatre Communications Group, 1992), 225.

6. *Ibid.*, 226.

7. Fabio Cleto, "Introduction: Queering the Camp," in *Camp: Queer Aesthetics and the Performing Subject—A Reader* (Edinburgh: Edinburgh University Press, 1999), 24.

8. Ludlam, "Camp," in *Scourge of Human Folly*, 227.

9. Charles Ludlam, personal notes, found in the Charles Ludlam Papers in the Billy Rose Theatre Collection at the New York Public Library for the Performing Arts, call number 8-MWEZ+n.c. 29.256, folder #5.

10. Quinton, interview, February 27, 2014.

11. Charles Ludlam, *Scourge of Human Folly*, 157. Incidentally, Jack Smith believed it was so-called "landlordism," or the need to pay rent, that destroyed art.

12. Charles Ludlam, "The Avant-Garde," in *Scourge of Human Folly*, 223.

13. *Ibid.*, 224.

14. Stephen J. Bottoms discusses this fissure in *Playing Underground* (Ann Arbor: University of Michigan Press, 2006). I further discuss this important moment in Ridiculous history in this book's third chapter.

15. http://www.ronaldtavel.com/about.html.

16. Charles Ludlam and Gautam Dasgupta, "Interview: Charles Ludlam," *Performing Arts Journal* 3, no. 1 (1978): 69–70.

17. Andrew Ross, "Uses of Camp," in *Camp*, 323.

18. This notebook is held in the collection of Charles Ludlam Papers in the Billy Rose Theatre Collection at the New York Public Library for the Performing Arts, call number 8-MWEZ+n.c. 29.256, folder #2.

19. Charles Ludlam, *The Grand Tarot*, in *The Complete Plays of Charles Ludlam* (New York: Harper & Row, 1989), 85.

20. Charles Ludlam's notebook, found in the Charles Ludlam Papers in the Billy Rose Theatre Collection at the New York Public Library for the Performing Arts, call number 8-MWEZ+n.c. 29.157, folder #6.

21. Quinton, interview, February 27, 2014.

22. Frank Rich, "A Mad and Busy Day in Ludlam's First Venture: The Guests Include Norma Desmond and Svengali" *New York Times*, September 29, 1989, C9 Accessed June 10, 2013. http://search.proquest.com.ezproxy.gc.cuny.edu/docview/110248240/fulltextPDF/13F4D7BD2616B8AF2FE/9?accountid=7287

23. Rick Roemer, *Charles Ludlam and the Ridiculous Theatrical Company: Critical Analyses of 29 Plays* (Jefferson, NC: McFarland, 2010), 85–86.

24. Charles Ludlam, *Big Hotel*, in *The Complete Plays of Charles Ludlam* (New York: Harper & Row, 1989), 4.

25. Marvin Carlson, *The Haunted Stage: The Theatre as Memory Machine* (Ann Arbor, MI: University of Michigan Press, 2003), 2.

26. Robert Mills, [qm]Queer Is Here? Lesbian, Gay, Bisexual, and Transgender Histories and Public Culture,[qm] *History Workshop Journal*, no. 62 (Autumn 2006): 253–63, 262.

27. Roemer, *Charles Ludlam*, 85.

28. Rich, "A Mad and Busy Day in Ludlam's First Venture," in *New York Times*, September 19, 1989, C9.

29. Roemer, *Charles Ludlam*, 85.

30. Transcript of Unidentified Interview, page 10, included in the Charles Ludlam Papers in the Billy Rose Theatre Collection at the New York Public Library for the Performing Arts, call number 8-MWEZ+n.c. 29.277, folder #19.

31. One could also see resonances of Maria Montez's *Cobra Woman* in the recent Red Bull Theatre production of *The Mystery of Irma Vep*, directed by Everett Quinton. The play's second act takes place in Egypt and includes a seductive, albeit silly, dance by a supposedly ancient mummy. Quinton's production styled

the mummy and her dance moves in such a way that it felt reminiscent of the sacrifice sequence of Montez's film.

32. David Kaufman, *Ridiculous!: The Theatrical Life and Times of Charles Ludlam* (New York: Applause Theatre and Cinema Books, 2002), 82.

33. *Ibid.*

34. Joseph LeSueur, "Theatre: Big Hotel," *Village Voice*, February 9, 1967 Accessed June 10, 2013. http://news.google.com/news papers?nid=1299&dat=19670209&id=NxA QAAAAIBAJ&sjid=KYwDAAAAIBAJ&pg= 5958,681787

35. Ludlam, *Big Hotel*, in *The Complete Plays of Charles Ludlam*, 22.

36. Ludlam, *Scourge of Human Folly*, 18.

37. *Ibid.*

38. Roemer, *Charles Ludlam*, 87.

39. Ludlam, *Scourge of Human Folly*, 19.

40. Carlson, *The Haunted Stage*, 48.

41. Roemer, *Charles Ludlam*, 90.

42. Carlson, *The Haunted Stage*, 167.

43. Notebook of Charles Ludlam, found in the Charles Ludlam Papers, in the Billy Rose Theatre Collection at the New York Public Library for the Performing Arts, call number 8-MWEZ+n.c. 29.257, folder #17.

44. From an article entitled "Ludlam Profile: Ridiculous," March 25, 1976, page 2, found in the Charles Ludlam Papers in the Billy Rose Theatre Collection at the New York Public Library for the Performing Arts.

45. J. David Bolter and Richard Grusin, *Remediation: Understanding New Media* (Cambridge: MIT Press, 2000), 20.

46. Robert K. Logan, *Understanding New Media: Extending Marshall McLuhan* (New York: Peter Lang, 2010), 70.

47. Quinton, interview, February 27, 2014.

48. In the Charles Ludlam Papers at the Billy Rose Theatre Collection at the New York Public Library for the Performing Arts, there are numerous drafts of this script, both typed and handwritten, as well as annotated pages from Molière's original. These materials are all filed under 8-MWEZ+n.c. 29.268.

49. Sam Shirakawa, "The Eccentric World of Charles Ludlam," *New York Times*, July 3, 1983, H3, accessed July 7, 2013, http://search.proquest.com.ezproxy.gc.cuny.edu/docview/122160530/13F4D7BD2616B8AF2FE/1?accountid=7287.

50. Certificate from the *Villager* awarded to Charles Ludlam and the Ridiculous Theatrical Company in honor of their contributions and *Le Bourgeois Avant-Garde*, dated June 6, 1983. Found in the Charles Ludlam Papers in the Billy Rose Theatre Collection at the New York Public Library, call number 8-MWEZ+n.c. 29.277, folder #1.

51. Ludlam, *Le Bourgeois Avant-Garde*, in *The Complete Plays*, 699.

52. Personal note of Charles Ludlam in the Charles Ludlam Papers in the Billy Rose Theatre Collection at the New York Public Library for the Performing Arts, call number 8-MWEZ+n.c. 29.268, folder #1.

53. Ludlam, "The Avant-Garde," in *Scourge of Human Folly*, 221.

54. Roemer, *Charles Ludlam*, 124.

55. Ludlam, *Le Bourgeois Avant-Garde*, 707.

56. *Ibid.*, 708.

57. Frank Rich, "Stage: 'Le Bourgeois,' Comedy After Molière," *New York Times*, April 15, 1983, C3, ccessed July 1, 2013, http://search.proquest.com.ezproxy.gc.cuny.edu/docview/122168449/13F4DA3465362FC4414/2?accountid=7287.

58. *Ibid.*

59. Kaufman, *Ridiculous!*, 362.

60. Galas was a drag role that Ludlam had recently performed. The play focused on an opera singer named Galas, who was loosely based on Maria Callas.

61. Ludlam, *How to Write a Play*, in *The Complete Plays*, 817.

62. *Ibid.*, 827.

63. Kaufman, *Ridiculous!*, 394.

64. Frank Rich, "A Ludlam Legacy: New Drummer, Same Beat: How to Write a Play a Legacy Is Updated," *New York Times*, November 9, 1993, C17, accessed June 10, 2013, http://search.proquest.com.ezproxy.gc.cuny.edu/docview/109160195/13F4DAD8689484CA18A/1?accountid=7287.

65. Patricia Waugh, *Metafiction* (2002; New York: Routledge, 2013), 2.

66. *Ibid.*

67. Ludlam, *Scourge of Human Folly*, 157.

68. Ludlam, *How to Write a Play*, 843.

69. Frank Rich, "Theater: Ludlam's 'Artificial Jungle,'" *New York Times*, September 23, 1986, C13, accessed July 7, 2013, http://search.proquest.com.ezproxy.gc.cuny.edu/docview/

111039075/13F4DB9CB362ECD0FEB/1?acco-
untid=7287.

70. Charles Ludlam, "Ridiculous Theatre,
Scourge of Human Folly," *TDR* 19, no. 4 (1975).

71. Charles Ludlam, *The Artificial Jungle*,
in *The Complete Plays* (New York: Harper &
Row, 1989), 905.

72. Ronald Tavel claimed to have created
the Ridiculous Theatre as a reaction to the
Theatre of the Absurd. See Chapter Three for
more.

73. Ludlam, *Scourge of Human Folly*, 32.

74. *Ibid.*, 31–32.

75. Joseph N. Straus, "Disability and 'Late
Style' in Music," *Journal of Musicology* 25, no.
1 (2008), 6.

76. *Ibid.*, 6.

77. *Ibid.*, 8–11.

78. *Ibid.*, 11–12.

79. Kaufman, *Ridiculous!*, 436.

80. *Ibid.*, 431.

81. Ronald Argelander, "Charles Ludlam's
Ridiculous Theatrical Company: A Way of
Working in the Theatre," page 9, found in the
Charles Ludlam Papers in the Billy Rose The-
atre Collection at the New York Public Library
for the Performing Arts, call number 8-
MWEZ+n.c. 29.277, folder #3.

82. Brett O'Connor, *del.icio.us Mashups*
(Somerset, NJ: John Wiley & Sons, 2007), xx.

83. *Ibid.*

84. Unpublished interview of Charles Ludlam by Lola Pashalinski. Found in the Charles
Ludlam Papers in the Billy Rose Theatre Collection at the New York Public Library for the
Performing Arts, call number 8-MWEZ+n.c.
29.277, folder #15.

85. Ludlam, *Scourge of Human Folly*, 22.

86. Quinton, interview, February 27, 2014.

87. *Ibid.*

88. Mary Ann Frese Witt, *Metatheater and
Modernity: Baroque and Neobaroque* (Madison, NJ: Fairleigh Dickinson University Press,
2012), 14.

89. Kaufman, *Ridiculous!*, 186.

90. Mel Gussow, "Ludlam Star of 'Camille
in Title Role," *New York Times*, May 4, 1973,
L4, accessed June 7, 2013, http://search.pro
quest.com.ezproxy.gc.cuny.edu/docview/
119625618/fulltextPDF/13F4DC0FDA
35A7DDA2C/1?accountid=7287.

91. Ludlam, qtd. in Kaufmann, *Ridiculous!*,
187.

92. Charles Ludlam, qtd. in Elenore
Lester, "The Holy Foolery of Charles Ludlam,"
New York Times, July, 14, 1974, 1, 16.

93. Ludlam, *Scourge of Human Folly*, 241.

94. Quinton, interview, February 27, 2014.

95. Charles Ludlam, *Camille*, in *The
Complete Plays*, 251.

96. Alexander Dumas, Jr., *Camille*, translated by Matilda Heron (New York: Books for
Libraries Press, 1971), 64.

97. Linda Hutcheon, *A Theory of Adaptation* (New York: Routledge, 2006), 9.

98. Lester, "Holy Foolery," 1.

99. Alan Sinfield, *Out on Stage: Lesbian
and Gay Theatre in the Twentieth Century*
(New Haven: Yale University Press, 1999), 299.

100. Roemer, *Charles Ludlam*, 99.

101. Chesley, "Dialogue with the Ridiculous," from the Charles Ludlam Papers at the
Billy Rose Theatre Collection, 25.

102. Ludlam, *Scourge*, 42.

103. Chesley, "Dialogue with the Ridiculous," 29, courtesy Charles Ludlam Papers in
the Billy Rose Theatre Collection, call number
8-MWEZ+n.c. 29.277, folder #2.

104. Savran, *A Queer Sort of Materialism*, 60.

105. *Ibid.*, 45.

106. Ludlam, *Scourge of Human Folly*, 45.

107. Ludlam, *Camille*, 229.

108. *Ibid.*, 246.

109. Charles Ludlam, quoted in Kaufman,
Ridiculous!, 193.

110. Charles Ludlam, personal notes,
found in the Charles Ludlam Papers at the
Billy Rose Theatre Collection in the New York
Public Library for the Performing Arts, call
number 8-MWEZ+n.c. 29.256, folder #5.

111. Interview conducted by Ted Castle for
ArtForum, March 30, 1981, page 3, transcript
found in the Charles Ludlam Papers in the
Billy Rose Theatre Collection at the New York
Public Library for the Performing Arts, call
number 8-MWEZ+n.c. 29.277, folder #12.

112. Notebook kept by Charles Ludlam,
found in the Charles Ludlam Papers in the
Billy Rose Theatre Collection at the New York
Public Library for the Performing Arts, call
number 8-MWEZ+n.c. 29.257, folder #6.

Chapter Two

1. Max Gold, "Eastern Meets West:
1944's Cobra Woman," *PopMatters*, July 21,

2010, http://www.popmatters.com/post/128 101-cobra-woman/.

2. Jack Halberstam, *In a Queer Time and Place* (New York: New York University Press, 2005), 186.

3. Richard Dyer, *The Culture of Queers* (New York: Routledge, 2002), 33–34.

4. Todd J. Ormsbee, *The Meaning of Gay: Interaction, Publicity, and Community among Homosexual Men in 1960s San Francisco* (Lanham, MD: Lexington Books, 2012), 259.

5. Rachel Joseph, "Glittering Junk: Jack Smith and the Vast Landfill of Identity," *The Journal of American Drama and Theatre* 25, no. 2 (2013): 77–90.

6. Uzi Parnes, http://uziny.com/Uzi_Parnes_on_Jack_Smith-94.pdf, 163.

7. Christopher Gair, *The American Counterculture, 1945–1975* (Edinburgh: Edinburgh University Press, 2007), 113.

8. Jack Smith, *What's Underground About Marshmallows?*, I.A.2086, Museum of Modern Art P.S.1 Archives, New York.

9. Ronald Tavel, "Maria Montez: Anima of an Antediluvian World," in *Flaming Creature* (London: Serpents Tail, 1997), 12.

10. Jack Smith, "Art and Art History," I.A.208.7, Museum of Modern Art P.S.1 Archives, New York.

11. Jack Sargeant, *Naked Lens: Beat Cinema* (Berkeley: Counterpoint Press, 2009), 104.

12. *Ibid.*

13. Steven Watson, *Factory Made: Warhol and the Sixties* (New York: Random House, 2003), 52.

14. Sargeant, *Naked Lens*, 102.

15. Jack Smith, qtd. in *Experimental Cinema: The Film Reader*, edited by Wheeler W. Dixon, Gwendolyn Audrey Foster (New York: Psychology Press, 2002), 164.

16. Richard Dyer, *Heavenly Bodies: Film Stars and Society* (New York: Psychology Press, 2004), 143.

17. See Jack Halberstam, *The Queer of Art Failure* (Durham: Duke University Press, 2011).

18. Tavel, "Maria Montez," *Flaming Creature*, 95.

19. Some of these pieces, particularly the male brassieres, were on display at the Whitney Museum, New York City, as part of the 2013–2014 exhibit *Rituals of Rented Island*.

20. Tavel, "Maria Montez," 100.

21. Watson, *Factory Made*, 52.

22. Internet Movie Database Entry on Maria Montez, http://www.imdb.com/name/nm0599688/bio?ref_=nm_ov_bio_sm, accessed March 3, 2013.

23. Tavel, *Jack Smith and the Destruction of Atlantis* documentary.

24. Douglas Crimp, *"Our Kind of Movie": The Films of Andy Warhol* (Cambridge: MIT Press, 2012), 133.

25. *Jack Smith and the Destruction of Atlantis* documentary.

26. Jeffreys, "An Outré Entrée," 108.

27. Jack Smith, "Actavistic, Action Packed, Action Acting of PFA," in *Wait for Me at the Bottom of the Pool* (London: Serpent's Tale, 2008), 165.

28. *Ibid.*, 166.

29. Sargeant, *Naked Lens*, 105–60.

30. Halberstam, *In a Queer Time and Place*, 178.

31. Julie Kristeva, "Word, Dialogue, and Novel," in *The Kristeva Reader* (New York: Columbia University Press, 1986), 66.

32. Marvin Carlson, *The Haunted Stage: The Theatre as Memory Machine* (Ann Arbor: University of Michigan Press, 2003), 17.

33. Sean F. Edgecomb, "The Ridiculous Performance of Taylor Mac," *Theatre Journal* 64, no. 4 (2012): 553.

34. Carlson, *The Haunted Stage*, 2.

Chapter Three

1. Charles Ludlam quoted on the back cover of Jack Smith, J. Hoberman and Edward Leffingwell, eds., *Wait for Me at the Bottom of the Pool: The Writings of Jack Smith* (London and New York: Serpent's Tail Press, 1997).

2. Uzi Parnes, interview with the author, October 8, 2013.

3. Gary Indiana, *Andy Warhol and the Can That Sold the World* (ReadHowYouWant. com: Limited, 2010), 60.

4. *Jack Smith and the Destruction of Atlantis*, directed and written by Mary Jordan, produced by Tongue Press, 2006, accessed via YouTube, http://www.youtube.com/watch?v=8AWRGH8jIJY.

5. C. D. Innes, *Holy Theatre: Ritual & the Avant-Garde* (New York: Cambridge University Press, 1981), 7.

6. Jack Smith was a key influence on Andy Warhol, which I discuss in a later section of this chapter. In terms of durationality, Smith's impact is clear; films like Warhol's *Empire* (1964) are entirely preoccupied with long stretches of time and the things that happen, and do not happen, during that time.

7. Sally Banes, *Subversive Expectations: Performance Art and Paratheater in New York, 1976–85* (Ann Arbor: University of Michigan Press, 1998), 278.

8. Rachel Joseph, "Glittering Junk: Jack Smith and the Vast Landfill of Identity," *The Journal of American Drama and Theatre* 25, no. 2 (2013): 77–90.

9. Joe Pogostin Transcript, I.A.2087, Museum of Modern Art PS1 Archives, New York.

10. Uzi Parnes, "Jack Smith: Legendary Filmmaker, Theatrical Genius, and Exotic Art Consultant," *New York* (1994): 163, accessed from http://uziny.com/Uzi_Parnes_on_Jack_Smith-94.pdf, accessed September 1, 2013.

11. Susan Slater, *Jack Smith and the Destruction of Atlantis* documentary.

12. *Ibid.*

13. Gary Comenas, "Jack Smith," on warholstars.org, http://www.warholstars.org/jack_smith.html, accessed March 3, 2013.

14. *Ibid.*

15. *Ibid.*

16. *Ibid.*

17. Sargeant, *Naked Lens*, 105–6.

18. Stefan Brecht, *Queer Theatre* (Berlin: Suhrkamp, 1978), 13.

19. Jack Smith, *Rehearsal for the Destruction of Atlantis*, 13 Film Culture, I.A.2086, Museum of Modern Art P.S.1 Archives, New York.

20. *Ibid.*

21. Jack Smith, *Rehearsal for the Destruction of Atlantis.*

22. Ronald Tavel, "Maria Montez," in *Flaming Creature*, 12.

23. Jack Smith, *Brassieres of Atlantis*, I.A.2104, Museum of Modern Art P.S.1 Archives, New York.

24. Smith, *Brassieres of Atlantis.*

25. *Ibid.*

26. *Ibid.*

27. Jack Halberstam, *The Queer Art of Failure* (Durham: Duke University Press, 2011), 89.

28. *Ibid.*, 88.

29. *Ibid.*

30. Laurence Senelick, "Text and Violence: Performance Practices of the Modernist Avant-Garde," in *Contours of the Theatrical Avant-Garde*, edited by James Harding (Ann Arbor: University of Michigan Press, 2000), 32–33.

31. Jack Smith, *Secrets of the Brass. Mus.* I.A.2102, Museum of Modern Art P.S.1 Archives, New York.

32. Jack Smith, *What's Underground About Marshmallows?*

33. Richard Foreman, "During the Second Half of the Sixties," in *To Free the Cinema: Jonas Mekas and the New York Underground*, edited by David E. James (Princeton: Princeton University Press, 1992), 143–44.

34. Ron Vawter, *What's Underground About Marshmallows?*, directed by Jill Godmillow, released by Facets Limited Edition DVD, 2010.

35. *Ibid.*

36. *Ibid.*

37. *Ibid.*

38. *Ibid.*, emphasis mine.

39. James Harding and Cindy Rosenthal, *Restaging the Sixties: Radical Theaters and their Legacies* (Ann Arbor: University of Michigan Press, 2006), 8.

40. Brecht, *Queer Theatre*, 16.

41. Brecht, "The Sheer Beauty of Junk," in *Flaming Creature: Jack Smith*, 43.

42. Judith Jerome, *Creating the World Waiting to Be Created: Jack Smith and D.W. Winnicott Performing Themselves* (Ann Arbor: ProQuest, 2007), 312.

43. *Ibid.*

44. Parnes, interview, October 8, 2013.

45. Richard Foreman, "During the Second Half of the Sixties," 26–27.

46. Jonas Mekas, in *Jack Smith: Flaming Creature*, 48.

47. Based on ideas in Stephen J. Bottoms's *Playing Underground: A Critical History of the 1960s Off-Off-Broadway Movement* (Ann Arbor: University of Michigan Press, 2006).

48. Parnes, interview, October 8, 2013.

49. Pogostin transcript.

50. J. Hoberman, *Flaming Creature*, 2.

51. Naomi Fiegelson, *Underground Revolution: Hippies, Yippies, and Others* (New York: Funk & Wagnalls, 1970), 171.

52. *Ibid.*

53. *Ibid.*, 172.
54. Elizabeth Freeman, "Preface," in *Time Binds: Queer Temporalities, Queer Histories* (Durham: Duke University Press, 2010), xxii.
55. Pogostin, transcript.
56. Jack Smith quoted in *The East Village Other* 1, no. 24 (1966), accessed via http://www.beatbooks.com/shop/beatbooks/32099.html, accessed October 13, 2013.
57. Pogostin, transcript.
58. Bottoms, *Playing Underground*, 216.
59. Susan Sontag, "Jack Smith's *Flaming Creatures*," in *Against Interpretation: And Other Essays* (New York: Macmillan, 1966), 229–30.
60. Mark C. Carnes, *The Columbia History of Post-World War II America* (New York: Columbia University Press, 2013), 113.
61. *Ibid.*
62. Arnold Aronson, *American Avant-Garde Theatre: A History* (New York: Psychology Press, 2000), 182.
63. Bottoms, *Playing Underground*, 216.
64. Jack Smith, *Secrets of the Brass. Mus.* I.A.2102, Museum of Modern Art P.S.1 Archives, New York, 12.
65. *Jack Smith and the Destruction of Atlantis* documentary.
66. For my purposes, I am only concerning myself with his connection to Jack Smith, but Victor Bockris, for one, claims that "one of the key points of Andy's character was his ability to share his life with whoever he spent time with. There was an openness towards others that let them feel as if they were doing something equally with him and were in a sense part of him" (*Warhol: The Biography* [Cambridge: Da Capo Press, 2009], 98). In a sense, those who worked with Warhol felt as though they were a part of him and had contributed to who he would become. Some felt good about this connection; others, like Smith, felt abused by it.
67. Andy Warhol and Pat Hackett, *POPism: The Warhol Sixties* (New York: Penguin Adult, 2007), 32.
68. Performers like Candy Darling and Holly Woodlawn would be referred to as Warhol Superstars.
69. Carlson, *The Haunted Stage*, 4–5.
70. Craig Highberger, *Superstar in a Housedress: The Life and Legend of Jackie Curtis* (New York: Chamberlain Bros., 2005), 70.

71. *Ibid.*
72. *Ibid.*, 94.

Chapter Four

1. Jay Sanders, "Love Is an Object," in *Rituals of Rented Island: Object Theater, Loft Performance, and the New Psychodrama—Manhattan, 1970–1980* (New Haven: Yale University Press, 2013), 28.
2. Lawrence Lessig, *Remix: Making Art and Commerce Thrive in the Hybrid Economy* (New York: Penguin, 2008), 20.
3. Paul D. Miller aka DJ Spooky That Subliminal Kid and Peter Lunenfeld, *Rhythm Science* (Cambridge: MIT Press, 2004), 5.
4. Linda Hutcheon, *The Politics of Postmodernism* (New York: Routledge, 2002), 1.
5. Stephen J. Bottoms, *Playing Underground: A Critical History of the 1960s Off-Off-Broadway Movement* (Ann Arbor: University of Michigan Press, 2006), 3.
6. *Ibid.*, 7.
7. Gary Comenas, "Conquest of the Ridiculous: Ronald Tavel, John Vaccaro, and Charles Ludlam," last modified November 2009, accessed December 4, 2012, http://www.warholstars.org/ridiculous.html.
8. Dan Isaac, "Ronald Tavel," *TDR* 13, no. 1 (Autumn, 1968): 108.
9. Comenas, "Conquest of the Ridiculous," http://www.warholstars.org/ridiculous.html.
10. Mary Ann Caws, "The Poetics of the Manifesto: Nowness and Newness," in *Manifesto: A Century of Isms*, edited by Mary Ann Caws (Lincoln: University of Nebraska Press, 2001), xx. Emphasis in original. Interestingly, the only artist associated with the Ridiculous to create a manifesto was Charles Ludlam. His manifesto, entitled "Scourge of Human Folly," is both a how-to guide for creating a Ridiculous play and a mockery of the practice of creating a manifesto simultaneously.
11. *Ibid.*, xix.
12. Comenas, "Conquest of the Ridiculous," http://www.ronaldtavel.com/about.html, accessed December 4, 2012.
13. *Ibid.*
14. Bottoms, *Playing Underground*, 220.
15. http://www.ronaldtavel.com/about.html.
16. *Ibid.*

17. Ronald Tavel, *Gorillia Queen*, originally performed in 1967, reprinted on http://www.ronaldtavel.com/documents/gorilla_queen.pdf.

18. Legs McNeil and Gillian McCain, *Please Kill Me: The Uncensored Oral History of Punk*, Tenth Anniversary Edition (New York: Grove Press, 2016), 88.

19. *Ibid.*, 99.

20. Bruce Weber, "John Vaccaro, Whose Playhouse of the Ridiculous Gave Anarchy a Stage, Dies at 86," *New York Times*, August 11, 2016, https://www.nytimes.com/2016/08/12/theater/john-vaccaro-iconoclastic-director-dies-at-86.html.

21. *Ibid.*

22. Stefan Brecht, *Queer Theatre* (Berlin: Suhrkamp, 1978), 30.

23. *Ibid.*, 31.

24. Note to Tavel's play, qtd. in Bottoms, *Playing Underground*, 220.

25. Brecht, *Queer Theatre*, 42.

26. Bottoms, *Playing Underground*, 222.

27. This is not to suggest that playwriting and the creation of play texts was not a goal of other artists associated with the Ridiculous, most notably Charles Ludlam.

28. Bottoms, *Playing Underground*, 35.

29. Arnold Aronson, *American Avant-Garde Theatre: A History* (New York: Psychology Press, 2000), 79.

30. George Rickey, "Preface," in *Constructivism: Origins & Evolutions* (New York: G. Braziller, 1995), vii.

31. Bonnie Marranca, "Introduction," *Theatre of the Ridiculous*, edited by Bonnie Marranca and Gautum Dasgupta (New York: Performing Arts Journal, 1979), 16.

32. David Savran, *A Queer Sort of Materialism: Recontextualizing American Theatre* (Ann Arbor: University of Michigan Press, 2003), 4.

33. *Ibid.*, 3.

34. *Ibid.*

35. *Ibid.*, 4–5.

36. *Ibid.*, 5.

37. Clement Greenberg, "Avant-Garde and Kitsch," in *Art and Culture: Critical Essays* (1936; Boston: Beacon Press, 1971), 5.

38. *Ibid.*, 4.

39. *Ibid.*, 5.

40. *Ibid.*

41. Celeste Olalquiaga, *The Artificial Kingdom: On The Kitsch Experience* (Minneapolis: University of Minnesota Press, 1998), 297.

42. Ronald Tavel, "The Theatre of the Ridiculous," quoted in Dan Isaac, "Ronald Tavel: Ridiculous Playwright," *TDR* 13.1 (Autumn 1968), 107.

43. Savran, *Queer Sort of Materialism*, 6.

44. Michael Kammen, *American Culture, American Tastes: Social Change and the 20th Century* (New York: Random House, 2012), 133.

45. Marvin J. Taylor, "Playing the Field: The Downtown Scene and Cultural Production, An Introduction," in *The Downtown Scene* (Princeton: Princeton University Press, 2006), 20.

46. *Ibid.*, 21.

47. Brandon Stosuy, "Introduction," in *Up Is Up, But So Is Down: New York's Downtown Literary Scene, 1974–1992* (New York: New York University Press, 2006), 15.

48. *Ibid.*

49. Marvin J. Taylor, "Playing the Field: The Downtown Scene and Cultural Production, An Introduction," in *The Downtown Book: The New York Art Scene 1974–1984*, edited by Marvin J. Taylor, 17–40 (Princeton: Princeton University Press, 2006), 20–21.

50. *Ibid.*

51. Allan Antliff, *Anarchist Modernism: Art, Politics, and the First American Avant-Garde* (Chicago: University of Chicago Press, 2007), 2.

52. *Ibid.*

53. Bottoms, *Playing Underground*, 224.

54. *Ibid.*

55. Michael Smith, "Theatre Journal: *The Life of Lady Godiva*," *Village Voice*, March 17, 1966, 19, quoted in Stephen J. Bottoms, *Playing Underground: A Critical History of the 1960s Off-Off-Broadway Movement* (Ann Arbor: University of Michigan Press, 2006), 225.

56. Everett Quinton, interview with the author, February 27, 2014, via telephone 2–3 p.m.

57. Bottoms, *Playing Underground*, 224.

58. Simon Langford, *The Remix Manual* (New York: Taylor & Francis, 2011), 6.

59. Langford, *Remix Manual*, 6.

60. See intro to Langford's book for more on the variations of remix in musical construction.

61. https://www.sensepublishers.com/media/2734-remix-and-life-hack-in-hip-hop.pdf, 16.

62. Ronald Tavel, *The Life of Lady Godiva* in *The Theatre of the Ridiculous*, edited by Bonnie Marranca and Gautum Dasgupta (New York: Performing Arts Journal, 1979), 15. All subsequent references from the play will be noted parenthetically.

63. Robert Lacey, *Great Tales from English History: The Truth About King Arthur, Lady Godiva, Richard the Lionheart, Volume 1* (New York: Hachette Digital, 2004), 63.

64. *Ibid.*, 63–64.

65. Eva Gruber, *Humor in Contemporary Native North American Literature: Reimagining Nativeness* (Rochester: Camden House, 2008), 63.

66. *Ibid.*

67. Bottoms, *Playing Underground*, 225.

68. Lacey, *Great Tales from English History*, 65.

69. *Ibid.*

70. "Bristol Meyer Squibb Co.," *Advertising Age*, last modified September 15, 2003, http://adage.com/article/adage-encyclopedia/bristol-myers-squibb/98360/, accessed August 1, 2012.

71. Marranca, "Introduction," *Theatre of the Ridiculous*, 6–7.

72. *Ibid.*, 8.

73. Matei Calinescu, *Five Faces of Modernity: Modernism, Avant-Garde, Decadence, Kitsch, Postmodernism* (Durham: Duke University Press, 1987), 228.

74. Calinescu, *Five Faces of Modernity*, 230.

75. Bottoms, *Playing Underground*, 323.

76. *Ibid.*, 322.

77. *Ibid.*, 323.

78. *Ibid.*, 234.

79. Chris Barker, *Cultural Studies: Theory and Practice* (Thousand Oaks, CA: Sage, 2011), 206.

80. *Ibid.*

81. Michael Smith, "Theatre Journal: The Magic Show of Dr. Ma-Gico," *Village Voice*, March 22, 1973, 64.

82. Marranca, "Introduction," *Theatre of the Ridiculous*, 9–10.

83. Eduardo Navas, *Remix Theory: The Aesthetics of Sampling* (New York: Springer, 2012), 3.

84. Kenneth Bernard, *The Magic Show of Dr. Ma-Gico*, in *Theatre of the Ridiculous*, edited by Gautum Dasgupta and Bonnie Marranca (1972; New York: Performing Arts Journal, 1979), 110. All subsequent references from the play will be noted parenthetically.

85. Marranca, "Introduction," *Theatre of the Ridiculous*, 10.

86. David Kaufman, *Ridiculous! The Theatrical Life and Times of Charles Ludlam* (New York: Applause Books, 2005), 69.

87. Bottoms, *Playing Underground*, 232.

88. Kaufman, *Ridiculous!*, 72.

89. Gary Garrison, "Charles Ludlam," http://www.press.umich.edu/pdf/0472098586-ludlam.pdf, 258, accessed December 13, 2012.

90. Navas, *Remix Theory*, 8.

91. *Ibid.*, 3.

92. Brecht, *Queer Theatre*, 58.

93. *Ibid.*, 57.

94. Bottoms, *Playing Underground*, 233.

95. Brecht, *Queer Theatre*, 56.

96. Elizabeth Freeman, "Preface," *Time Binds: Queer Temporalities, Queer Histories* (Durham: Duke University Press, 2012), xix.

97. Charles Ludlam, *Conquest of the Universe or When Queens Collide* in *The Complete Plays of Charles Ludlam* (New York: Harper & Row, 1989), 34. All subsequent references from the play will be noted parenthetically.

98. Kaufman, *Ridiculous!*, 67.

99. James M. Harding, Jr., and Cindy Rosenthal, "Introduction," in *Restaging the Sixties: Radical Theatres and Their Legacies* (Ann Arbor: University of Michigan Press, 2006), 3.

100. Bottoms, *Playing Underground*, 234.

Chapter Five

1. Jay Sanders, "Love Is an Object," in *Rituals of Rented Island: Object Theater, Loft Performance, and the New Psychodrama—Manhattan, 1970–1980* (New Haven: Yale University Press, 2013), 39.

2. Ethyl Eichelberger quoted in Uzi Parnes, 281–82, quoted in Joe E. Jeffreys, "An Outré Entrée into the Para-Ridiculous Histrionics of Drag Diva Ethyl Eichelberger" (PhD diss., New York University, 1996), 104.

3. Uzi Parnes, interview with the author, October 8, 2013.

4. Joe E. Jeffreys, personal correspondence with the author, March 31, 2018, email.

5. Robert Mills, "Queer Is Here? Lesbian, Gay, Bisexual, and Transgender Histories and Public Culture," *History Workshop Journal* 62 (Autumn 2006): 253–63, 262.

6. Roselee Goldberg, "Art After Hours: Downtown Performance," in *The Downtown Book: The New York Art Scene, 1974–1984*, edited by Marvin J. Taylor (New York: Grey Art Gallery and Study Center, Fales Library, 2006), 98.

7. *Ibid.*, 100.

8. *Ibid.*, 99.

9. *Ibid.*, 114.

10. Ethyl Eichelberger, *Minnie the Maid*, qtd. in Jeffreys, "An Outré Entrée," 90–91.

11. For more on this topic, see this book's second chapter, which covers Jack Smith and his Maria Montez idol worship in more detail.

12. Rudolf Kuenzli, *Dada (Themes and Movements)* (London: Phaidon Press, 2011), 18.

13. *Ibid.*

14. Tim Miller and David Román, "Preaching to the Converted," in *The Queerest Art: Essays on Lesbian and Gay Theatre* (New York: New York University Press, 2002), 173.

15. For a comprehensive introduction to queer theory, see Annamarie Jagose's 1996 *Queer Theory: An Introduction*. Other key theorists, besides those directly mentioned in this chapter, include Michael Warner, Teresa de Lauretis, and Adrienne Rich.

16. Judith Butler, *Gender Trouble* (New York: Routledge, 1990; reprinted with new preface 1999), 95.

17. See Butler, "Preface (1999)."

18. Butler, "Preface," *Gender Trouble*, xxiv.

19. Jose Muñoz, *Cruising Utopia: The Then and There of Queer Futurity* (New York: New York University Press, 2009), 1.

20. Some would argue that Jack Smith's commitment to undoing "landlordism" and his pro-marijuana stance were political activism.

21. Heather Love, *Feeling Backward: Loss and the Politics of Queer History* (Cambridge: Harvard University Press, 2007), 24.

22. Jack Halberstam, *The Queer Art of Failure* (Durham: Duke University Press, 2011), 3.

23. Eve Shapiro, "Drag Kinging and the Transformation of Gender Identities," *Gender and Society* (2007): 251.

24. Mel Gussow, *Theatre on the Edge: New Visions, New Voices* (New York: Applause, 1998), 191.

25. *Ibid.*

26. For a more detailed account of the life and times of Eichelberger, see Joe E. Jeffrey's "An Outré Entrée into the Para-Ridiculous Histrionics of Drag Diva Ethyl Eichelberger" (PhD diss., New York University, 1996). Because that information is so well covered in that document, I did not see the need to belabor repeating it all here.

27. Jeffreys, "An Outré Entrée," 192.

28. Aram Sinnreich, *Mashed Up: Music, Technology, and the Rise of Configurable Culture* (Amherst: University of Massachusetts Press, 2010), 112.

29. Stefan Sonvilla-Weiss, *Mashup Cultures* (New York: Springer, 2010), 9.

30. From *Minnie the Maid*, available via YouTube, at http://www.youtube.com/watch?v=YNMry53o_GU.

31. *Minnie the Maid* as performed at P.S. 122 is also available via YouTube, at http://www.youtube.com/watch?v=e1CetndjCqA.

32. Marvin Carlson, *The Haunted Stage: The Theatre as Memory Machine* (Ann Arbor: University of Michigan Press, 2003), 5.

33. *Ibid.*, 140.

34. Esther Newton, *Mother Camp: Female Impersonators in America* (Chicago: University of Chicago Press, 1972), 4.

35. Jeffreys, "An Outré Entrée," 243–44.

36. George Plasketes, *Play It Again: Cover Songs in Popular Music* (London: Ashgate, 2010), 206.

37. Miller and Román, "Preaching to the Converted," 173.

38. Brett Beemyn, "Introduction," in *Creating a Place for Ourselves: Lesbian, Gay and Bisexual Community Histories*, edited by Brett Beemyn (New York: Routledge, 2013), 3.

39. Ethyl Eichelberger, *Minnie the Maid*, qtd. in Jeffreys, "An Outré Entrée," 89.

40. This description is based on what firsthand accounts, such as Jeffreys' dissertation, record, as well as the clips on YouTube, cited earlier.

41. Joe E. Jeffreys, "Introduction to *Neferet-iti*" in *Extreme Exposure: An Anthology of Solo Performance Texts from the Twentieth Century* (New York: Theatre Communications Group, 2000), 72.

42. *Ibid.*, 73.

43. Ethyl Eichelberger, *Nefert-iti*, in *Extreme Exposure: An Anthology of Solo Performance Texts from the Twentieth Century* (New York: Theatre Communications Group, 2000), 75–76. All subsequent references will be made parenthetically.
44. Plasketes, *Play It Again*, 205.
45. Jeffreys, "Introduction to *Nefert-iti*," in *Extreme Exposure*, 73.
46. Plasketes, *Play It Again*, 205–06.
47. Ethyl Eichelberger, *Dasvedanya Mama*, in *Grove New American Theater: An Anthology*, edited by Michael Feingold (New York: Grove Press, 1993), 268. All subsequent references will be made parenthetically.
48. Eichelberger quoted in George Cottingham, "Outside the Fold," August 22, 1988, 20.
49. Butler, *Gender Trouble*, 20.
50. Judith Butler, *Bodies that Matter: On the Discursive Limits of "Sex"* (New York: Routledge, 1993), 21.
51. *Jack Smith and the Destruction of Atlantis*, directed and written by Mary Jordan, produced by Tongue Press, 2006, accessed via YouTube, http://www.youtube.com/watch?v=8AWRGH8jIJY.
52. Moe Meyer, *The Politics and Poetics of Camp* (New York: Routledge, 1993), 3.
53. *Ibid.*, 2.
54. David Halperin, "Saint Foucault," qtd. in Nikki Sullivan, *Introduction to Queer Theory* (New York: New York University Press, 2003), 62.
55. *Jack Smith and the Destruction of Atlantis* documentary.
56. Jack Halberstam, *The Queer Art of Failure* (Durham: Duke University Press, 2011), 11–12.
57. Jeffreys, "An Outré Entrée," 98.
58. Ethyl Eichelberger, qtd. in Uzi Parnes, p. 287, qtd. in Jeffreys, "An Outré Entrée," 98.
59. Jeffreys, "An Outré Entrée," 101.
60. Ann Cooper Albright, *Traces of Light: Absence and Presence in the Work of Loïe Fuller* (Middletown, CT: Wesleyan University Press, 2007), 140.
61. Michael Feingold, "Editor's Note to *Dasvedanya Mama*," in *Grove New American Theatre*, 261.
62. Michael Moon, "Tragedy and Trash: Yiddish Theater and Queer Theater, Henry James, Charles Ludlam, Ethyl Eichlberger," in *Queer Theory and the Jewish Question*, edited

by Daniel Boyarin, Daniel Itzkovitz, and Anne Pelligrini (New York: Columbia University Press, 2003), 280.
63. *Ibid.*, 262.
64. For more on H. M. Koutoukas and the goings on at the Caffe Cino, see Wendell Stone's definitive account of this important pre-Ridiculous site, *Caffe Cino: The Birthplace of Off-Off-Broadway* (Carbondale: Southern Illinois University Press, 2005).
65. Kuenzli, *Dada*, 17.
66. *Ibid.*, 31.
67. https://performancespacenewyork.org/eichelberger/.

Chapter Six

1. Ethyl Eichelberger, qtd. in https://performancespacenewyork.org/eichelberger/.
2. Uzi Parnes, interview with the author, October 8, 2013.
3. Royal Young, "Review: A Post-Modern Christmas Carol at Abrons," thelowdownny.com, posted December 13, 2012, accessed December 10, 2013, http://www.thelodownny.com/leslog/tag/everett-quinton.
4. LaMaMa.org archives, http://www.lamama.org/archives/year_lists/1970page.htm, accessed January 15, 2014.
5. Charles Busch, telephone interview with the author, March 3, 2014.
6. *Ibid.*
7. *Ibid.*
8. *Ibid.*
9. *Ibid.*
10. *Ibid.*
11. *Ibid.*
12. Don Shewey, "The Tale of Charles Busch: From Drag Diva to Broadway Farceur," http://www.donshewey.com/theater_articles/charles_busch.htm, accessed January 20, 2014.
13. In his biography of Ludlam, David Kaufman narrates that after seeing *Vampire Lesbians of Sodom*, "Ludlam returned from the performance enraged, griping that superficial elements of his work had indeed been stolen, but without any of their substance" (361).
14. Frank Rich, "Scene: Europe 1940. Subject: True Kitsch," *New York Times*, July 26, 1989, accessed February 11, 2014, http://www.charlesbusch.com/Review%20-%20The%20Lady%20In%20Question%20-%20NY%20Times.htm.

15. Busch, interview, March 3, 2014.

16. *Ibid.*

17. *Ibid.*

18. *Ibid.*

19. See Sally Banes, "Junk Alchemy" for a description of this piece.

20. Charles Busch, *Vampire Lesbians of Sodom and Sleeping Beauty or Coma* (New York: Samuel French, 1985), 81. All subsequent references to the play will be made parenthetically.

21. Roemer explores this term in *Charles Ludlam and the Ridiculous Theatrical Company.*

22. Tom Smith, "Charles Busch (1954–)," in *Contemporary Gay American Poets and Playwrights: An A-to-Z Guide,* edited by Emmanuel Sampath Nelson (Westport, CT: Greenwood Publishing Group, 2003), 64.

23. Charles Busch, *Judith of Bethulia* (New York: Samuel French, 2013), back cover.

24. Busch, *Judith of Bethulia,* 5. All subsequent references to the play will be made parenthetically.

25. Ben Brantley, "A Woman on the Verge of Another Breakdown," *New York Times,* March 1, 2000, accessed January 15, 2014, http://www.nytimes.com/2000/03/01/theater/theater-review-a-woman-on-the-verge-of-another-breakdown.html.

26. John Simon, "'The Tale of the Allergist's Wife,'" *New York,* March 13, 2000, accessed February 1, 2014, nymag.com/nymetro/arts/theater/reviews/2317/.

27. Charles Busch, *The Tale of the Allergist's Wife* in *The Tale of the Allergist's Wife and Other Plays* (New York: Grove Press, 2001), 276. All subsequent references to the play will be made parenthetically.

28. Charles Busch, *The Tribute Artist,* 2014, unpublished script courtesy of Busch, 5. All subsequent references to the play will be made parenthetically.

29. "The Tribute Artist/Almost, Maine," Interview with Charles Busch and Julie Halston for *Theater Talk* with Michael Riedel and Susan Haskins, CUNY TV, February 8, 2014.

30. Frank Scheck, "A Way with Women," *New York Post,* February 10, 2010, 34.

31. Marilyn Stasio, "Off-Broadway Review: 'The Tribute Artist,'" accessed February 11, 2014, http://variety.com/2014/legit/reviews/off-broadway-review-the-tribute-artist-1201094951/.

32. "The Tribute Artist/Almost, Maine," Interview with Charles Busch and Julie Halston for *Theater Talk* with Michael Riedel and Susan Haskins, CUNY TV, February 8, 2014.

33. Scheck, "A Way with Women," 34.

34. Tony Kushner, "A Fan's Foreword," in *The Mystery of Irma Vep and Other Plays,* by Charles Ludlam (New York: Theatre Communications Group, 2001), vii.

35. Michael Cunningham, "Thinking About Fabulousness," in *Tony Kushner in Conversation,* edited by Robert Vorlicky (Ann Arbor: University of Michigan Press, 1998), 74.

36. *Ibid.,* 63.

37. Tony Kushner, "Foreword: Notes Toward a Theater of the Fabulous," in *Staging Gay Lives: An Anthology of Contemporary Gay Theater,* edited by John M. Clum (Boulder: Westview Press, 1996), vii–viii.

38. *Ibid.,* 74.

39. Ben Brantley, "This Time, the Angel Is in the Details," *New York Times,* October 28, 2010, accessed February 8, 2014, http://www.nytimes.com/2010/10/29/theater/reviews/29angels.html?pagewanted=all&_r=0.

40. Frank Rich, "Review/Theater: Angels in America; Millennium Approaches; Embracing All Possibilities in Art and Life," *New York Times,* May 5, 1993, accessed January 13, 2014, http://www.nytimes.com/mem/theater/treview.html?res=9F0CE2DC1431F936A35756C0A965958260.

41. Ken Neilsen, *Tony Kushner's Angels in America* (New York: Bloomsbury, 2013), 47.

42. Tony Kushner, *Angels in America* (New York: Theatre Communications Group, 1995), 280.

43. See Charles Ludlam, "The Avant-Garde," in *Scourge of Human Folly* (New York: Theatre Communications Group, 1992), 222.

Chapter Seven

1. Charles Isherwood, "Among the Huddled Masses, Doing Good Can Come with a High Price," *New York Times,* October 29, 2013, accessed January 20, 2014, http://www.nytimes.com/2013/10/30/theater/reviews/brechts-good-person-of-szechwan-opens-at-public-theater.html?pagewanted=1.

2. Peggy Shaw, email message to author, February 27, 2014. Sue-Ellen Case's book on

Split Britches covers the company's connections with Hot Peaches and Spiderwoman. Stefan Brecht discusses Hot Peaches in *Queer Theatre*, contrasting it with Ludlam's Ridiculous, while Spiderwoman contributor Ana Maria Simo dismissed the radical qualities of the Ridiculous (see "From the Invisible to the Ridiculous" in *The Queerest Art*). These companies suggest important connections—and counterpoints—to the Ridiculous discussion that I conduct in this book.

3. Shaw, email, February 27, 2014.

4. Peggy Shaw, *Ruff*, unpublished play script, 3–4.

5. *Ibid.*, 28.

6. *Ibid.*

7. For more on Split Britches, see books such as Sue-Ellen Case's *Split Britches: Lesbian Practice/Feminist Performance* (New York: Routledge, 2013).

8. Alexis Clements, "I Am an Archive: Tracking the Continuing Legacy of Peggy Shaw and Lois Weaver," *American Theatre Magazine*, January 14, 2014, 74–78, 74.

9. Shaw, email, February 27, 2014.

10. Clements, "I Am an Archive," 77.

11. *Ibid.*

12. Mary F. Brewer, *Race, Sex, and Gender in Contemporary Women's Theatre* (Toronto: Sussex Academic Press, 1999),160.

13. Case, *Split Britches: Lesbian Practice/Feminist Performance*, 27.

14. *Ibid.*, 28.

15. Sean F. Edgecomb, "The Ridiculous Performance of Taylor Mac," *Theatre Journal* 64 (December 2012), 549–63.

16. Angelos, et al., "From the Invisible to the Ridiculous: The Emergence of an Out Theater Aesthetic," in *The Queerest Art: Essays on Lesbian and Gay Theatre*, edited Alisa Solomon and Framji Minwalla (New York: New York University Press, 2002), 147.

17. James Wilson, "'Ladies and Gentlemen, People Die': The Uncomfortable Performances of Kiki and Herb," in *We Will Be Citizens: New Essays on Gay and Lesbian Theatre*, edited by James Fisher (Jefferson, NC: McFarland, 2006), 201.

18. Kiki and Herb, vocal performance of "The Revolution Medley," by Kiki and Herb, released February 8, 2005, on *Kiki and Herb Will Die for You: Live at Carnegie Hall*, Evolver, 2 discs, CD.

19. The film, 2004's *Imaginary Heroes*, features Kiki and Herb as the entertainment at a party.

20. Ben Brantley, "'Kiki and Herb': The Road to Catharsis with Those 2 Immortals," *New York Times*, August 16, 2006, accessed October 20, 2013, http://www.nytimes.com/2006/08/16/theater/reviews/16kiki.html?adxnnl=1&adxnnlx=1393252243-rnDW4dxGgdxflUzm1bvedg.

21. *Ibid.*

22. *Ibid.*

23. John Cameron Mitchell, *Hedwig and the Angry Inch*, text by John Cameron Mitchell, music and lyrics by Stephen Trask (New York: The Overlook Press, 1998), 14.

24. *Ibid.*, 9.

25. Peter Marks, "THEATRE REVIEW; How to Be Captivating Without a Sense of Self," *New York Times*, February 16, 1998, accessed January 20, 2014, http://www.nytimes.com/mem/theater/treview.html?res=9504E3DC1F3CF935A25751C0A96E958260.

26. *Ibid.*

27. Stephen Holden, "Hedwig and the Angry Inch (2001) FILM REVIEW; Betwixt, Between on a Glam Frontier," *New York Times*, July 20, 2001, accessed January 20, 2014, http://www.nytimes.com/movie/review?res=9C05EEDF143AF933A15754C0A9679C8B63.

28. *Ibid.*

29. Neil Patrick Harris, quoted in Patrick Healy, "As Far as Possible from His Sitcom," *New York Times*, February 19, 2014.

30. *Kinky Boots* performance at the Macy's Thanksgiving Day Parade, November 28, 2013, NBC.

31. Ben Brantley, "High Spirits, Higher Heels," *New York Times*, April 4, 2013, accessed November 30, 2013, http://www.nytimes.com/2013/04/05/theater/reviews/kinky-boots-the-harvey-fierstein-cyndi-lauper-musical.html?_r=0&pagewanted=1.

32. "'Kinky Boots' Performance at Macy's Day Parade Provokes Outrage," *The Huffington Post*, posted November 29, 2013, updated December 1, 2013, http://www.huffingtonpost.com/2013/11/29/kinky-boots-macys_n_4360035.html. The aforementioned tweets came from @ChanRussell22 and @stevemcgrew among others. The article reproduces the tweets via screenshots.

33. Todrick Hall to Andrew Isaac Burrill

for "Todrick Hall Discusses His Return to Broadway After YouTube Stardom," *HuffPost*, January 13, 2017, http://www.huffingtonpost.com/entry/todrick-hall-discusses-return-to-broadway-after-achieving_us_5876a368e4b065be69099140.

34. This occurs during the memorial scene that precedes "I'll Cover You (Reprise)" in Jonathan Larson's *Rent* developed for New York Theatre Workshop and which ran on Broadway from 1996 to 2008.

35. Certainly cross-dressing has a long tradition on Broadway stages, and vaudeville ones before that. What these musicals add to that presentation is the evocation of sexual identity or sexuality being linked to the cross-dressed representations. Unlike Mae West's 1927 play *The Drag*, these musicals have led to little in the way of raids or riots, despite the occasional angry tweets.

36. "I Am What I Am," from *La Cage aux Folles*, book by Harvey Fierstein, lyrics and music by Jerry Herman, originally produced on Broadway in 1983.

37. Ben Brantley, "Through Hot Pink Glasses, a World That's Nice," *New York Times*, August 16, 2012, accessed December 20, 2013, http://www.nytimes.com/mem/theater/treview.html?res=9F0CE1DA173DF935A2575BC0A9649C8B63&_r=0.

38. Charles Isherwood, "With Song in Heart, Pompoms on Head," *New York Times*, March 20, 2011, accessed November 30, 2013, http://www.nytimes.com/2011/03/21/theater/reviews/priscilla-queen-of-the-desert-on-broadway-review.html?_r=0.

Conclusion

1. Everett Quinton, telephone interview with the author, March 3, 2014.

2. Gregory J. Seigworth and Melissa Gregg, "An Inventory of Shimmers," in *The Affect Theory Reader*, edited Melissa Gregg and Gregory J. Seigworth (Durham: Duke University Press, 2010), 3.

3. *Ibid.*, 10.

4. *Ibid.*

5. Eve Kosofsky Sedgwick, *Touching Feel-ing: Affect, Pedagogy, Performativity* (Durham: Duke University Press, 2003), 38.

6. *Ibid.*

7. Ethyl Eichelberger, *Dasvedanya Mama*, in *Grove New American Theatre: An Anthology*, edited by Michael Feingold (New York: Grove Press, 1993), 296.

8. Dialogue by Charles Ludlam, reprinted in *Ridiculous! The Theatrical Life and Times of Charles Ludlam*, by David Kaufman (New York: Applause Theatre and Cinema Books, 2002), 450. Of the one-page scene, Kaufman notes that it "was based on a conversation that actually transpired between Quinton and himself [Ludlam]. Ludlam probably wrote it sometime in March, at a moment when he was feeling ill and realized his days might be numbered."

9. For more on Quinton's leadership of the RTC, see James Fisher, *Historical Dictionary of Contemporary American Theatre, 1930–2010* (New York: Scarecrow Press, 2011), 653.

10. Under the "History" tab of their website, the Axis Company provides a brief but thorough overview of the site's storied past. http://www.axiscompany.org/history.htm.

11. Christopher Mele, *Selling the Lower East Side: Culture, Real Estate, and Resistance in New York City* (Minneapolis: University of Minnesota Press, 2000), 284.

12. Wendell Stone, *Caffe Cino: The Birthplace of Off-Off-Broadway* (Carbondale: Southern Illinois University Press, 2005), 2.

13. Uzi Parnes, interview with the author, October 8, 2013.

14. Edgecomb, *Ludlam Lives!*, 174.

15. *Ibid.*, 175.

16. *Ibid.*, 176.

17. See Chapter Three.

18. Charles Ludlam, "Broadway," in *Ridiculous Theatre: Scourge of Human Folly, the Essays and Opinions of Charles* Ludlam, edited by Samuel Stevens (New York: Theatre Communications Group, 1992), 198.

19. Sally Banes, "Junk Alchemy (Jack Smith)," in *Subversive Expectations: Performance Art and Paratheater in New York, 1976–85* (Ann Arbor: University of Michigan Press, 1998), 278.

Bibliography

Libraries, Archives, Exhibits

Billy Rose Theatre Division
Museum of Modern Art
New York Public Library for the Performing Arts
P.S. 1 Archive
Rituals of Rented Island: Object Theater, Loft Performance, and the New Psychodrama—Manhattan, 1970–1980
Whitney Museum of American Art; October 31, 2013–February 2, 2014

Newspapers and Magazines

American Theatre
New York Magazine
New York Post
New York Times
Village Voice
Villager

Interviews

Charles Busch, playwright. Interviewed by Kelly Aliano. March 3, 2014.
Joe E. Jeffreys, Ridiculous scholar. Responded to manuscript via email. March 31, 2018.
Uzi Parnes, collaborator of Jack Smith and expert on Pop Performance. Interviewed by Kelly Aliano. October 8, 2013.
Everett Quinton, former member of the Ridiculous Theatrical Company and actor. Interviewed by Kelly Aliano. February 27, 2014.
Peggy Shaw, member of Split Britches and performer of *Ruff* at LaMaMa E.T.C. in early 2014. Interviewed via email by Kelly Aliano. February 27, 2014.

Published Plays

Bernard, Kenneth. *The Magic Show of Dr. Ma-Gico.* 1972. In *Theatre of the Ridiculous*, edited by Gautum Dasgupta and Bonnie Marranca, 107–33. New York: Performing Arts Journal, 1979.
Busch, Charles. *Judith of Bethulia.* New York: Samuel French, 2013.

195

_____. *The Tale of the Allergist's Wife*. In *The Tale of the Allergist's Wife and Other Plays*, 267–344. New York: Grove Press, 2001.

_____. *The Tribute Artist*. New York: Samuel French, 2014.

_____. *Vampire Lesbians of Sodom and Sleeping Beauty or Coma*. New York: Samuel French, 1985.

Dumas, Alexander, Jr. *Camille*. Translated by Matilda Heron. New York: Books for Libraries Press, 1971.

Eichelberger, Ethyl. *Dasvedanya Mama*. In *Grove New American Theater: An Anthology*, edited by Michael Feingold, 259–96. New York: Grove Press, 1993.

_____. *Nefert-iti*. In *Extreme Exposure: An Anthology of Solo Performance Texts from the Twentieth Century*, edited by Jo Bonney, 72–81. New York: Theatre Communications Group, 2000.

Kushner, Tony. *Angels in America*. New York: Theatre Communications Group, 1995.

_____. *A Bright Room Called Day*. New York: Theatre Communications Group, 1994.

Ludlam, Charles. *The Artificial Jungle*. In *The Complete Plays of Charles Ludlam*, by Charles Ludlam, 877–905. New York: Perennial Library, 1989.

_____. *Big Hotel*. In *The Complete Plays of Charles Ludlam*, by Charles Ludlam, 1–24. New York: Perennial Library, 1989.

_____. *Le Bourgeois Avant-Garde*. In *The Complete Plays of Charles Ludlam*, by Charles Ludlam, 697–730. New York: Harper & Row, 1989.

_____. *Camille*. In *The Complete Plays of Charles Ludlam*, by Charles Ludlam, 221–52. New York: Harper & Row, 1989.

_____. *Conquest of the Universe or When Queens Collide*. In *The Complete Plays of Charles Ludlam*, by Charles Ludlam, 25–48. New York: Harper & Row, 1989.

_____. *The Grand Tarot*. In *The Complete Plays of Charles Ludlam*, by Charles Ludlam, 83–114. New York: Harper & Row, 1989.

_____. *How to Write a Play*. In *The Complete Plays of Charles Ludlam*, by Charles Ludlam, 815–44. New York: Harper & Row, 1989.

Mitchell, John Cameron. *Hedwig and the Angry Inch*. Script by John Cameron Mitchell. Music and lyrics by Stephen Trask. New York: The Overlook Press, 1998.

Smith, Jack. *Rehearsal for the Destruction of Atlantis. Film Culture*. I.A.2086, Museum of Modern Art P.S. 1 Archive, New York. Published in *Wait for Me at the Bottom of the Pool*, edited by J. Hoberman and Edward Leffingwell, 90–96. New York: Serpent's Tail, 1997.

_____. *What's Underground About Marshmallows?* I.A.2086, Museum of Modern Art P.S. 1 Archive, New York. Published in *Wait for Me at the Bottom of the Pool*, edited by J. Hoberman and Edward Leffingwell, 137–44. New York: Serpent's Tail, 1997.

Tavel, Ronald. *Gorilla Queen*. Originally performed in 1967. Reprinted at http://www.ronaldtavel.com/documents/gorilla_queen.pdf.

_____. *The Life of Lady Godiva*. In *The Theatre of the Ridiculous*, edited by Gautum Dasgupta and Bonnie Marranca, 13–50. New York: Performing Arts Journal, 1979.

Unpublished Plays

Eichelberger, Ethyl. "Minnie the Maid." Quoted in Jeffreys, Joe E. "An Outré Entrée into the Para-Ridiculous Histrionics of Drag Diva Ethyl Eichelberger." PhD Diss., New York University, 1996.

Shaw, Peggy. "Ruff." Unpublished play script. Courtesy Jonathan Slaff, 2013. Accessed digitally.

Smith, Jack. "Brassieres of Atlantis." I.A.2104, Museum of Modern Art P.S.1 Archives, New York.

_____. "Secrets of the Brass. Mus." I.A.2102, Museum of Modern Art P.S.1 Archives, New York.

Films and Recordings

Brooks, Richard, and Gene Lewis. *Cobra Woman*. Directed by Robert Siodmak. Universal Pictures, 1944. Running time: 71 minutes.

Eichelberger, Ethyl. *Minnie the Maid*. YouTube video, 1:41, from a performance recorded February 8, 1987 at P.S. 122, New York. http://www.youtube.com/watch?v=elCet ndjCqA.

Eichelberger, Ethyl. *Minnie the Maid*. YouTube video, 5:59, from a performance at the Pyramid Club. Video by Nelson Sullivan. http://www.youtube.com/watch?v= YNMry53o_GU.

"I Am What I Am." From *La Cage aux Folles*. Book by Harvey Fierstein, Lyrics and music by Jerry Herman. Originally produced on Broadway in 1983.

Jordon, Mary. *Jack Smith and the Destruction of Atlantis*. YouTube video, 1:35:05. Produced by Tongue Press, 2006. http://www.youtube.com/watch?v=8AWRGH8jIJY.

Kiki and Herb. *Kiki and Herb Will Die for You: Live at Carnegie Hall*. Evolver. Released February 8, 2005, 2 discs.

Kinky Boots. Original Broadway Cast Recording. Masterworks Broadway. Released May 28, 2013, 1 disc.

Lady Gaga. "Applause." *Artpop*. Interscope Records. Released 2013, 1 disc.

"The Tribute Artist/Almost, Maine." Interview with Charles Busch and Julie Halston for *Theater Talk* with Michael Riedel and Susan Haskins, CUNY TV, February 8, 2014.

Vawter, Ron. *What's Underground About Marshmallows?* Directed by Jill Godmillow. Facets Limited Edition DVD, 2010.

Books, Articles, Websites

Albright, Ann Cooper. *Traces of Light: Absence and Presence in the Work of Loïe Fuller*. Middletown, CT: Wesleyan University Press, 2007.

Angelos, Moe, et al. "From the Invisible to the Ridiculous: The Emergence of an Out Theater Aesthetic." In *The Queerest Art: Essays on Lesbian and Gay Theatre*, edited by Alisa Solomon and Framji Minwalla, 135–51. New York: New York University Press, 2002.

Antliff, Allan. *Anarchist Modernism: Art, Politics, and the First American Avant-Garde*. Chicago: University of Chicago Press, 2007.

Argelander, Ronald. "Charles Ludlam's Ridiculous Theatrical Company: A Way of Working in the Theatre." Found in the Charles Ludlam Papers in the Billy Rose Theatre Collection at the New York Public Library for the Performing Arts, call number 8-MWEZ+n.c. 29.277, folder #3. Published in *The Drama Review* 18 no. 2 (1974): 81–86.

Aristotle. *Poetics*. In *Theatre, Theory, Theatre*, edited by Daniel Gerould, 43–67. New York: Applause Books, 2003.

Aronson, Arnold. *American Avant-Garde Theatre: A History*. New York: Psychology Press, 2000.

Axis Theatre Company. http://www.axiscompany.org/history.htm.

Banes, Sally. *Subversive Expectations: Performance Art and Paratheater in New York, 1976–85*. Ann Arbor: University of Michigan Press, 1998.

Barker, Chris. *Cultural Studies: Theory and Practice*. Thousand Oaks, CA: Sage, 2011.

Beemyn, Brett. *Creating a Place for Ourselves: Lesbian, Gay and Bisexual Community Histories*. Edited by Brett Beemyn. New York: Routledge, 2013.

Bentley, Eric. *Thinking About the Playwright*. Evanston: Northwestern University Press, 1987.

Bockris, Victor. *Warhol: The Biography*. Cambridge: Da Capo Press, 2009.

Bolter, J. David, and Richard Grusin. *Remediation: Understanding New Media*. Cambridge: MIT Press, 2000.

Bond, Justin Vivian. "New Year, New Name, New Gender." In *Justin Vivian Bond: A User's Guide*. Posted January 1, 2011, http://justinbond.com/?p=537.

Bottoms, Stephen J. *Playing Underground: A Critical History of the 1960s Off-Off-Broadway Movement*. Ann Arbor: University of Michigan Press, 2006.

Brantley, Ben. "High Spirits, Higher Heels." *New York Times*, April 4, 2013. Accessed November 30, 2013. http://www.nytimes.com/2013/04/05/theater/reviews/kinky-boots-the-harvey-fierstein-cyndi-lauper-musical.html?_r=0&pagewanted=1.

_____. "'Kiki and Herb': The Road to Catharsis with Those 2 Immortals." *New York Times*. August 16, 2006. Accessed October 20, 2013. http://www.nytimes.com/2006/08/16/theater/reviews/16kiki.html?adxnnl=1&adxnnlx=1393252243-rnDW4dxGgdxf1Uzm1bvedg.

_____. "This Time, the Angel Is in the Details." *New York Times*, October 28, 2010. Accessed February 8, 2014. http://www.nytimes.com/2010/10/29/theater/reviews/29angels.html?pagewanted=all&_r=0.

_____. "Through Hot Pink Glasses, a World That's Nice." *New York Times*, August 16, 2012. Accessed December 20, 2013. http://www.nytimes.com/mem/theater/treview.html?res=9F0CE1DA173DF935A2575BC0A9649C8B63&_r=0

_____. "A Woman on the Verge of Another Breakdown." *New York Times*, March 1, 2000. Accessed January 15, 2014. http://www.nytimes.com/2000/03/01/theater/theater-review-a-woman-on-the-verge-of-another-breakdown.html.

Brecht, Stefan. *Queer Theatre*. Berlin: Suhrkamp, 1978.

_____. "The Sheer Beauty of Junk," in *Flaming Creature: Jack Smith, His Amazing Life and Times*, edited by Edward Leffingwell, 43–47. New York: Serpent's Tail, 1997.

Brewer, Mary F. *Race, Sex, and Gender in Contemporary Women's Theatre*. Toronto: Sussex Academic Press, 1999.

"Bristol Meyer Squibb Co." *Advertising Age*. Last modified September 15, 2003. Accessed August 1, 2012. http://adage.com/article/adage-encyclopedia/bristol-myers-squibb/98360/.

Brockett, Oscar G., and Franklin J. Hildy. *History of the Theatre, Tenth Edition*. New York: Pearson, 2008.

Burrill, Andrew Isaac. "Todrick Hall Discusses His Return to Broadway After YouTube Stardom." *HuffPost*. January 13, 2017. Accessed August 28, 2017. http://www.huffingtonpost.com/entry/todrick-hall-discusses-return-to-broadway-after-achieving_us_5876a368e4b065be69099140.

Butler, Judith. *Bodies That Matter: On the Discursive Limits of "Sex."* New York: Routledge, 1993.

_____. *Gender Trouble: Feminism and the Subversion of Identity*. New York: Routledge, 2011.

Calinescu, Matei. *Five Faces of Modernity: Modernism, Avant-Garde, Decadence, Kitsch, Postmodernism*. Durham: Duke University Press, 1987.

Carlson, Marvin. *The Haunted Stage: The Theatre as Memory Machine*. Ann Arbor: University of Michigan Press, 2003.

Carnes, Mark C. *The Columbia History of Post-World War II America*. New York: Columbia University Press, 2013.

Case, Sue-Ellen. *Split Britches: Lesbian Practice/Feminist Performance*. New York: Routledge, 2013.

Caws, Mary Ann. "The Poetics of the Manifesto: Nowness and Newness," in *Manifesto:*

A Century of Isms, edited by Mary Ann Caws, xix–xxxii. Lincoln: University of Nebraska Press, 2001.

Chesley, Robert. "Dialogue with the Ridiculous." *Omega One*, January 19, 1979. Found in the Charles Ludlam Papers in the Billy Rose Theatre Collection at the New York Public Library for the Performing Arts, call number 8-MWEZ+n.c. 29.277, folder #2.

Clements, Alexis. "I Am an Archive: Tracking the Continuing Legacy of Peggy Shaw and Lois Weaver." *American Theatre Magazine*, January 14, 2014.

Cleto, Fabio. "Introduction: Queering the Camp," in *Camp: Queer Aesthetics and the Performing Subject: A Reader*, edited by Fabio Cleto, 1–42. Ann Arbor: University of Michigan Press, 1999.

Comenas, Gary. "Conquest of the Ridiculous: Ronald Tavel, John Vaccaro, and Charles Ludlam." Last modified November 2009. Accessed December 4, 2012. http://www.warholstars.org/ridiculous.html.

_____. "Jack Smith." Accessed November 30, 2012. http://www.warholstars.org/jack_smith.html.

Cottingham, George. "Outside the Fold." August 22, 1988. Cited in Jeffreys, Joe E. "An Outré Entrée into the Para-Ridiculous Histrionics of Drag Diva Ethyl Eichelberger." PhD Dissertation. New York University, 1996.

Crimp, Douglas. *"Our Kind of Movie": The Films of Andy Warhol*. Cambridge: MIT Press, 2012.

Cunningham, Michael. "Thinking About Fabulousness," in *Tony Kushner in Conversation*, edited by Robert Vorlicky, 62–76. Ann Arbor: University of Michigan Press, 1998.

Dixon, Wheeler W., and Gwendolyn Audrey Foster, Editors. *Experimental Cinema: The Film Reader*. New York: Psychology Press, 2002.

Dolan, Jill. "Building a Theatrical Vernacular: Responsibility, Community, Ambivalence, and Queer Theatre," in *The Queerest Art: Essays on Lesbian and Gay Theatre*, edited by Alisa Solomon and Framji Minwalla. New York: New York University Press, 2002, 1–8.

Dyer, Richard. *The Culture of Queers*. New York: Routledge, 2002.

_____. *Heavenly Bodies: Film Stars and Society*. New York: Psychology Press, 2004.

Edgecomb, Sean F. *Charles Ludlam Lives! Charles Busch, Bradford Louryk, Taylor Mac and the Queer Legacy of the Ridiculous Theatrical Company*. Ann Arbor: University of Michigan Press, 2017.

_____. "The Ridiculous Performance of Taylor Mac." *Theatre Journal* 64, no. 4 (2012): 549–63.

"Ethyl Eicherlberger." Accessed March 31, 2018. https://performancespacenewyork.org/eichelberger/.

Feingold, Michael. "Editor's Note to Dasvedanya Mama," in *Grove New American Theatre: An Anthology*, edited by Michael Feingold, 261–62. New York: Grove Press, 1993.

Fiegelson, Naomi. *Underground Revolution: Hippies, Yippies, and Others*. New York: Funk & Wagnalls, 1970.

Firat, Begüm Özden, and Aylin Kuryel, eds. *Cultural Activism: Practices, Dilemmas, and Possibilities*. New York: Rodopi, 2011.

Fisher, James. *Historical Dictionary of Contemporary American Theatre, 1930–2010*. New York: Scarecrow Press, 2011.

Foreman, Richard. "During the Second Half of the Sixties," in *To Free the Cinema: Jonas Mekas and the New York Underground*, edited by David E. James, 138–44. Princeton: Princeton University Press, 1992.

Freeman, Elizabeth. *Time Binds: Queer Temporalities, Queer Histories*. Durham: Duke University Press, 2010.

Gair, Christopher. *The American Counterculture, 1945–1975.* Edinburgh: Edinburgh University Press, 2007.

Garrison, Gary. "Charles Ludlam." Accessed June 1, 2013. http://www.press.umich.edu/pdf/0472098586-ludlam.pdf.

Gillespie, Benjamin. "Theatre Review: *Ruff.*" *Theatre Journal* 65, no. 4 (2013): 576–77.

Gold, Max. "Eastern Meets West: 1944's Cobra Woman." *PopMatters*, July 21, 2010. http://www.popmatters.com/post/128101-cobra-woman/.

Goldberg, Roselee. "Art After Hours: Downtown Performance," in *The Downtown Book: The New York Art Scene, 1974–1984*, edited by Marvin J. Taylor, 97–103. New York: Grey Art Gallery and Study Center, Fales Library, 2006.

Greenberg, Clement. "Avant-Garde and Kitsch." 1939. In *Art and Culture: Critical Essays.* Boston: Beacon Press, 1971. http://books.google.com/books?id=OZEDAQAAQBAJ&pg=PT4&dq=art+and+culture:+critical+essays&source=gbs_selected_pages&cad=2#v=onepage&q=art%20and%20culture%3A%20critical%20essays&f=false.

Gregg, Melissa, and Gregory J. Seigworth. "An Inventory of Shimmers," in *The Affect Theory Reader*, edited by Melissa Gregg and Gregory J. Seigworth. Durham: Duke University Press, 2010.

Gruber, Eva. *Humor in Contemporary Native North American Literature: Reimagining Nativeness.* Rochester: Camden House, 2008.

Gussow, Mel. "Ludlam Star of 'Camille in Title Role.'" *New York Times*, May 4, 1973, L4. Accessed June 7, 2013. http://search.proquest.com.ezproxy.gc.cuny.edu/docview/119625618/fulltextPDF/13F4DC0FDA35A7DDA2C/1?accountid=7287.

_____. *Theatre on the Edge: New Visions, New Voices.* New York: Applause, 1998.

Halberstam, Judith. *The Queer Art of Failure.* Durham: Duke University Press, 2011.

Halperin, David. *Saint Foucault: Toward a Gay Hagiography.* New York: Oxford University Press, 1995.

Harding, James, and Cindy Rosenthal. *Restaging the Sixties: Radical Theaters and their Legacies.* Ann Arbor: University of Michigan Press, 2006.

Harding, James M., and John Rouse, eds. *Not the Other Avant-Garde: The Transnational Foundations of the Avant-Garde.* Ann Arbor: University of Michigan Press, 2006.

Healy, Patrick. "As Far as Possible from His Sitcom." *New York Times*, February 19, 2014. Accessed February 23, 2014. http://mobile.nytimes.com/2014/02/23/theater/neil-patrick-harris-prepares-for-hedwig-and-the-angry-inch.html?hpw&rref=arts&_r=1&referrer=.

Highberger, Craig. *Superstar in a Housedress: The Life and Legend of Jackie Curtis.* New York: Chamberlain Bros., 2005.

Hoberman, J. *On Jack's Smith's Flaming Creatures (and Other Secret-Flix of Cinemaroc).* New York: Granary Books/Hips Road, 2001.

Holden, Stephen. "Hedwig and the Angry Inch (2001) FILM REVIEW; Betwixt, Between On a Glam Frontier." *New York Times*, July 20, 2001. Accessed January 20, 2014. http://www.nytimes.com/movie/review?res=9C05EEDF143AF933A15754C0A9679C8B63.

Hutcheon, Linda. *The Politics of Postmodernism.* New York: Routledge, 2002.

_____. *A Theory of Adaptation.* New York: Routledge, 2006.

Indiana, Gary. *Andy Warhol and the Can That Sold the World.* ReadHowYouWant.com: Limited, 2010.

Innes, C. D. *Holy Theatre: Ritual & the Avant-Garde.* New York: Cambridge University Press, 1981.

Internet Movie Database Entry on Maria Montez, http://www.imdb.com/name/nm0599688/bio?ref_=nm_ov_bio_sm.

Isaac, Dan. "Ronald Tavel." *TDR* 13, no. 1 (1968): 106–15.

Isherwood, Charles. "Among the Huddled Masses, Doing Good Can Come with a High

Price." *New York Times*, October 29, 2013. Accessed January 20, 2014. http://www.nytimes.com/2013/10/30/theater/reviews/brechts-good-person-of-szechwan-opens-at-public-theater.html?pagewanted=1.

_____. "With Song in Heart, Pompoms on Head." *New York Times*, March 20, 2011. Accessed November 30, 2013. http://www.nytimes.com/2011/03/21/theater/reviews/priscilla-queen-of-the-desert-on-broadway-review.html?_r=0.

Jagose, Annamarie. *Queer Theory: An Introduction*. New York: New York University Press, 1996.

Jeffreys, Joe E. "Introduction to *Neferet-iti*," in *Extreme Exposure: An Anthology of Solo Performance Texts from the Twentieth Century*, edited by Jo Bonney, 72–73. New York: Theatre Communications Group, 2000.

Jerome, Judith. *Creating the World Waiting to Be Created: Jack Smith and D. W. Winnicott Performing Themselves*. Ann Arbor: ProQuest, 2007.

Joseph, Rachel. "Glittering Junk: Jack Smith and the Vast Landfill of Identity." *The Journal of American Drama and Theatre* 25, no. 2 (2013): 77–90.

Kammen, Michael. *American Culture, American Tastes: Social Change and the 20th Century*. New York: Random House, 2012.

Kaufman, David. *Ridiculous! The Theatrical Life and Times of Charles Ludlam*. New York: Applause Theatre and Cinema Books, 2002.

Kershaw, Baz. *The Radical in Performance: Between Brecht and Baudrillard*. New York: Routledge, 1999.

"'Kinky Boots' Performance at Macy's Day Parade Provokes Outrage." *The Huffington Post*. Posted November 29, 2013. Updated December 1, 2013. Accessed February 8, 2014. http://www.huffingtonpost.com/2013/11/29/kinky-boots-macys_n_4360035.html.

Kristeva, Julie. *The Kristeva Reader*. New York: Columbia University Press, 1986.

Kuenzli, Rudolf. *Dada (Themes and Movements)*. London: Phaidon Press, 2011.

Kushner, Tony. "A Fan's Foreword." In *The Mystery of Irma Vep and Other Plays*, by Charles Ludlam, vii–ix. New York: Theatre Communications Group, 2001.

_____. "Foreword: Notes Toward a Theater of the Fabulous," in *Staging Gay Lives: An Anthology of Contemporary Gay Theater*, edited by John M. Clum, vii–x. Boulder: Westview Press, 1996.

_____. "Notes about Political Theater." *Kenyon Review* 19, no. ¾ (1997): 19–34.

Lacey, Robert. *Great Tales from English History: The Truth About King Arthur, Lady Godiva, Richard the Lionheart, Volume 1*. New York: Hachette Digital, 2004.

La MaMa E.T.C. Archives. "Play List 1970." Accessed September 17, 2013. http://www.lamama.org/archives/year_lists/1970page.htm.

Langford, Simon. *The Remix Manual*. New York: Taylor & Francis, 2011.

Lessig, Lawrence. *Remix: Making Art and Commerce Thrive in the Hybrid Economy*. New York: Penguin Press, 2008.

Lester, Elenore. "The Holy Foolery of Charles Ludlam." *New York Times*, July 14, 1974, 16.

LeSueur, Joseph. "Theatre: Big Hotel." *Village Voice*, February 9, 1967. Accessed June 10, 2013. http://news.google.com/newspapers?nid=1299&dat=19670209&id=NxAQAA AAIBAJ&sjid=KYwDAAAAIBAJ&pg=5958,681787.

Logan, Robert K. *Understanding New Media: Extending Marshall McLuhan*. New York: Peter Lang, 2010.

Love, Heather. *Feeling Backward: Loss and the Politics of Queer History*. Cambridge: Harvard University Press, 2007.

Ludlam, Charles. Interview with *Life* magazine, December 1985. Found in the Charles Ludlam Papers in the Billy Rose Theatre Collection at the New York Public Library for the Performing Arts, call number 8-MWEZ+n.c. 29.277, folder #14.

_____. *Ridiculous Theatre: Scourge of Human Folly*. Edited by Steven Samuels. New York: Theatre Communications Group: 1992.

_____. "Ridiculous Theatre, Scourge of Human Folly." *TDR* 19, no. 4 (1975): 70.

Ludlam, Charles, and Ted Castle. "Interview," *ArtForum*, March 30, 1981. Transcript found in the Charles Ludlam Papers in the Billy Rose Theatre Collection at the New York Public Library for the Performing Arts, call number 8-MWEZ+n.c. 29.277, folder #12.

Ludlam, Charles, and Gautam Dasgupta. "Interview: Charles Ludlam," *Performing Arts Journal* 3, no. 1 (1978): 69–80.

Ludlam, Charles, and Lola Pashalinski. Unpublished Interview. Found in the Charles Ludlam Papers in the Billy Rose Theatre Collection at the New York Public Library for the Performing Arts, call number 8-MWEZ+n.c. 29.277, folder #15.

"Ludlam Profile: Ridiculous." Published March 25, 1976. Found in the Charles Ludlam Papers in the Billy Rose Theatre Collection at the New York Public Library for the Performing Arts, call number 8-MWEZ+n.c. 29.277, folder #6.

Marks, Peter. "THEATRE REVIEW; How to Be Captivating Without a Sense of Self." *New York Times*, February 16, 1998. Accessed January 20, 2014. http://www.nytimes.com/mem/theater/treview.html?res=9504E3DC1F3CF935A25751C0A96E958260.

Marranca, Bonnie. Introduction to *Theatre of the Ridiculous*, edited by Bonnie Marranca and Gautum Dasgupta, 5–11. New York: Performing Arts Journal, 1979.

McNeil, Legs, and Gillian McCain. *Please Kill Me: The Uncensored Oral History of Punk*. Tenth Anniversary Edition. New York: Grove Press, 2016.

Mekas, Jonas. "Jack Smith or the End of Civilization," in *Jack Smith: Flaming Creature*, edited by Edward Leffingwell, 48–64. New York: Serpent's Tail, 1997.

Mele, Christopher. *Selling the Lower East Side: Culture, Real Estate, and Resistance in New York City*. Minneapolis: University of Minnesota Press, 2000.

Meyer, Moe. *The Politics and Poetics of Camp*. New York: Routledge, 1993.

Miller, Paul D., aka DJ Spooky That Subliminal Kid and Peter Lunenfeld. *Rhythm Science*. Cambridge: MIT Press, 2004.

Miller, Tim, and David Román. "Preaching to the Converted." In *The Queerest Art: Essays on Lesbian and Gay Theatre*. New York: New York University Press, 2002.

Mills, Robert. "Queer Is Here? Lesbian, Gay, Bisexual, and Transgender Histories and Public Culture." *History Workshop Journal* 62 (Autumn 2006): 253–63.

Moon, Michael. "Tragedy and Trash: Yiddish Theater and Queer Theater, Henry James, Charles Ludlam, Ethyl Eichlberger," in *Queer Theory and the Jewish Question*, edited by Daniel Boyarin, Daniel Itzkovitz, and Anne Pelligrini. New York: Columbia University Press, 2003.

Muñoz, Jose. *Cruising Utopia: The Then and There of Queer Futurity*. New York: New York University Press, 2009.

Navas, Eduardo. *Remix Theory: The Aesthetics of Sampling*. New York: Springer, 2012.

Neilsen, Ken. *Tony Kushner's Angels in America*. New York: Bloomsbury, 2013.

Newton, Esther. *Mother Camp: Female Impersonators in America*. Chicago: University of Chicago Press, 1972.

Noble, Jean Bobby. *Sons of the Movement: FtMs Risking Incoherence on a Post-Queer Cultural Landscape*. Toronto: Women's Press, 2006.

O'Connor, Brett. *del.icio.us Mashups*. Online Resource: Wrox, 2007. Digital.

Olalquiaga, Celeste. *The Artificial Kingdom: On The Kitsch Experience*. Minneapolis: University of Minnesota Press, 1998.

Ormsbee, Todd J. *The Meaning of Gay: Interaction, Publicity, and Community among Homosexual Men in 1960s San Francisco*. Lanham, MD: Lexington Books, 2012.

Parnes, Uzi. "Jack Smith: Legendary Filmmaker, Theatrical Genius, and Exotic Art Consultant." New York, 1994. Accessed September 1, 2013. http://uziny.com/Uzi_Parnes_on_Jack_Smith-94.pdf,

Plasketes, George. *Play It Again: Cover Songs in Popular Music*. London: Ashgate Publishing, Ltd., 2010.

Reich, June L. "Genderfuck: The Law of the Dildo," in *Camp: Queer Aesthetics and the Performing Subject: A Reader*, edited By Fabio Cleto, 250¬–65. Ann Arbor: University of Michigan Press, 1999.

Rich, Frank. "A Ludlam Legacy: New Drummer, Same Beat: How to Write a Play a Legacy Is Updated." *New York Times*, November 9, 1993. Accessed June 10, 2013. http://search.proquest.com.ezproxy.gc.cuny.edu/docview/109160195/13F4DAD8689484CA18A/1?accountid=7287.

_____. "A Mad and Busy Day in Ludlam's First Venture: The Guests Include Norma Desmond and Svengali." *New York Times*, September 29, 1989. Accessed June 10, 2013. http://search.proquest.com.ezproxy.gc.cuny.edu/docview/110248240/fulltext PDF/13F4D7BD2616B8AF2FE/9?accountid=7287.

_____. "Making History Repeat, Even Against Its Will." *New York Times*, January 8, 1991. Accessed January 15, 2014. http://www.nytimes.com/1991/01/08/theater/review-theater-making-history-repeat-even-against-its-will.html.

_____. "Review/Theater: Angels in America; Millennium Approaches; Embracing All Possibilities in Art and Life." *New York Times*, May 5, 1993. Accessed January 13, 2014. http://www.nytimes.com/mem/theater/treview.html?res=9F0CE2DC1431F 936A35756C0A965958260.

_____. "Scene: Europe 1940. Subject: True Kitsch." *New York Times*. July 26, 1989. Accessed February 11, 2014. http://www.charlesbusch.com/Review%20-%20The%20Lady%20In%20Question%20-%20NY%20Times.htm.

_____. "Stage: 'Le Bourgeois,' Comedy After Moliere." *New York Times*, April 15, 1983. Accessed July 1, 2013. http://search.proquest.com.ezproxy.gc.cuny.edu/docview/122168449/13F4DA3465362FC4414/2?accountid=7287.

_____. "Theater: Ludlam's 'Artificial Jungle.'" *New York Times*. September 23, 1986. Accessed July 7, 2013. http://search.proquest.com.ezproxy.gc.cuny.edu/docview/111039075/13F4DB9CB362ECD0FEB/1?accountid=7287.

Richards, David. "Tale of One City Set in Two Times—Both Fearful." *New York Times*, January 13, 1991. Accessed August 1, 2013. http://www.nytimes.com/1991/01/13/theater/sunday-view-tale-of-one-city-set-in-two-times-both-fearful.html.

Rickey, George. *Constructivism: Origins & Evolutions*. New York: G. Braziller, 1995.

Roemer, Rick. *Charles Ludlam and the Ridiculous Theatrical Company: Critical Analyses of 29 Plays*. Jefferson, NC: McFarland, 2010.

Salandra, Adam. "'Queer Ghost Hunters' Is Back to Wake the LGBT Dead for Second Season." *Logo*, June 27, 2017. http://www.newnownext.com/queer-ghost-hunters-season-two/06/2017/.

Sanders, Jay. "Love Is an Object." In *Rituals of Rented Island: Object Theater, Loft Performance, and the New Psychodrama—Manhattan, 1970–1980*. New Haven: Yale University Press, 2013.

Sargeant, Jack. *Naked Lens: Beat Cinema*. Berkeley: Counterpoint Press, 2009.

Savran, David. *A Queer Sort of Materialism: Recontextualizing American Theatre*. Ann Arbor: University of Michigan Press, 2003.

Scheck, Frank. "A Way with Women." *New York Post*, February 10, 2010, 34. Print.

Sedgwick, Eve Kosofsky. *Touching Feeling: Affect, Pedagogy, Performativity*. Durham: Duke University Press, 2003.

Senelick, Laurence. "Text and Violence: Performance Practices of the Modernist Avant-Garde," in *Contours of the Theatrical Avant-Garde*, edited by James Harding, 15–42. Ann Arbor: University of Michigan Press, 2000.

Shapiro, Eve. "Drag Kinging and the Transformation of Gender Identities." *Gender and Society* (2007): 250–71.

Shewey, Don. "The Tale of Charles Busch: From Drag Diva to Broadway Farceur." *New York Times*, October 29, 2000. Accessed November 3, 2013, on donshewey.com. http://www.donshewey.com/theater_articles/charles_busch.htm.

Shirakawa, Sam. "The Eccentric World of Charles Ludlam." *New York Times*, July 3, 1983. Accessed July 7, 2013. http://www.nytimes.com/1983/07/03/theater/the-eccentric-world-of-charles-ludlam-by-sam-h-shirakawa.html.

Simon, John. "'The Tale of the Allergist's Wife." *New York*. March 13, 2000. Accessed February 1, 2014. nymag.com/nymetro/arts/theater/reviews/2317/.

Sinfield, Alan. *Out on Stage: Lesbian and Gay Theatre in the Twentieth Century*. New Haven: Yale University Press, 1999.

Sinnreich, Aram. *Mashed Up: Music, Technology, and the Rise of Configurable Culture*. Amherst: University of Massachusetts Press, 2010.

Smith, Jack. "Actavistic, Action Packed, Action Acting of PFA." In *Wait for Me at the Bottom of the Pool*. London: Serpent's Tale, 2008.

Smith, Jack, J. Hoberman, and Edward Leffingwell, eds. *Wait for Me at the Bottom of the Pool: The Writings of Jack Smith*. London: Serpent's Tail, 1997.

Smith, Michael. "Theatre Journal: *The Life of Lady Godiva*." *Village Voice*, March 17, 1966. Quoted in Stephen J. Bottoms, *Playing Underground: A Critical History of the 1960s Off-Off-Broadway Movement*. Ann Arbor: University of Michigan Press, 2006.

_____. "Theatre Journal: The Magic Show of Dr. Ma-Gico." *Village Voice*. March 22, 1973. Accessed September 10, 2012. http://news.google.com/newspapers?nid=1299&dat=19730322&id=5tNHAAAAIBAJ&sjid=4IsDAAAAIBAJ&pg=6376,5518977.

Smith, Tom. "Charles Busch (1954–)," in *Contemporary Gay American Poets and Playwrights: An A-to-Z Guide*, edited by Emmanuel Sampath Nelson, 61–68. Westport, CT: Greenwood Publishing Group, 2003.

Stasio, Marilyn. "Off-Broadway Review: 'The Tribute Artist.'" *Variety*, February 9, 2014. Accessed February 11, 2014. http://variety.com/2014/legit/reviews/off-broadway-review-the-tribute-artist-1201094951/.

Sontag, Susan. "Jack Smith's *Flaming Creatures*." In *Against Interpretation: And Other Essays*, by Susan Sontag, 226–31. New York: Macmillan, 1966.

Sonvilla-Weiss, Stefan. *Mashup Cultures*. New York: Springer, 2010.

Stone, Wendell. *Caffe Cino: The Birthplace of Off-Off-Broadway*. Carbondale: Southern Illinois University Press, 2005.

Stosuy, Brandon. *Up Is Up, But So Is Down: New York's Downtown Literary Scene, 1974–1992*. New York: New York University Press, 2006.

Straus, Joseph N. "Disability and 'Late Style' in Music." *The Journal of Musicology* 25, no. 1 (2008), 3–45.

Sullivan, Nikki. *A Critical Introduction to Queer Theory*. New York: New York University Press, 2003.

Tavel, Ronald. "Maria Montez: Anima of an Antediluvian World," in *Flaming Creature*, edited by Edward Leffingwell, 88–139. New York: Serpent's Tail, 1997.

Taylor, Marvin J. "Playing the Field: The Downtown Scene and Cultural Production, an Introduction," in *The Downtown Book: The New York Art Scene 1974–1984*, edited by Marvin J. Taylor, 17–40. Princeton: Princeton University Press, 2006.

Warhol, Andy, and Pat Hackett. *POPism: The Warhol Sixties*. New York: Penguin Adult, 2007.

Watson, Steven. *Factory Made: Warhol and the Sixties*. New York: Random House, 2003.

Waugh, Patricia. *Metafiction*. 2002. New York: Routledge 2013.

Wilson, James. "'Ladies and Gentlemen, People Die': The Uncomfortable Performances of Kiki and Herb," in *We Will Be Citizens: New Essays on Gay and Lesbian Theatre*, edited by James Fisher, 194–224. Jefferson, NC: McFarland, 2006.

Witt, Mary Ann Frese. *Metatheater and Modernity: Baroque and Neobaroque*. Madison, NJ: Fairleigh Dickinson, 2012.
Young, Royal. "Review: A Post-Modern Christmas Carol at Abrons." December 13, 2012. Accessed December 10, 2013. http://www.thelodownny.com/leslog/tag/everett-quinton.

Unpublished Documents

Jeffreys, Joe E. "An Outré Entrée into the Para-Ridiculous Histrionics of Drag Diva Ethyl Eichelberger." PhD Diss., New York University, 1996. Accessed via ProQuest.
Ludlam, Charles. Personal Notebook. In the Charles Ludlam Papers in the Billy Rose Theatre Collection at the New York Public Library for the Performing Arts, call number 8-MWEZ+n.c. 29.256, folder #2.
_____. Personal Notebook. Found in the Charles Ludlam Papers in the Billy Rose Theatre Collection at the New York Public Library for the Performing Arts, call number 8-MWEZ+n.c. 29.157, folder #6.
_____. Personal Notebook. Found in the Charles Ludlam Papers in the Billy Rose Theatre Collection at the New York Public Library for the Performing Arts, call number 8-MWEZ+n.c. 29.257, folder #17.
_____. Personal Note. Found in the Charles Ludlam Papers in the Billy Rose Theatre Collection at the New York Public Library for the Performing Arts, call number 8-MWEZ+n.c. 29.268, folder #1.
_____. Personal Notes. Found in the Charles Ludlam Papers in the Billy Rose Theatre Collection at the New York Public Library for the Performing Arts, call number 8-MWEZ+n.c. 29.256, folder #5.
_____. Transcript of Unidentified Interview, page 10, included in the Charles Ludlam Papers in the Billy Rose Theatre Collection at the New York Public Library for the Performing Arts, call number 8-MWEZ+n.c. 29.277, folder #19.
Pogostin, Joe. Transcript of Article. I.A.2087, Museum of Modern Art P.S. 1 Archives, New York.
Smith, Jack. "Art and Art History." I.A.2087, Museum of Modern Art P.S.1 Archives, New York.
_____. Quoted in *East Village Other* 1, no. 24 (1966). Accessed March 10, 2013 via http://www.beatbooks.com/shop/beatbooks/32099.html.
Villager. Certificate awarded to Charles Ludlam and the Ridiculous Theatrical Company in honor of their contributions and *Le Bourgeois Avant-Garde*, dated June 6, 1983. Found in the Charles Ludlam Papers in the Billy Rose Theatre Collection at the New York Public Library, call number 8-MWEZ+n.c. 29.277, folder #1.

Index